Firefights of the Mind

When the Demons of War Follow You Home

Ed Kugler

OTHER BOOKS AVAILABLE BY ED KUGLER

Dead Center
A Marine Sniper's Two Year Odyssey in the Vietnam War

Poems of a Rogue
A Marine Sniper's Reflections on War

My Vietnam
Montana Veterans Stories Straight from the Heart

Marine Sniper Wisdom
A Dozen Things I Learned About Life as a Marine Sniper in Vietnam

Obamunism
The Enemy Within

The Well House
A Story of Love, Peace, War and Forever

Through the Darkness Comes the Light
A Marine Sniper, An Atheist, A Love Story, An Unlikely and Powerful Conversion to the Gospel of Jesus Christ; the Challenge and Sacrifice and the Continuing Daily Battle to Stay the Course

A special thanks to my friend
Robert Fraser for his great editing.

And to my friend Steve Alexander
of Swassworks for the cover design.

Copyright 2014 by Ed Kugler

*All rights reserved by SparrowHawk, Inc.
Permission granted to quote from this book;
just give credit where credit is due. Enjoy.*

ISBN: 1499152507
ISBN 13: 978-1499152500
Library of Congress Control Number: 2014909826
CreateSpace Independent Publishing Platform
North Charleston, South Carolina

Dedicated to all those who served
& fought for America throughout its history.
A special recognition to our Korean War vets;
they are America's true forgotten heroes.
And our young brothers and sisters, veterans of OIF & OEF.
Make sure you reach out for help. We are here.
Welcome home!

THOUGHTS ON WAR

"The true soldier fights not because he hates what is in front of him, but because he loves what is behind him".
G. K Chesterton

"I am in awe of war, its permanent role in biological and social evolution, its capture of psychology, philosophy, and theology, its role in historical, political, and technological progress.
Through its own independent organic growth, war creates its own culture.
War creates and uses the state monopoly on, and protection from, killing.
I am susceptible to the mind-altering extremes of war.
Exoticism, eroticism, excitement. Big guns and explosive afterburners.
I have an appetite for the spectacular. Awesome power, hot technology, and volcanic emotional intensity. Rapidly expanding highs and paralyzing lows.
I feel a strong, hideous fascination and embrace the thrill of the proximity of death. There is a certain pleasure in demolition, a mania of complete autonomy and a freedom from social contracts."

John A. Parish, M.D.
Author of Autopsy of War

"Only the dead have seen the end of war."
Plato

"In Peace, Sons bury their Fathers. In War, Fathers bury their Sons."
Herodotus

"It is only those who have neither fired a shot nor heard the shrieks and groans of the wounded who cry aloud for blood, more vengeance, more desolation. War is hell."
William T. Sherman

"Ours is a world of nuclear giants and ethical infants. We know more about war
than we know about peace, more about killing than we know about living.
We have grasped the mystery of the atom and rejected the Sermon on the Mount."
General Omar Bradley

FOREWORD

The eyes of my brothers give it away. Their pupils are dilated, pulsing, pounding, telegraphing the situation we're in. The toughest of the tough are trying to mask their fear so the others will not see. But even the best magicians fail at the slight of hand. The enemy knows these mountains, and they always have the advantage, but this time is different, dire. I watch beads of sweat on my brother turn to crimson. His eyes are no longer focused; they're fading. I can see his agony. I can smell his pain; that's my trigger. I open my eyes that were never closed.

"Are you ok baby?" my wife asks. I put my knife and fork down on the table. I get up and leave the dinner table without saying a word. Certain smells remind me of the past, of firefights gone by. Tonight's dinner has triggered it. I have slipped into a memory that I desperately try to suppress. Hopeless.

I originally wrote this for my Marine brothers that could potentially be suffering from PTSD, or just trying to find direction in civilian life. I posted it on Facebook and a friend of mine, Ed Kugler, contacted me and asked if he could use it to open his new book. I was surprised and honored. Ed and I met while I was serving in the Marine NCO School, in Hawaii. Ed and a few of his fellow Vietnam Vets, Marine snipers, were visiting the 3rd Marine Division Scout Sniper School in Kaneohe Bay.

After being in a Marine combat arms occupation, life after that can be a little dull, a little drab, and a little meaningless at times. A coworker of mine, an Army Grunt, and I talk all the time, about why this is and how to overcome it. I read the book "War", by Sebastian Junger. In it Sebastian chronicles his time embedded on a journalistic tour with an Army unit in the Korengal Valley, Afghanistan. Reaching the last few chapters of the book, I started to read a few paragraphs that portray, in my opinion, exactly why civilian life for grunts is so hard to adapt to. The below excerpts are the work of Sebastian Junger, a civilian journalist. His points are spot on and a testament to how combat changes a man's roadmap – a man's purpose. You are never the same.

Excerpt: In the civilian world almost nothing has lasting consequences, so you can blunder through life in a 'kind of daze'. You never have to take inventory of the items in your possession, and you never have to calculate the ways in which mundane circumstances can play out. As a result, you lose a sense of the importance of things, the gravity of things. Back home mundane details also have the power to destroy you, but the cause and effect, are often spread so far apart that you don't even make a connection; in combat, that connection is impossible to ignore. It is tedious, but it gave the stuff of one's existence - the dirty weapon, low water, no food - a riveting importance. Frankly, after you got used to living that way it was hard to go home.

Excerpt: There was carelessness and then there were real mistakes, and it all came down to one fact - discipline. Individuals who are exposed to prolong combat do not miss getting shot at or escaping death, you would have to be deranged, it's that they miss being in a world where everything is important, and nothing is taken for granted. They miss being in a world where human relations are entirely governed by whether you can trust the other person with your life.

Excerpt: It's such a pure, clean standard that men can completely remake themselves in war. You could be anything back home - shy, ugly, rich, poor, unpopular, it doesn't matter in combat because it's of zero consequence in a firefight, and, therefore, of no consequence, period. The only thing that matters is your level of dedication to the rest of the group, and that is almost impossible to fake. That is why the men say impossibly vulgar things about each other's sisters, mothers, fathers - nothing is off limits. It is one more way to prove they're not alone out there.

Excerpt: War is a big and sprawling word that brings a lot of human suffering into the conversation, but combat is a different matter. Combat is the smaller game that young men fall in love with, and any solution to the human problem of war will have to take into account the psyches of these young men. For some reason, there is a profound and mysterious gratification to the reciprocal agreement to protect another person with your life, and combat is virtually the only situation in which that happens regularly. These hillsides of loose shale and cedar trees are where the men feel not most alive - that you can get skydiving - but the most utilized, the most necessary, the most clear and certain and purposeful. If young men could get that feeling at home, no one would ever want to go to war again.

Excerpt: Most returning combat vets feel as if they have no "life skills". For most combat vets, life skills are skills that literally keep you alive. Those are far simpler and more compelling than the skills required at home. In the Korengal Valley and all other battlefields, almost every problem could get settled by getting violent faster than the other guy. Do that at home, and it's not going to go so well. It's a stressful way to live but once you experience combat almost everything else looks boring.

Excerpt: Civilians balk at recognizing that one of the most traumatic things about combat is having to give it up. War is so obviously evil and wrong that the idea that there could be anything good to it almost feels like a profanity. And yet throughout history vets have come home to find that they are desperately missing what should have been the worst experience of their lives. To a combat vet war is simple - necessary - understood.

Fast forward six years. I'm living what most consider the American dream. Beautiful wife, perfect house, baby on the way, I have worked hard for this white picket fence, and I will be damned if PTSD will take that away. Or so I tell myself. The truth is, that everyday is a constant struggle, a constant battle. No enemy ever hit me as hard as PTSD. I was definitely not warned, or ready for this. It has been the single hardest part of my transition into the civilian world. My family, my brothers, and my constant dedication to find out exactly what PTSD is, and how it effects individuals has given me purpose, and the drive to love life again.

Too many times when the topic of PTSD is brought up, vets become quiet, shy or ashamed. I look at it this way; I am not suffering from PTSD, I am living with PTSD. I have PTSD because I willingly placed myself into situations that a normal man would cower and hide. PTSD is no longer a disorder for me; it is a tool that I use to remember the men that I had the opportunity to serve alongside. Without these men, the memories, the experiences and the brotherhood that we share, I would not have PTSD. I will gladly go through hell again with my brothers for another serving of PTSD.

I highly recommend Ed's new book, Firefights of the Mind, because that is the essence of living with PTSD.

Semper Fi,

Sergeant Andrew Farlaino, USMC
Echo 2nd Battalion, 3rd Marines

Kunar Province, Afghanistan; Haditha, Iraq

A VIETNAM WAR POEM

When youth was a soldier,
And we fought across the sea,
We were young and cold hearts,
Of bloody savagery.

Born of Indignation,
Children of our time,
We were orphans of creation,
And dying in our prime.

***Ned Broderick 1966**
The poem is in the book *Cat From Hue*
by correspondent John Laurence.

PROLOGUE

The demons of war come in all shapes and sizes, and even clever disguises. In my case, they were disguised for over twenty-five years. It would take another fifteen years for me to admit it, and begin to deal with it. My family knew though, probably more than a few people around me, but not me. Society tends to think of what was lost in war. Some lost their limbs, some of their manhood, others their lives, and all our innocence. But until the current wars, in Iraq and Afghanistan, society didn't fully recognize what survivors secretly bring home from war. Firefights of the Mind is a glimpse into the life of one Marine, successful in most ways, and the impact of the unseen travelers who followed me home.

It would be many years before I would admit the impact Vietnam had on my life. I chronicled my time in Vietnam in a previous book, Dead Center - A Marine Sniper's Two Year Odyssey in the Vietnam War. This book is very different. I came home from Nam with all my limbs and most of my faculties. I came home to a world very different from the one I left. The streets were full of long haired hippies; girls with skirts that left little to the imagination and college campuses ablaze in protest. Being in the military was no longer in vogue, and young people were having fun destroying all that America valued. I felt like I'd returned to a place I'd never been.

I wasn't returning to Cleveland, New York or Chicago, where Marines got spit on. I was returning to small town Ohio, as middle America as you can get. I grew up in a little town called Lock Seventeen. By my count, there were 75 people living there. Today they'd call it a bedroom community to Gnadenhutten, where we all went to school. Gnaden, as we called it, had 2,500 people on a good day and sat a mile away. Our rural area was fine when I returned, but the world at large had gone bonkers.

This book represents a year in my life, twenty-five years after I returned from Nam. I wrote the diary part before Dead Center. I've been sitting on it for several years. As I watched, and talked with returning veterans, I knew the time was right to bring it back to life. It's part diary, a little biography, and hopefully, a warning shot, and helpful guide for everyone out there with a loved one who 'came home' from war. Today, we have thousands of vets returning from Iraq, Afghanistan, and other places around the world. The War on Terror is real, even if Mr. Obama insists it no longer exists. And with war, comes casualties.

My demons officially boiled to the surface when we invaded Iraq. One night, while watching the action on Fox News, imbedded reporter, Rick Leventhal was interviewing a young Marine. He was with a Marine Reserve Unit based in Las Vegas and Salt Lake City. They referred to themselves as the Saints and the Sinners.

Leventhal was interviewing a very young Marine. He was excitedly describing how he'd knocked out six Iraqi tanks that day. He was talking about it, just as we did years ago, as if it was a Friday night football game. Then he asked, "Are you a Saint or a Sinner?" The young Marine smiled, and proudly said he was a Saint, from Kaysville, Utah. The next question got right to the heart of what this book is about. Leventhal asked, "Tell me, what did you do before the war?" The kid, who was celebrating his nineteenth birthday that very day, proudly said, "I worked at Walmart, Sir!" And you know what, you can never go back to Walmart.

Once you've experienced life in combat, you are never the same. In the end, that might be bad, or it might be good, but it is never the same. You will not come back the same person who left. To some it's horror, to some exciting, to all it's frightening. It's a human experience like no other. It's responsibility at a level you may never experience again. It's a feeling of brotherhood that binds you forever, in ways you can't explain because you don't fully understand it yourself. You feel that others don't understand what you've experienced, and why should they? But you know what, it's okay. You're not the Lone Ranger. You're not the only one to ever feel the way you do. You're not the only one to struggle with what you struggle with today. It's okay. There is life after combat. I'm living proof.

The idea for what became the diary part of this book came from one of my brothers from Nam. He asked me to pass on what it was like, what we live with, what we see. He was a Marine sniper partner of mine. Stepped on a mine and came home less one leg, and an arm heavily damaged. We remained friends for life. Vacationed together, raised kids together, I even spoke at his Mothers funeral. And within two weeks of his asking me to pass on our struggles, his ended, I delivered his eulogy. He died of lung cancer in December of 1992, at the age of forty-five.

As I stood to deliver his eulogy, I experienced a Technicolor burst from Vietnam. Three weeks after the funeral began the new year, 1993. I was working for Pepsi Cola in their headquarters in Somers, New York. We had just moved there, our second move in as many years. I decided to keep a journal that year, documenting my year, more importantly, documenting the impact of our war so long ago on my daily life. I had lost a brother and ripped open my soul.

I was happily married, enjoying a successful corporate career with a Fortune 50 company, succeeding in life using the very principles I'd learned on the battlefields of Vietnam. Although I never admitted or accepted it, my family reminded me often, when I was retreating to my 'bad place' as they called it. At the time, I wasn't sure there were demons of war, but if there were I was sure mine were neatly, and tightly, tucked away, sealed in an airtight compartment, never to be opened again. Little did I know, standing before the congregation at my friend's funeral, the first crack in my compartment appeared, and a couple ghosts crept out.

I'm no exception; my story could be that of many a vet returning from war. My heart goes out to the young men and women fighting a Vietnam-like war in Iraq and Afghanistan. It's Vietnam-like, in that we have a clueless government playing politics with the lives of our young people, who valiantly sign up to serve this great nation. It is my hope and prayer, that my experience may serve to let them, and their loved ones, know, that they are not alone in their feelings, their struggles, or their journey to understand the person you have unwittingly become.

When I volunteered for my second consecutive year in Vietnam, my Mother wrote and said, I should, 'see someone'. When I returned to sleepy little Lock Seventeen, she told me face to face. I was 'different'. My journey to being 'different' began early. Lock Seventeen was a proud little place. Every Memorial Day, the old ladies of the DAR, the Daughters of the American Revolution, had a big ceremony. All dozen of us kids in town were dragged down to the local cemetery, with graves dating back to the Civil War, to recite patriotic poems.

If that wasn't enough, several of the men in town would routinely take us kids on the front porch and share stories of their times in World War II. The stories weren't of glory; rather the price others paid to keep America free. It's no wonder then, in the Fifth Grade, after doing a book report on *The Story of the U.S. Marines*, I decided to be a U.S. Marine. Two weeks after high school graduation I was standing front and center in Parris Island, South Carolina, Marine Boot Camp.

Being a Marine didn't come easy. Less than a year after graduating Boot Camp, we were fighting for our lives in the dirty streets of Santo Domingo, Dominican Republic. In what our politicians dubbed a 'police action', my company of Marines lost four killed and thirty-six wounded in the space of thirty minutes. I was one of the wounded. One Marine next to me took two machine gun rounds to the chest and died in front of me. Another took rounds in the throat and would spend the rest of his life as a quadriplegic. It wasn't quite as romantic as my book report made it out to be.

I'm sure I was a little 'different' after that experience, but I didn't feel like I was. I was high on adrenaline for months, blinded to the dangers since I was still standing. Vietnam was heating up, and I longed for another chance to do what Marines do. My Mother wondered about me, but I was a Marine, and that's what Marines do. I volunteered to go to Vietnam. The adrenaline high I'd felt in Santo Domingo returned and I was pumped, and ready to go.

After thirty days jungle training on the bare hills of Camp Pendleton and a thirty day ride aboard ship, I was standing ten-thousand miles away in a place called Vietnam. I was a replacement. Each one of the nine hundred Marines onboard, was replacing a Marine either rotating home, wounded or dead, the last two didn't sound so good. Before being assigned as replacements, they came around looking for volunteers to be scout-snipers. It would be the first time since World War II that the Marines formally fielded sniper teams. Out of nine hundred Marines, a couple dozen held up their hands; eleven of us were chosen to become snipers, I was one of them.

We flew an old chopper north to a place called Phu Bai, an old French base at one time. We trained there. We shot specially equipped rifles from sun up to sun down, seven days a week, for a month. Our targets were 105 artillery canisters, measuring about eight inches wide by twenty inches tall. Dead center for a mans chest. We trained hitting targets at four hundred meters to a thousand, and every hundred meters in between. Then, they wished us well, sent us out in pairs, and told us to do good. We were an eclectic group of young men. From cities large and small, families rich and poor, fueled by varying degrees of patriotism, but all, with a high desire for the adventure of a lifetime.

Our normal tour in Vietnam was thirteen months. I would end up staying twenty four months. Some snipers stayed the normal thirteen months, others I knew stayed as long as thirty-three months. It was the wild west. After two years, I returned with a lot of 'different' experiences and a few ghosts tagged along.

Marines kill in a flash, a firefight, an ambush, a fight for survival. A Marine sniper stalks his prey, hides, deprives himself, stares down the enemy, and silently pulls the trigger. He sees him drop. He sees him die, and the target never heard the crack of the sniper's rifle. In another place and time, the enemy is a person, just like you. Not today though. We live in the jungles of Vietnam. We're in the business of death; business is good, and we're good at what we do. We deliver death. It has a smell, a stench, driven by the heat that takes its toll on the dead and the living. Once you get used to it, your veins fill with adrenaline, and you'll soon be addicted to your unnatural high. Before long, you're numb to the carnage around you. It happens to somebody else, not you. An arm here, a leg there, so what, body count rules. There they are, Marine grunts exiting the jungle. Cover them. Eye to my scope, nothing but fire and smoke. A blast, a boom the size of Texas. Trees fly, ears ring, heads hurt, and bodies fly. Corpsman up! Dirt and debris drop like a monsoon rain. Poor bastard stepped on a five hundred pounder. A dud dropped from an F-4 Phantom, no doubt. Gooks made it into a massive booby trap. Vaporized five Marines before our eyes. One flash, they're gone; found only a rib cage, in a tree. Wounded others. Chaos ruled. It's a bitch, but it's just Nam. We won't be here forever, going home soon. Back to the world, back to normal, can't wait, life, just like it used to be.

Back to normal for me was an assignment to the Marine Reserve Center as part of the Inspector Instructor Staff. After two years in Nam this was great duty, except with four months left in the Corps, and not reenlisting, there was only one thing for me to do. Handle the firing squad for military funerals, for my Brothers killed in Nam. For my four months at the Reserve Center, we averaged four Marine funerals a week. You do the math, not just funeral math, the math on the pain. It was excruciating, and yes, 'different'.

A few months and many funerals later, four years after it started, it was over. I was home, out of the Marines, and expected to get back to normal, whatever 'normal' was? One of the first problems you'll stumble on is that 'your normal' is not the same 'normal' as those around you. My normal was a black and white world full of death and destruction, of kills and body count, of rifle stocks with notches and necklaces with ears. It was a world of violence, deprivation and hard living. It was also a world of brotherhood.

One of the challenges you'll find returning from war is that all your points of reference have changed dramatically. You leave a world behind where you enjoyed incredible responsibility, and rejoin a new world where being lackadaisical is rewarded and celebrated. You leave behind a world of adventure and excitement; your adrenaline's still pumps day and night and rejoin one that's frivolous, one you no longer recognize, nor want to. You're new world's filled with 'make believe', anything to avoid reality. You try to cope with video games, reality shows and political correctness, at a level unimaginable. You no longer relate to those around you, and you no longer want to either. The power of the life you left behind, is, intoxicating. You long for your brothers in arms, for the feeling you once had, and for an adrenaline fix. People around you say they 'understand' and what you're feeling is just 'normal'. How would they know? Reentry is a bitch.

When I woke up my first day home, in my old bed, I nearly punched my dear Aunt in the face. She was in my bedroom, trying to close my drapes so I could sleep late. My Aunts good intentions were missed on me. I just heard shuffling, saw a figure that appeared to me to be sneaking along the bottom of my bed. Adrenaline shot me into a red rage. I flew out of bed; arm cocked, fist at the ready as she ran from my room. And you know what, I didn't feel bad, because that was my reality. Don't sneak in my room.

I went back to sleep and got up about noon. Went down the hall to take a shower, as I'd done many times before, and it had the same cold water I'd left four years before. Apparently no one bothered to fix it. My adrenaline pump went off once again. I stormed out of the house, amidst the gasps of my Aunt and Grandmother, who lived with us. My Mom stood staring at the ground, as I left and drove to a local flea bag motel, rented a room, took a shower and went out and got drunk.

I'd come home to a place I'd never been before. In three plane rides, four days, and the most powerful experiences of my life, now this? No one understands. Even people who love you, who care about you, are lost for a time, some forever. You wake up and smell the napalm, while they smell flowers. You wake up looking for the enemy, they're looking for some fun and games. They walk out and see a beautiful garden, you see crispy critters from the latest bombing and hear a car backfire, that you hear as a close rifle shot. You're different, but there's a good reason for it.

When I laid down that night, I should have been happy. I was safe; I was home, surrounded by loved ones, but I was miserable. I wanted to get on a plane and fly straight back to my friends, my brothers, my Marines, and the war I'd left behind. I had a brief moment that night, where I realized the demon of anger, back then called the red rage, had followed me home. But I blew it off. It was 'their' problem, whoever they were. My Mothers words, 'you should see someone', echoed in my soul. As you'll read in the pages ahead, there were many demons who'd followed me home. Unfortunately, I didn't 'see someone' for forty years after the war. Marines didn't do that; they just sucked it up and kept moving.

While all that's true, there is hope. That's what I hope to accomplish with this book, to give my young Brothers and Sisters in arms, hope. It's important to understand you aren't alone; you can live a normal and successful life, and learn to use the positive from your experiences to do good. Demons come in all colors, shapes and sizes. They can be a tough enemy. But they can be tamed.

As you read this 'year in my life', twenty-five years after the war, you'll see my demons weren't nightmares, guilt, or agonizing memories, as so many of you experience. My demons are reliving the experiences, chasing the adrenaline and longing for the brotherhood, because I missed it. My demons came out in anger, in prejudice to certain types of people and circumstances, and in depression. Yes, I said it, depression. For years, I wouldn't acknowledge depression was even a remote possibility. Thanks to the late Stephen Covey I learned that we cannot change that which we don't acknowledge. It's important to come clean with yourself. Only then, can you move forward and deal with your demons.

I've had the opportunity, the privilege, to be friends with, counsel with, love and encourage, many of today's veterans returning from our current wars. I have the utmost respect for our military today. They're professionals, and the character of the men and women who serve is impeccable. Many of you come home with no issues, others have many of the problems I describe. Some of you have major, life threatening problems. Regardless, everyone returning from war is impacted by their experience, we are indeed, 'different'.

Come with me on an eye opening journey. A journey many of you may have traveled, perhaps your loved ones, or friends too. And as you do, keep in mind that I've overcame alcoholism, learned to live with my PTSD, and still done reasonably well. I've stayed married to the same woman for nearly five decades, raised three productive kids, all, in spite of my demons. You'll see that sometimes, if it weren't for flashbacks, we wouldn't have any memory at all. I've written my flashbacks as they happened, in italics, so they are easier to follow. Come with me on a journey most can't understand, unless they've been there. Read what Counsul Lucius Aemilius said in 168 BC ...

"I am not, fellow citizens, one who believes that no advice may be given to leaders; nay rather I judge him to be not a sage, but haughty, who conducts everything according to his own opinion alone. What, therefore, is my conclusion? Generals should receive advice, in the first place from the experts, who are both specially skilled in military matters and have learned from experience;

Secondly, from those who are on the scene of action, who see the terrain, the enemy, the fitness of the occasion, who are sharers in the danger, as it were, aboard the same vessel.

Thus, if there is anyone who is confident that he can advise me as to the best advantage of the state in this campaign which I am about to conduct, let him not refuse his services to the state, but come with me into Macedonia. I will furnish him with his sea-passage, with a horse, a tent, and even travel-funds. If anyone is reluctant to do this and prefers the leisure of the city to the hardships of Campaigning, let him not steer the ship from on shore. The city provides enough subjects for conversation; let him confine his garrulity to these; and let him be aware that I shall be satisfied with the advice originating in camp."

Come with me my fellow warriors on a journey of hope and change. To my friends, come to our Macedonia, and begin to understand what the men and women, those who protect us each day, endure, after they've stared the tiger in the eye.

"Please don't tell me about Vietnam, I've been there"
Found on a Zippo lighter from the War

One Year - 1993

JANUARY

1 January, Friday - Brookfield, CT. Home

New Years day 1993. Festive, friends over, kids home. Good day to be alive. Fun day, football all day, everyone's bored except me. New Year in Connecticut. Second time we've lived here, a surprise this time. Loved it in Eastern Connecticut in the early eighties. Now, ten plus years later, we're back. This time around we're living in Western Connecticut. Danbury area to be exact.

New Year. New state, new job. This time I'm moving Pepsi instead of potato chips. I'm a Headquarters puke now, and I hate it. I guess it's my ego wrestling with old tapes from Nam. The headquarters pukes here are just as worthless and out of touch as they were in Nam. They cost lives in Nam and money and careers here. God help me not to be that way. Let me stay real.

Hopeful for a day without Nam. Losing Greek was a setback. We have friends we haven't seen in ten years, visiting for the weekend. Chris goes off with my wife, Kurt with me. He's not a sports fan. Bummer. I can see this may not be my day. We sit down and talk about our problems. His are tougher than mine. A teenage daughter with some big struggles. My day will come. Then he tells me he's now into hunting. That's a surprise.

"Hey Ed, you were a sniper in Nam, a Marine weren't you?" I nod my head while trying to watch football. "You loved it, didn't you?" he asks. I admit that I did. He thinks I'm weird and tells me so. But he's still raining questions regarding his new hunting hobby. The interrogation seems to have no end. "How far did you shoot? What rifle did you use? What grain bullets? What about windage? Weight? Anxiety crept into the room as football vanished.

Technical questions are usually comfortable, but they lead to the always inevitable question, "What was it like, you know, to, a kill someone?" I turn away, sliding into my bad place, "I felt nothing". That ends the discussion.

Truth was; it was a game. Them or me, and here I am. The remainder of the day was a blur, as my mind slithered deeper into my bad place. I can go there, even in the midst of people, chattering away. It's not that I haven't tried to change, and leave it all behind, I have. My journey has traveled from life as an Atheist, then an Agnostic in Nam to a few years ago finding Christ. I try; I try every day. But living with Nam is like scratching an old piece of furniture, once burnt in a fire. As you scratch the surface, you're hit with an overwhelming stench of fire, old fire that penetrates your being. That's a flashback. It's always there, just beneath the surface.

If it weren't for my wife, my love, my original therapist, I don't know where I'd be today? She hates all this but tolerates it well. She just wishes it weren't so alive, hiding right beneath the surface of our lives. She likes to tell people after twenty-four years of marriage she has sexually transmitted PTSD. I don't know how she could; I don't. It's a great line though.

Years ago, slipping into my bad place, it would hold on to me like quicksand, for days. My first five years out of Nam, I'd get a buzz that would trip me out for a week or two straight. My trips were alcohol fueled, turbocharged with adrenaline, blinded me to life taking place around me. Even so, it's such a small price to pay, compared to the Greeks leg, Perl's life, Crud's suicide and the nameless thousands of others missing arms and legs, and the countless body bags of good guys and bad.

Everyone's in bed. I hung out physically with everyone, but mentally, I'm still ten-thousand miles away. I'm thankful that Mother Time, and the patience and encouragement of a great wife changed my buzz from a few weeks to a week, then a couple days, to a day, then an hour or two. Maybe someday, it will be minutes, or seconds, or not at all? But not tonight. It's bedtime. I'm in my bad place. It's dark here. Sleep may have to wait. *I'm back in Nam; it's New Years 1966 in the Co Bi Than Tan Valley.*

We're humping in from the valley and a week long patrol. Our biggest worry? Will there be any beer left on Hill 51 when we made it in from patrol. The patrol was a bitch. Hot, sometimes wet, and the four of us had all the fun we could stand for awhile. We'd been running four man patrols for too long. We were burned out. Gone. We had a click, click and a half, to reach our grunt outpost.

Co Bi Than Tan Valley was a free-fire zone. All non-combatants were removed. The valley was an infiltration route out of the Laotian mountains. We lived there and did our thing. We trudged along in the baking sun. We'd been shot at and missed for a week. Their snipers weren't as good as us. In our cynicism, it seemed a joke. Hood was on point. I walked second, Stu behind me and Crud as tail end Charlie.

We headed across the dilapidated paddies under cover of the tanks on Hill 51 where the grunts were. We walked about fifty, maybe seventy-five yards towards a tree line surrounding a small, vacant, old village. With beer on our minds we heard the distinct crack, crack, crack, of a carbine zing bullets over our heads. They weren't going to hit us, but they were close enough to get our attention.

Without a word from me, we're all down on the ground, spread out, leap frogging our way to the village edge, covering each other as we went. I thought, 'this, is a beautiful thing'. Hood's pissed. "Kug, if we don't beat the last chopper to Hill 51 we're gettin' no holiday beer. Screw these assholes!" Crud's laughing, as usual. I take the 7 x 50's and scan the tree line, about twenty-five yards from our trail. I know the dude is in there somewhere. I just don't know where.

We sat tight, taking turns listening, scanning trees until Hood and Bu were about to boil over. "Screw em!" We moved out. Hood led, as we cautiously moved ahead. Fifteen yards out we heard the now familiar 'crack, crack, crack'. The bullets were closer but still missed by a few yards. We stopped, turned left, facing the tree line. Without a word, we started walking on line across the paddy, towards the tree line. The trees formed a U in front of us. We walked towards the closed end, rifles at the ready. About half way in we stopped. It was quiet, surreal. We were disgusted, tired and pissed off. Nothing was happening; we didn't see or hear anyone.

Standing there in our tiger stripes, M-14's on full auto, our sniper rifles strapped on our backs, sweatin' our balls off, hallucinating in the heat, this fool cranked off a round that hit the dirt near Stu. I couldn't believe the balls of the little bastard. We took off running, straight at the tree where we'd heard the crack of his rifle. We screamed shooting at the one tree we knew this little turd could be hiding. We leaped a small fence as hurdlers, busted through a hedgerow and there he was, in a heap on the ground, dead. An old M-1 next to his body. We were high as kites, adrenaline pumping hard through our veins.

We gathered our spoils of war and headed up to Hill 51. The grunt Lieutenant met us, and assured us he'd saved us two beers each. Hood was happy and disappeared as did Crud and Bu. The Lieutenant said, "Sergeant Kugler, I watched you guys through the scope in one of our tanks. What's wrong with you?" What's wrong with me? Nothing.

Sleep was nowhere to be found.

2 January, Saturday - Brookfield, CT. Home

Slept in, way in. It felt great. New year, new goals, plans I'll work on today. I laid in bed thinking of the year ahead, 1993. I'm a meticulous planner. Learned that in Nam. I have an overwhelming need for control.

I thought I'd get up, watch the Pro Playoffs and work on my plan. I have to do more than one thing at a time. Right now, enjoying time alone, relaxing, then WHAM! The Black Bastard hits me with a right hook. Depression. No warning. No reason. I fell off the cliff without taking a step. Anxiety smothered me. Not now, not today. But it's here. The blackness, the mood, Lord, please let me beat it. I need today. I need the security of knowing what we're doing, where we're going, and how we're going to get there. I need today Lord. It hits me. This year won't be the same as last. My best friend is gone. Died a month ago. Dead. Six years in a row, our families, vacationed at our cottage on the French River. Our annual therapy. No therapy this year. He's gone and so am I. Alone in bed; *I'm back at the 3rd Med Tent in Phu Bai. "Kug, looks like I'm about three feet shorter, and listing to the starboard side." I was kneeling beside my point man, holding his hand. He'd just got out of surgery to remove what remained of his left leg. The Greek. Robert Charles Devoti, Corporal, United States Marine Corps. Merrick, Long Island, New York. My partner and my friend. He stepped on a mine and got launched.*

"Greek, you're gonna' be fine. We've got lots of living yet to do." I tried to reassure him. I didn't want to tell him he looked like a dead man on an old green cot. He smiled, drifting in and out of consciousness. The Corpsman nearby waved signaling my time was up. I squeezed his hand to keep him awake. He motioned me down closer so I could hear. His voice was scratchy, weak. "Kug. I think my dancin' days are over." I smiled. "See you stateside my man". He weakly replied, "Stateside", and immediately drifted off.

My wife called me back to reality. It was time for brunch with our friends. I got up, dressed, my mind shaky with anxiety, anger and frustration. For the first time, I even felt guilt. I'd heard of it, read of it, but never felt it before. I now felt alone, all alone amidst my wonderful family, and friends.

They talked, laughed and reminisced. My family is a great blessing to me. I sat quietly, still thinking of my friend. I heard the words of my eulogy. I saw the Marine Honor Guard fold the flag, and present it to his widow, Bobbie. And I saw her, and her two, young boys, crying softly. I saw myself crying, as part of me went with Greek into the cold, December ground of Calverton National Cemetery on Long Island.

Gloria eventually dragged me out of the muddy rice paddies of my mind. Her love and inspiration kept me on the straight and narrow. We laughed. Gradually, the black receded. I was again comfortably home in Connecticut, where I belonged. The phone rang; it was our Bishop from church. He asked if I would speak tomorrow at a Joint Youth meeting. He said I could speak on whatever I felt inspired to share? My energy came back; I was excited. I love the youth. They're not damaged goods yet. We still have a chance to make a difference in their lives. I hung up with a new mission. Prepare my talk. I decided on "The Power of Choice". I feel strongly that we're the sum, total of our choices. I prepared into the night.

3 January, Sunday - Newtown, CT. Church

I love Sundays. I used to love them because I raced fast go-karts and motocross bikes on Sunday. Now, I worship Jesus Christ. The Sabbath works for me. I finally got the memo. It's a weekly break from the storms of everyday life. I love the peace I feel. I love to sit quietly and feel the soothing spirit of a Sunday morning service.

Today is our fast and testimony meeting. One of the things that attracted me to the faith was our welfare program. We're each expected to fast the first Sunday of each month and donate the value of two meals to our church welfare program. Makes sense to me. Take care of your own. On the same Sunday, the members have the floor to stand and bear their testimonies of the gospel to other members. It's very strengthening to me.

I sat listening to others, I knew I must stand and share my thoughts, as well. I needed to keep my word to Greek, and share his dying message. I waited for a break in speakers, stood, and made my way to the front. When I looked across the congregation, I could see the surprise on Gloria and my daughter's faces. I hadn't told them what I was doing.

Besides my personal testimony of Jesus Christ, I shared Greek's message, the one he'd shared with me, only a couple days before he died. His voice was weak, as it had been years ago after surgery. I explained who he was and what had happened. *He said, "Life is so fragile, Kug. Five months ago, I had everything going for me. I had my family but didn't appreciate them. Now, my life is in the Lords's hands. My days are numbered. I had everything Kug. I can see that now. I don't want one more day to work. I don't want to sell one more, damned house. I'm on my deathbed. I beg for one more day with Bobbie and the kids. Just one more day, just the smell of one more rose. One more day to make amends for all of my wrongs, but I can't have it Kug!" I can't have it! Tell people to live their lives now. Tell them today might be their last."*

I returned to my seat with tears in my eyes, and a heart so heavy it was difficult to carry. When Sacrament meeting ended, many people came up and thanked me for sharing my friend's message. The Bishop was waiting for me in the class I'd agreed to teach. "Here's Brother Kugler, I've asked him to address you today. He's had some unique experiences in Vietnam. I'd like him to share them with you".

Vietnam, one more time. I shared my journey from Atheist to Agnostic, then finally coming to Christ. I weaved in a small message about the power of choice. It's a good experience, but tough. It stirs the stale jungle hidden in my bad place. The odor of my past often seeps out, displayed in my bad behavior. Hopefully, not today.

As I leave class a nice man about my age came up and introduced himself. I recognize him as the piano player in our church service. Turns out he's a Marine chopper pilot and a Nam vet. He flew CH-46 Sea Knights. He even flew insertions of Force Recon teams. We're brothers; the feeling is there. We trip out on our adrenaline fueled past. He flies corporate jets for American Express these days. We agree to get our families together.

On the way home, my wife shares her conversation with the guy's wife. She told Gloria she was amazed how quickly he 'bonded' with me. Said he doesn't do that with men. He just likes to stay home with his family. I can relate.

4 January, Monday - Somers, NY. Pepsi Headquarters

First workday of the new year. New project to deliver in the next few months. Interesting. Working with two consultants my boss handed me. Seem to be good guys. Sharp. At least they're hands-on types. I don't need any wire rim glasses and red suspender types.

We finished up late. They asked where I lived. Turns out one lives near me, an hour commute, on a good day. They tell me to watch out for the State Police speed traps on I-84. I wanted done. I want to go home. I guess the consultant in them; they went back and forth about how the State Police could more efficiently conduct their speed traps. I listened for awhile, *then took out a piece of paper. I laid out how we used to execute double ambushes in Nam. Simple.* As I did, I realized my analogies, even twenty-five years later, still revolve around my life in Nam.

We finish. Always a relief to head home to family.

5 January, Tuesday - Brookfield, CT. Home to Work

Wake up early. Tired. Didn't sleep well, stayed up too late. I can't seem to sleep. Noises bother me. Early this morning it was heavy rain. It's pouring outside. If the rain were snow, I could stay in bed. But it's not snow, the pounding rain *takes me back to 1966.*

My first monsoon in Nam. Its rained hard, drizzled, and its poured. Twenty-seven days and nights of rain. Never stopped. Eternal wetness. The ground is mud and muck, so thick it pulls your boots off as you walk. Cold. Never knew how cold, but cold enough to make you shiver. Nights in slop holes, sleeping with your bush hat over your face, flat on your back in the goo. So tired, the flood around you doesn't matter.

Cortney, my fifteen year old daughter, asks for a ride to the bus stop. I'm home again. No worries, it's three or four blocks. I get up, dress, and head out to the car. Our driveway isn't paved. By the time I reach the car, my dress shoes look like snow shoes. The muck caked onto my soles, making my shoes heavy as a cement block. I see my jungle boots in Nam. Inside the car, Cortney asks, "Is this like a real monsoon?" Indeed it is.

My commute was longer than the usual hour. I joined the gridlock on I-84 as I headed west to New York state. The rain is blinding; the wipers aren't keeping up. I turned on Imus in the Morning, on

WFAN in New York City. He's crazy. He's also my morning therapy. He breaks up the commute.

I hate to listen to the news. It's often hard to believe. The State of Pennsylvania's changing their school curriculum. They're beginning to teach that the gay lifestyle is okay, normal even. Our nation's going down. Our friends, who just visited from Connecticut, told us about our church there. Girls pregnant, one with Aids. Hard to see that happening. Bad for my attitude. We inched our way into New York, and through the junction where I go south on I-684 to Somers. The hillsides, normally gorgeous and green, are bare and brown. It's winter; its a driving rain, and today, the hills are shrouded in a low, gray mist, which tightly hugs the ground. Visibility is dangerously low. *I see a monsoon morning in the DMZ.*

I drive into the parking lot of Pepsi North America, which brings me back from Nam. A giant American flag is gently waving in the rain. It has a red, white and blue Pepsi flag, flying right below it. *My mind's like a set of flash cards right now. Life is flipping the cards fast. Here one minute, gone the next. I'm used to it.* I park and step out into the rain. *The choppers will never get in for us today.* I smile to myself, as I pop my red, white and blue Pepsi umbrella. It's about a fifty yard walk to the main entrance. I take my time. *Strangely, I enjoy the rain.*

Today is a good day. I'm walking ten-thousand miles and twenty-five years from the other monsoons in my life. *I'm laying in my rack. Camp Evans. My second monsoon in Nam. The red water is rushing under our racks and through our tent. Misery lays next to me.* As I reached the marble framed main entrance, a roar passed close overhead. An unseen plane whooshes through the foggy mist, leaving nearby White Plains Airport. I stop, looking up, but not seeing the plane. *My flashcards flip. I'm in Dong Ha on a monsoon resupply. Ah, mail call, C-rats, dry clothes. A kaleidoscope of emotions shakes my soul.* I step inside. *The rain stops, so does my battle for reality.* The lobby is upbeat, the gentle background music that's playing changes the motion picture playing in my mind. Today, I walk into a new war, the Cola Wars. It's all good.

6 January, Wednesday - Brookfield, CT. Home

My usual. Up late, wake early and off to work. Cortney's up with me. Her bus comes early. We chatted for awhile. Then I remembered my promise to Whitney, who is turning eight. When I tucked her into bed last night, she reminded me; I hadn't been leaving her notes in the morning.

She picked it up from my wife and me. We'd been writing each other notes for years. I penned her a quick note, laid it on her school clothes and headed to work. As I pulled out of the driveway, *I realized I sign my notes to the kids, Papasan. A ghost pops up, but I turn on Imus and knock it down,* and quickly leave it behind.

At least my trip to Fresno was cancelled today. Instead, I'm driving to Cranston, Rhode Island, for a meeting this morning. Then to Jersey for another this afternoon.

7 January, Thursday - Brookfield, CT. Home

Home. Work was great. A grand day overall. Let it continue.

8 January, Friday - Brookfield, CT. Home

At home with the family after a good week at work. Here in New England, it's cold. Last year this time, we were living in Pasadena, Maryland, just outside Baltimore. Winter was on vacation there. Our Christmas snow here in Connecticut has disappeared in all the rain this week. Earlier tonight, we put up a new mailbox up. Gloria bought it today to replace the one we lost over the Holidays. It's our second mailbox in the six weeks we've lived here. Apparently, somebody thinks it's funny to destroy other's property. I don't.

We were watching TV when we saw car lights through the drapes. Cortney jumped up to check. A car was sitting out front. Before I could get to the door, I hear, WHACK! I open the door to tires squealing, as the car raced down the street. My new mailbox, replaced today, is laying crushed, at the end of our sidewalk, in one of the remaining patches of snow still surviving. It looks like it died a quick death, probably from a baseball bat.

It should have been a small thing, *but my red rage exploded, and my head was ablaze. The doors burst off my bad place as adrenaline rushed out. I'm in Nam. I'll handle it. Don't screw with me. As I walk back inside and I ran into my daughter.* "I'll booby trap the next one!" She says, "Dad; it's just a mailbox!" *I don't care. They're on my turf, inside my wire.* "Dad, you'll get the Mailman". She had a point. *I fought for control of the moment, but I was losing.*

My wife, who was upstairs, heard 'booby trap', and came running. We all sat in the kitchen while Cortney called her friends. "I'll ambush the little bastards next time." Gloria assures me that's not necessary or appropriate. Sitting with my wife, I begin to calm down, *to come home from Nam.* Cort walked in with the news her girlfriend knows who's doing it. They've been bragging about their exploits. *"Call back. Get an address!" I order.* She says she knows it. I'm up, heading out the door. "Where are you going?" my wife pleads.

"Come on Cort." At sixteen, she obeys, following me with a look of disbelief painted on her young face. She's knows my triggers. She's working on damage control. I told her to drive. *I wanted to be free to get out.* She pulls out of the driveway and says, "Dad; I'll show you where he lives, and then let's go home". *I told her to stop the car by the house.* She stopped down the street. It was pushing midnight. *I sat for a minute, firmly in my bad place, trying desperately to come home. I took several deep breaths, and* decide to write a note. *As quickly as I wrote it, I tore it up. My heart raced like I'd ran a mile. I look outside and see the bright of a full moon. As a sniper, I love moonlight nights. I can feel it. I can feel the warm flow of adrenaline. I think about booby traps. I think about gooks.*

"Dad, why are you waiting? I'm tired." *I don't know.* I know I need to go home and chill, *I don't want to. I want to hurt someone.* Then, an idea. "Cort, let's lay our mailbox on the porch. Let the parents sort it out". She thinks that's a better idea than booby traps. *I write a generic note to the kid, telling him I'm in a forgiving mood. Just knock it off.* I tear up the note. "Lets just drop off the box and go." She agrees. I sit there. "Dad, what are you waiting for, just drop it off". I continue to sit there. She looks at me. *"No way, go around for a different approach, we need more cover. Too much visibility here."* With a sigh belying her sixteen years, she said, "Dad, think about it, this ain't Nam!" She grabbed our dented mailbox and delivered it herself. *I sat in our Bronco II, staring at the silver lining of a brilliant moon. I was faraway, like so many nights before, in a faraway land no one understood. Now I was waiting to spend the adrenaline that filled my body.* Tonight I'm thankful for my bright young daughter, she knew how to handle Dad.

We drove the two blocks home in silence. She debriefed her Mom. I went straight to bed. Sleep was MIA. I lay silent, as my wife quietly came to bed. She rubbed my arm. I stared through the wood blinds of our window, *focusing on moonbeams that called me back to Nam. It was suddenly the summer of 1967, the Co Bi Than Tan Valley.*

Four Marine snipers, we're sneaking under cover of moonlight, to a place we called 'Johans'. It's 0400. We must be in the position before sunrise. It's hot; it's dark and it's dangerous. If it weren't for the silvery light of the moon, we couldn't see at all. My main man, Matt Hood, is walking point. He's cat like. He can smell a booby trap or a gook. He's foiled several ambushes, sniffed out countless booby traps and saved my young ass many times. I'd follow him anywhere.

We crossed the deserted valley, floated the river and were heading up the draw. I hated the draw; it was ambush alley. It was also the only practical way to Johan's. The trail headed up and over a short hill, lined with thick brush and short trees that pushed in on either side of eight foot steep banks. A perfect ambush spot and not for the faint of heart.

The draw was only about thirty yards long, but it was thirty slow, puckered tight yards. We counted every step, stopped at the slightest sound, and were alert to every smell. I walked with my finger tight on the trigger of my M-14 automatic. We make it through. Our biggest problem tonight was our own imaginations, fueled by past experiences; we're always ready for the ugly to jump.

We reached a small plateau with waist high grass. We're about thirty minutes behind schedule. We run the risk of being caught in the open at first light. I make the decision to abort our original objective. I stop Hood, exhale all the air from my lungs, and whisper our new destination. He nodded.

We turned off the planned trail and headed down the west slope. When daylight came, we'd have a good view of the valley. It was critical for us to be hidden by first light. It was a target rich environment. We loved it here. We started down the steep slope, me on Hoods ass. The thick grass was wet from the smothering humidity. Hood slipped, and began to slide down the hill. I reached out, grabbed his pack, and held him in place.

He's leaning back, his right leg straight out and down the hill, his left leg bent back under him. The moon shined on his face. He was trying to say something to me. I'd been holding him up with one hand, my rifle in the other. I handed my rifle to Stu, behind me. Free, I grabbed Hood's pack with both hands, crouched down, my ear to his mouth, and listened.

He gently whispered, "Kug, hold me up, don't move. There's a trip wire on my left foot!" We had a problem, a serious problem. If I let him slip we were both mincemeat. I'll have to disarm it. It's something we're trained to do, but it sucks. I motion with my head to Stu. He leans down. I tell him what's happening. He takes my place holding the pack and carefully lifts Hood a little higher. I'm glad he's doing the holding. He's a six foot-two; pure bred Iowa farmer and strong as an ox.

With Hood secure, I slide down on my butt, placing my legs around Hoods. Sitting, I slowly reach my hands down Hoods left leg, searching for the wire. I found it where he said I would, crossing the laces of his left jungle boot. Before I could tell him I found it, he leaned back, whispering,

"Your hand feels sooooo good on my leg". A little dark humor, in a dark moment, on a dark night.

Now that I'd found it, my race was with daylight. If we didn't get out of here soon, we'd be exposed on the hillside at first light. I touched the trip wire; we called it cat gut. It looked and felt like fine fishing line. Gently, I placed my fingertips on the wire and traced it to my right. It was tied to the limb of a bush. The prize was on the other side. Light was seeping into the east sky, and I needed to get this done.

I gently followed the trip wire to the left of the trail, away from Hoods leg. I hit the jackpot. I could feel the casing of a Chi-Com grenade. These were old Chinese armament, often used as booby traps on jungle trails. Now that I knew what I was dealing with, I had to get Hood out of his predicament without blowing this sucker and the three of us into the morning sky. I was too young to become raw meat. Besides, Crud would be pissed if we left him here all alone to deal with our body's.

There wasn't time, nor daylight enough, to disarm this baby properly. I carefully grasped the trip wire with my thumb and index finger, and lifted it slowly away. It had little slack. Crud, who'd been guarding our rear, came forward to pull Hood's foot back and away from the wire, while Stu was lifting him up, and backwards. Safely away from the Chi-Com, we gathered our things, crawled up the trail and into the underbrush. The day and our work is before us.

Before we leave the area, we'd have to set a charge and blow the booby trap so no one else would take a hit. Settled in for the morning, I lean over to Hood and said, "Hey man, you owe me a kiss for that one". He drew the line there.

My lucky star was still shining, and so was his.

I didn't sleep much. It's hard, when your mind's wired for sound, and you carry the war wherever you go.

9 January, - Saturday - Danbury, CT. A Friends House

Lazy day with the family, tired, I put the mailbox charades behind me. We were invited to a friend's house for the evening.

It was his birthday. We knew everyone from church, except one. An attractive Spanish woman. We're introduced, and soon realize she doesn't speak much, if any, English. She's from Brazil. It's fun meeting new people, especially those from a different country. The evening went well, although she was difficult to understand.

As the evening wound down, the conversation turned to her immigration status. She's in limbo. "I no understand America". She's very animated. Her arms and hands wave as she talks. She declares, "You no like America, you complain about cold, you complain about politics, inflation, then you leave! You no belong here!" My kind of girl.

I asked what the issue was with her immigration? She burst into another rant. "I love America, but I no understand government. If you are Brazilian or South American, they no want you. If you Vietnamese, they open arms. Bring you, and your family. I no understand. American and Vietnamese (making a gun with her hand and fingers) shoot each other, bang bang, and then you bring all of them here. I just no understand."

I had to agree; I didn't understand our government anymore either.

11 January, Monday - Brookfield, CT. Home

It's great to be home. Spent the day in meetings out in Pittsburg. Turned it. Flew out and back today. Too much US Scare can be a bad thing. At least my head is on straight, no invasions from Nam today. My wife set up our new bank accounts. Uneventful, which is good. She tells me our codes are still the same. The same is interesting. Guess I've thoroughly indoctrinated the family. The codes relate to things in Nam. Then I remember when Gloria and I got married. She wanted a poodle. We ended up with three. *We named them Co Bi Than Tan, Khe Sahn and Cam Lo.* We called them Cobi, Kasi and Cami. My wife is the best.

15 January, Friday - Somers, NY. Pepsi Headquarters

Long, but good week. Been able to live in the present most of the time. Haven't thought about Greek too much. Heavy travel schedule on the horizon. Don't look forward to it, but I have a great job. Do what you have to do. First time this year, I'm starting to feel run down. I feel the deterioration, physically and mentally. New projects with the usual 'have it done yesterday' expectations. PepsiCo is perfect for me. A travel week is just another patrol. I know how to suck it up and get it done. *The Marine Corps taught me to make commitments and deliver on your commitment. Take that hill. Simple.* The hills are different in Corporate America. Only your career might die here. I try to keep my reservoir of strength hidden in my bad place, until it's needed. I know I can do anything, I already have. Time to get home.

16 January, Saturday - Brookfield, CT. - Home

Easy weekend, if I hadn't received the card I got from the best boss I've ever had. Charlie Cotton. He was a weird dude, way ahead of his time. He's dying of cancer. We talk once a week. He's so organized; he has a list. Only positive people are allowed to talk with him. A fun guy in his late forties, divorced, raising his two kids. He was VP of Logistics at Frito Lay when I was there.

His card is touching and heartfelt. He told me goodbye and wished me a good life. First it's Greek, now Charlie. Greek and I went through a real war, Charlie and I the corporate wars. There's a bond in both, different, but it's there. He's one of a kind. He was a great manufacturing guy. Came to Frito from Proctor & Gamble. People thought he was 'out there', weird, flaky, even a flamer. He was, but what a great guy and future thinker. He and I became close.

It didn't start out that way. He was promoted to Vice President of Logistics right after I moved to Frito headquarters, in Dallas.

He immediately chose me to be his 'assistant'. That meant his bag carrier. When he traveled, I'd prepare his talks, speeches, make his travel and meeting arrangements, and do his analysis. I wasn't looking forward to it. My wife was pregnant with our last child, due the next month. Charlie was planning a big kick off meeting in Lake Tahoe the very same week my wife was due. He wanted me to speak at the meeting and handle all the details.

I told him I'd love to set everything up and prepare his presentations, but I couldn't be there. We had a baby coming. "Well, you're not one of those hand holders are you?", he asked, laughing. I confirmed that I indeed, was, one of those 'hand holders'. He laughed again, stood up, and said, "Just work it out". There wasn't any working it out; I'd be with my wife.

Every week for three weeks he'd stick his head in my office and ask, "Kug, you got it worked out yet?" I'd give him a quick review of the details of what I'd set up for him. He'd laugh, and always say the same thing. "Remember now, work it out". It was disturbing. My wife and I talked it over. I was going to be with her. If he fired me, he fired me. I'd be there for the birth of our daughter.

A week before the meeting, Charlie walked into my office, it was about noon. He had a big smile as he sat all six foot six of him into a chair, put his feet up on my desk and asked, "Well, did you get it all worked out Kug? You going to be there next week?" Half angry, and more than a little nervous, I stood my ground. "No Charlie. I told you. My daughter is being born next Tuesday, the first day of your meeting. If you have to fire me for not being there, fire me."

He burst out laughing, sat up, and slapped his hand on my desk as he said, "Kug, I knew I liked you. I love a man with conviction. I wish you and the wife the best. See you next Friday". He got up, still laughing to himself as he left my office. We became great friends. He was the real deal. He had my back. My two years with him were some of the best of my career. I went on to Pepsi; he left to start his own company. I'm going to miss talking with him. Of all the people I've worked with, he taught me more than anyone. Now, he too will be gone soon. Sometimes, life sucks.

18 January, Monday - Somers, NY. Pepsi Headquarters

I'm in a tough spot heading into this week. Been sleeping only four or five hours a night. Not good. Anxiety's knocking on my door like a Kirby vacuum cleaner salesman. I'm working on digging us out of a financial mess. We had a side business that failed. Started it a couple moves ago in Pennsylvania. Now I have lots of work to do in the evening when I get home.

It's morning, but still dark. I'm fighting my own darkness. It happens often, but I rarely know when. I'm packed, leaving this afternoon for a week on the road. When I prepare for these trips, *I always over prepare. Detailed travel plans for every minute of every day. I psych up for another patrol,* corporate style. Greek once looked at my Day Planner, and told me he hoped when the Martian's land, they didn't find me first and think everyone was like me. I took it as a compliment.

I got out of my car in a heavy fog that draped over the countryside. I can barely see our building. I grab my bag and start walking when I hear the whomp, whomp, whomp of chopper blades, breaking the wet morning silence somewhere in the gray mist above. *My first thought now, and always, 'ah, they're coming to get us out'. A Technicolor burst of yesteryear floods my mind, as adrenaline warmed my body with a gentle flow of energy. I could've been in Phu Bai, Dong Ha, Con Thein or the Rockpile.* I stepped into our beautiful lobby at Pepsi, and the chopper faded away. I've got a meeting in thirty minutes. A couple of coworkers step in the elevator with me and *help shake the jungle canopy from my morning.*

I'm rescued from myself.

20 January, Wednesday - Birmingham, AL. Airport

Just off the plane in Birmingham. Couple days work with a local Pepsi bottler. Meeting my boss here. Checked my voicemail, he's late. Plane delayed out of Atlanta. No problem. I love airport layovers. I love people watching. Chicago O'Hare is the best. Today, it's Birmingham International. Why does everyone have an international airport when they have no international flights?

I walked to the end of the concourse, to the gate where my boss will be landing. I sat down, did a little people watching, and dozed off. When I woke up, I finished the book I was reading. When I read, I'm disconnected from the world around me. I was zoned out, but reality came roaring back in the unmistakable roar of a plane blasting past us. *I'd know that sound anywhere.* An F-4 Phantom streaked by the end of our concourse as it landed in Birmingham.

Adrenaline shot through my body. The F-4 was a beautiful thing in Nam. They're the game changers in many a ground battle. I got up, quickly walking across the concourse, following the plane as it taxied to the other side of the airport. Looking out at the Phantom, I could see that one half of the airport was nothing but camouflage planes and choppers. I see a CH-53, several F-4's and my favorite, the workhorse, a C-130. I'm enjoying a reunion in my mind.

I walk back to my seat, heart pounding, sweating adrenaline as it fuels my emotions. I pick up my book off the floor, where I dropped it, and sit down. I'm no longer in Birmingham. *I'm twenty-five years away in Dong Ha. It's a hot summer day in 1966.*

We've been here long enough to melt. It's hot as an iron skillet on a wood fire. Crud and I've been hanging out here since 0700. It's late afternoon. We're still trying to hitch a ride out to Con Thien. The Dong Ha airstrip where we sit is 1,800 feet of steel matting the Seabee's laid down to make an instant airport. There's no control tower; just a ten by ten wooden shed made out of old pallets.

We've been watching choppers and C-130's come and go all day. I've also had to listen to Crud's ramblings on Plato and Aristotle. Worse, his incessant chatter about the time machine he's gonna' build. I told him to build that bitch right now, and spin us the hell out of here. Our Con Thein supply chopper is MIA, and I'm about to die listening to him.

A short walk from the airstrip is an Air Force radar compound. They have a damned kingdom in there. Their little world's surrounded by thirty feet of laced concertina wire, cement M-60 machine gun bunkers every thirty feet, no tents for them, they live in little house trailers with friggin' air conditioning. And they still whine. What tales they'll tell. In addition to their fortifications, they're protected by a couple of company's of Marines. Tough duty.

A couple months ago, when I was here with Marine Force Recon, we came off a ten day patrol in the mountains near Laos. We had a first light extraction and landed here at Dong Ha about 0600. The Recon commander told the seven of us he'd arranged for breakfast at the Flyboy chow hall. Chow hall? We'd been eating C-rats for months. The seven of us, still dressed in our grungy tiger stripes, faces painted, with ten days of sweat and dirt layering our body's, showed up for a hot breakfast.

The joke was on us; they refused to serve us, we're too 'dirty' to eat there. Pussy bastards! We didn't take the news too kindly. The Air Force MP's showed up just as we're about to level the place and everyone in it. He escorted us out of the compound. Walked us right by their damned swimming pool. There's something seriously wrong with this war. We're five miles south of the North Vietnamese border. Marines are dying by the truckload, and these candy asses get a swimming pool, air-conditioning and hot food? Life's not fair; then you come to Nam and live with this shit.

I laid back on my pack to catch some Z's. An F-4 Phantom woke me up. He was circling our little airstrip. About that time, several Flyboy's showed up. We rarely saw them outside their Princess Palace. What the hell did they want?

An Air Force Captain appeared next to me. He smiled, so I stood up and asked him what was up? Seems the F-4 was up North, above the DMZ, near Vihn, on a bombing mission, and took a hit from a missile. He couldn't make it back to Da Nang, so he was gonna' try and land it here.

As we talked, the jet made another pass. He flew by us, turned, and headed out east to the South China Sea. I figured common sense got the better of him, and he'd ditch it in the ocean. The Captain said no; he was dumping ordinance and was coming back here to land.

When Crud heard that, he burst into a loud laugh and said, "Kug, these guys are smokin' some of that Thai shit". I thought it sounded crazy, but then what did I know about landing a Phantom? The Phantom Show turned out to be the highlight of our day, albeit a brief highlight. One saving grace, for the pilot, was beyond the end of the runway, lay a few miles of dried up rice paddies. At least it was all flat, he could shoot across the paddies like a saucer when he landed.

Crud and I and about a dozen Flyboy's stood in a long line about fifty feet away from the steel matted runway. The F-4 came in about twenty feet off the ground and went by us in a blur. Boom! He was by us in a blink. Shot back up in the sky, made a hard left and another, heading east again towards the sea. The Captain said it was a dry run. I said, "His landing's going to be pretty dry too, Sir". He didn't seem to get my humor.

Coming in again from the sea, he headed in for a real crash landing. I was half deaf after the last pass, so I plugged my ears for the second one. Here he comes. When he landed that big boy it all happened in seconds. One loud boom, chute out when he hit the ground, with lots of metal noises. He went by us in a streak of camouflage that looked like one elongated jet. At the end of the runway was a five foot wall of dirt, leftover from grading the runway when they built it last year. The wall of dirt took off the landing gear and the plane shot across the old rice paddies, leaving a trail of dust in its wake a hundred feet high.

The Phantom skipped across the ground like a stone I used to love throwing across the Tuscarawas River as a kid. The jet came to rest, barely within sight of us. The Marines assigned to secure a perimeter around the plane were on their way. The pilot popped out, uninjured. I was damned impressed.

Crud and I still didn't have a ride to Con Thein, but the Flyboy's did have a new story to tell. I was shaken back to reality when someone touched my shoulder. *The flood waters of Nam receded.* My boss arrived and touched my shoulder. As we walked to baggage claim he said, "You were out there when I walked up Ed. Are you okay?" I took a deep breath, "I'm fine Steve, just a little tired". He wouldn't understand.

21 January, Thursday - Birmingham, AL. Wynfrey Hotel

Done with my work here. Just finished lunch with everyone. Going over what we'd learned. We ate in a bar with a TV blaring over us. We couldn't help but hear the rerun of the Inauguration of our 42nd President, William Jefferson Clinton. From Governor of Arkansas to President. Could it get any worse? I laughed to myself thinking of Ross Perot saying he'd run a company bigger than Arkansas. But there was no denying it, the liberals of the 60's had indeed won. Sad. We now had, as WFAN's Don Imus said, "President Bubba".

As the TV blared my *mind was in a tussle with the demons inside. It's infuriating; I can't listen. His liberal policies make me sick. Slick Willy will say and do anything to get elected, to gain more power. Gays in the military's one. This draft dodger doesn't have a clue what he's doing. Gays in the military are not a mission critical issue, it's a social issue.*

My lunch is ruined when I hear Slick Willy. I try to listen, to stay engaged in the conversation at the table, *but my mind's trying to sneak off to my bad place. I feel hapless and helpless at the same time. I can't believe where our country's headed. It hurts. I get angry. I see Marines zipped up in body bags, those who lost limbs and the cripples. For what? To elect this asswipe? I don't think so.*

I hear the President of the Pepsi franchise ask me, "What did you think of our operations?" Reality bites. "I'm impressed". And I was impressed. It was an outstanding operation. I engaged in the conversation at the table as best I could, *but my mind was ten-thousand miles away. I hoped the red rage I felt wasn't visible to those at the table. The background music of the Clinton Inauguration drove me further where I didn't want to go. An empty suit, with an Oxford education, was sending me there.*

Our lunch ended with the usual pleasantries. I grabbed a cab to the airport. It'd been a long day, but at least I'm heading home. Another corporate patrol down.

23 January, Saturday - New Canaan, CT. My Boss' Ho*me*

Weekends are always a welcome relief. Been in Birmingham, an unscheduled stop in Atlanta on Friday, then home Friday night. Gloria and I try and do something on Friday nights, but I got home too late last night. Spending time with her is my therapy. Instead of our time, tonight we had dinner with my co-workers at my boss' house. He had a buffet dinner party.

I hate crowds. We didn't want to go. When the corporate types get together with their spouses, there's too many 'who can piss highest contests'. People jockeying for position, it's disgusting. I've never been politically correct. Get togethers like this can go nowhere but down for me.

We were surprised; the evening wasn't bad. My co-workers and my boss are nice people. There were a few people engaged in a pissing contest, but not too many. And since it's Pepsi, we had to play some games for 'team building'. The game was to tell something that no one in the room knew about you. That's easy enough.

It's fun to shock people, especially corporate and college types. In Nam, we called it 'blowing minds'. When it's my turn I say, *"In 1973, I tried to enlist in the Israeli Army but was rejected"*. It was during the 1973 Arab and Israeli War. I love the Israelis and their fighting spirit. That shocked more than a few, who didn't know my background. I didn't have the luxury of the college thing; I'd made it to Director at Pepsi with no college degree and was proud of it.

My boss comes over while we're cleaning up and wants details. "How and why did you try to enlist? Why would they reject you?"

Why? It was simple. I'm not Jewish. I told him about my time in the Marines and Vietnam. He proceeds to tell me about his time at college, how he got deferments during Vietnam. *Why the hell tell me this? Get a clue. The inmates are running the asylum.*

I was seriously conflicted talking to him. I controlled myself, but I wanted to rip his face off. I feel bad. I like the guy. He's a decent human being. He seems to be a good boss. It bothered me for a fleeting moment. When Gloria and I got to the car, I let it go. Everything's better when I'm with her. I get my 'piss off' out, and we enjoy a pleasant ride for the hour drive home. She's my safe place. The storms of the night are behind me. All is good.

24 January, Sunday - Brookfield, CT. - Home

Started out a relaxing day. It's ending a tough one. Came home from church with lots of work to do. Tonight's problem started back in Pennsylvania, two moves and a few years ago. I knew I was on Frito's shit list. I wouldn't play the political game that took over the company in the late eighties. My boss at the time, Charlie, was let go. He called and told me I was on the list, too. In fact, his exact words were, "Kug, they fired me, your air cover's gone. Get ready". So I did.

I convinced my wife to roll our life savings into a chain of weight loss centers. We liked to help people and loved where we lived, so when the hammer came down, after 13 stellar years, we wouldn't have to move again. I researched the opportunity backwards and forwards. Talked to franchisees, ran the numbers and took the leap. And a fateful leap it was.

Our first center was a success. Then I bought another, in a town thirty miles away, that was run into the ground. Turning it around, proved to be tough. Some friendlies in Frito headquarters gave me the date of my impending demise. That prompted me to push too fast, and open a third center, sixty-five miles away. That's why I'm working late tonight.

Those were tough times. I don't know how we did it. I was working full time for Frito Lay, traveling around the northeastern states every week. I was in my sixth year serving as a Lay Minister in our church, and trying to manage three weight loss centers. I got fired, along with a couple thousand others, on what we called Black Monday. The very next week, I got a call from a former Frito VP, who was now at Pepsi, our sister company. He invited me to come over to Pepsi. I took the job, and we moved to Baltimore. Two years later, my weekends are still taken up managing the debt of my venture.

I always wondered if I could roll the dice, lose it all, and still laugh? I can still laugh; my wife can't. She didn't find losing our life savings, plus credit card debt, funny. My work is calling former members and asking them to trust me; I'll give them a refund, sometime soon. Every single member, over a 100 who were owed a refund, trusted me to pay them. I'm working on it every week, thankful to have landed another good job.

This year we have to skimp on everything, to get out of debt. Not to worry. *I learned in Vietnam; I can do anything.* Its only money; we'll just have to make more. *It's time; I suck it up.*

29 January, Friday - Brookfield, CT. Home

Up early, big meeting at work. It's still dark. Dawn struggled through the morning overcast, as I got in the car. The trees shielded my view, but *the gray mist sent me off to Nam. I bounced between my Connecticut home and the DMZ It was an eerie morning, we were sneaking up Dong Ha mountain for an early morning raid.*

A neighbor honked and waved, bringing me back to the world. Let it go Ed. Let it go.

30 January, Saturday - Brookfield, CT. Home

It's Saturday. The girls are out shopping. Football's over. I'm looking for something to watch on TV. I keep changing channels.

I see a PBS special on the 1968 Tet Offensive in Vietnam. I remember it well.

I click to the PBS program and settle in to see how they cover it. They paint the story with a broad brush, and yet try to cover Tet across the whole country. As I begin watching, *I'm back at Camp Carroll, the DMZ. It's 1968. We're cowering deep inside the bunker we just built. Rockets stream down, like a heavy monsoon rain. Camp Carroll is a Marine artillery base. The NVA hit us two or three times a day, dropping over a hundred rounds at a time.*

The explosions were deafening. The ground shook; dirt covered us, falling from our sandbagged ceiling. When the barrage ended, we crawled above ground like shaken moles. We find our hooch destroyed. The silence is eerie. The dead can't speak; the wounded begin to scream and the living shout Corpsman up! If you're still standing, it's a good day. We'd soon find out; this barrage was the start of what would become known as, the Tet Offensive. It was the ugliest of times. Thousands killed and wounded on both sides to the south of here, where we used to work, near Hue, the old Imperial Capital. The North Vietnamese wreaked death and destruction on the inhabitant's of the city. Summarily killing over one thousand civilians. Their crime? Supporting the fight for democracy in South Vietnam. It would take elements of the 5th Marines twenty days of close, house-to-house fighting, to retake the Citadel that was once the capital city.

We'd soon learn the North Vietnamese had infiltrated over two-thousand troops into Hue. Most of them came through the Co Bi Than Tan Valley, where my team, the Rogues, wreaked havoc for the past six months. The five of us lived there twenty-four, seven. As time went by, we'd encounter more and more enemy troops. In the beginning, we'd see ten to fifteen troops, and then thirty or forty at a time. Just before we moved up here to the DMZ, we encountered over a 150 North Vietnamese moving south toward Hue. They had giant packs, so heavy they were bent over, forward, almost falling face first. We ran into them in the middle of the afternoon.

Hidden 400 meters away, outmanned; I called for artillery fire. We'd fire our sniper rifles only when the Arty was in the air. We soon heard the faint boom, as our artillery fired. We fired in unison. The NVA column stretching out before us was instantly in chaos. Soldier's were disappearing, falling, running and screaming. We dropped a few with our rifles. They were scattered, running back and forth between the tree lines. It was absolutely, beautiful. As the artillery rained down its destruction, I was on the radio with the Colonel. He was scrambling a quick reaction force of Marines to fly to the scene and engage what was left of the enemy force. Choppers were soon on the scene, unloading a hundred Marines, who were now in hot pursuit of the fleeing NVA. The spotter plane on scene reported a body count of at least thirty-five enemy dead. We'd later receive the Vietnamese Cross of Gallantry for our actions. That and fifty cents will get us a beer. Who cares?

The reality of Tet, and life at Camp Carroll, was easy to grasp. As long as we sit here, we'll be playing Russian Roulette with the big NVA guns. Night time, day time, anytime, we had incoming rounds, lots of them. Sleep was only for the whacked out. We decided to spend more time in the bush.

The girls walked in from shopping and brought me home.

"Kill them all, let God sortem' out"
Found on a Zippo lighter from the War

FEBRUARY

2 February, Tuesday - Newburg, NY. on the way to Pittsburg

Early morning flight. Going out and back today. Tired. Restless night. Cortney is still struggling with our latest move. We've been cruel and unusual to her. She's in her Sophomore year, and her third high school. Not by our choice, rather, the chance of corporate life. My plans to keep her in Pennsylvania to graduate went up in the smoke of our weight loss venture. I have to laugh, I lost everything but weight. Time for my plane, later.

3 February, Wednesday - Somers, NY. Pepsi

I'm in for an early meeting today. The big guys want to talk about their change debacle. It's not raining today, but it's minus six degrees. Be glad when spring gets here. Be glad when I'm doing less traveling, too. My bonus check was on my desk this morning. That's good. Most of it's going to the money we owe on my failed business. I'll have everyone half paid with this one. Getting there.

4 February, Thursday - Merritt Parkway, near NYC

Time's flying by, it's already February. The turmoil in my head remains. Maybe it's the Holidays that dredged up the depths of my soul? *There were no holidays in Nam. Just the Marine Corps Birthday. We got a piece of cake and two beers.*

I had meetings today in New Jersey with UPS. My mind wandered as I drove home. I wanted to see the kids before they went to bed. Traffic was light. I was happy to find a new radio station that plays Sixty's music. I love the music and the melancholy of the past. 'Silence is Golden' came on. The Four Seasons. As Yogi Berra said, 'it's de je vu all over again'.

As I drove the Merritt Parkway, *my mind was walking point in Nam. When I walked point, my mind played that song over and over. I can still hear 'silence is golden, but my eyes can see' with each and every step. It was weird. It played a continuous loop, softening the high pucker factor, walking point carried. Your nerves wound tight; your ears tuned like a grand piano, to the slightest noise in the night. Your breathing's shallow, slow, your heart raced. Your nose sensitive to the slightest odd smell. Feelings? If we had any, buried deep, a Cat dozer couldn't dig deep enough to find them. Feelings buried so deep we wouldn't find them for years, maybe never. An experience indelibly burned in our young minds.*

When I pulled in the driveway, I realized I didn't remember the last hour of my trip. Scary. I pulled myself out of the car; it was cold outside and I shivered my way back into life at home. Everyone's asleep. Hopefully, I will be soon.

8 February, Monday - Brookfield, CT. Home

Great day today! Came home early for my youngest daughter's eighth birthday. Whitney's pumped about her party. That's great, except Gloria had to fly to Ohio Saturday. Her Mother had a heart attack. She'd planned the party a few weeks ago. I had seven little girls, between the age of six and eight, coming soon. The show must go on. At least Cort was here to help. I was hoping it wouldn't be too bad.

Cort decorated the house last night. Whit didn't want to open her presents without talking to her Mom first. We called, and she was happy. When the Mothers dropped off their kids, they all gave me an attaboy for bravely going forward without my wife. I couldn't disappoint my beautiful little daughter. We took the kids to a place called Sportland America. They skated, rode bumper cars and played games.

The decibel level was soon rivaling Yankee stadium. Man was it loud. They were cute little kids, but they never sat down or quit talking. It was fun, for a few minutes, *but the noise triggered a mental avalanche. I was soon careening into my bad place. I began barking orders at Cortney, telling her to take charge, control the chaos and stop the noise. I tried not to be mean, I'm learning my triggers but I want there yet. In the Corps we called the chaos, grab ass. I was never good at grab ass.*

I needed control and order. The little girls were great kids, *but the noise and constant activity unnerved me.* Cortney knew me well, and quickly told me to get a grip. I stepped outside for a little space. The cold winter air shocked my system. It sounds stupid, but *to me, chaos is a stateside ambush. My world goes to hell in a heartbeat. I get a shot of adrenaline that propels me back to Nam. It's often overwhelming, like an ambush, the fear, adrenaline, and rage, spin my life out of control, I have to have control. Through my eyes the only option is to attack.* Like Mencius, an old Chinese dude I love, said many centuries ago, *"Go to the heart of danger, for it is there you shall find safety".*

One of my 'hearts of danger' is being is being surrounded by chaos. The party ended, the kids were happy, and we headed home. Whitney went to bed a happy girl. Cortney had homework; I had a long night ahead. I laid down in Brookfield but *was soon in Santo Domingo; it was May, 1965. It's suffocating in here! Ten of us crammed in an armored Amtrak, heading who knows where? We've just been picked up, rescued from heavy automatic weapons fire that had our platoon pinned down in an open field. We're in the middle of a firefight to take back the radio station. I'm part of India Company, Third Battalion, Sixth Marines. We landed here two days ago, after a leftist uprising toppled the government.*

As we rumble somewhere, bullet's ping off our Amtrak. The rattle of a machine gun is getting closer. Without warning, we jerk to a stop, the iron coffin we're riding in spins around, dropping the exit gate. It's time to earn our title as United States Marines. Our Platoon Sergeant is screaming, "Get out! Get out! *We run into the burning sun, dirty streets, and a wall of machine gun fire. Bullets rake the ground around our feet as we sprint for cover. Survival leaves no room for fear, only action.*

As the machine gun chattered above us, I followed another Marine through a plate glass window. Inside, a family of four huddled in the corner. We try hand signals to let them know we're friendlies. Our Squad Leader is outside yelling commands, organizing us for movement to the radio station a block away. We step back through the window onto the sidewalk, as shell casings rain down from the machine gun above us.

We're in a bad, filthy, poor part of Santo Domingo. We start advancing around a nearby corner. A rebel appears on a rooftop, above and across the street from me. I blast away with my M-14. He disappears, falling backwards, his rifle crashing to the sidewalk. I probably killed my first person. Cool.

At the corner, we take a left. Two blocks ahead is our objective, the radio station. Our Fire Team splits. My partner and I start up the near side of the street. Two other Marines cross to the other side along a wooden wall. They were a few feet apart, inching their way towards the radio station. We'd cover each other as we advanced. We didn't know where the machine gun was now, but we knew it couldn't be far.

It suddenly came to life, etching holes down the wall where our two fellow Marines stood exposed. The gun was now down the street, about thirty feet in front, still on the rooftop above us. We couldn't get a shot from our angle. My Squad Leader jumped in the street, blazing up at the machine gunner. My partner and I followed him into the street, blazing away to provide cover for our teammates. Lead filled the air in both directions.

In the chaos, the machine gun again walked down the wall, stitching the life out of one Marine, and mortally wounding the other. One took two rounds in the throat; the other took two in the chest. Life as we knew it died a quick death right along with our fellow Marine. The first Marine hit, lay on his back, gurgling, blood spewing from his mouth, drowning in his own blood. The second, a short Danny DeVito like character from upstate New York, was dead. When the two bullets slammed into his chest, it stood him up against the wall like he was standing at attention. As he died, he slid down the wall where he now sat, eyes wide open, an almost sly smile on his face, blood dripping from his lips.

My squad leader kept firing, another ran and dragged the wounded Marine to cover. My partner and I grabbed the dead Marine. We picked him up, one on each arm, and started across the street. Easy targets, the *machine gunner drew a bead on us. With another burst coming our way, life shifted into slow motion. The smells the sounds, the heat, grenades exploding, all maddening to the mind and deadly to the soul, were all slowed to a crawl. We were both wounded, his were life threatening. I helped him to safety while our Squad Leader returned for our brother's body.*

The fight for the radio station heated up, as my partner lay dying. He was bleeding out. The flip side of his elbow was nothing but raw meat. The machine gun rounds blew a massive hole in his arm, nearly cutting it in two. I tried a Battle Bandage, but the flesh and blood swallowed it up, as it did my hand disappeared in blood. If I didn't do something, he was going to die. I took a bandolier of M-79 ammo from around his neck, removed the ammo and used the web material as a tourniquet. I wrapped it around his upper arm, took my K-bar, stuck it through the webbing and twisted it tight The bleeding stopped.

The cries for Corpsman up rose above the chaos. Before the firefight was over, we'd lose four dead and thirty-six wounded. Our evacuation came by the same Amtrak's that brought us to battle. The wounded and dead were gathered at the Polo Grounds and eventually airlifted to the USS Wasp. A day we'd all like to forget, but will always remember.

11 February, Thursday - White Plains, NY. Airport

Cold, gray, February day. I stood in the arrival's area of Westchester County Airport in White Plains, waiting for Gloria to return from her Ohio trip. The airport building still surprises me. Westchester County is the land of milk and money, home to a large number of 'high rolling' corporate executives. The airport looks like it's in a Third World country. *It reminds me of the old French hanger in Phu Bai. Go figure?*

I'm not feeling well today. Fighting depression. Just had a meeting with my boss about one of my projects. He's a good guy, but a politician. That's the price of entry to make VP at PepsiCo. Tell 'em what they wanna' hear. He loves my work. No issue there. But he says he has to 'massage' my presentation a bit before I present it to SET. The corporate world loves acronyms. SET stands for Senior Executive Team. The President and his merry direct reports.

I'm no politician. *I know first hand what happens when you're not straight with people. I learned it in Nam. They die.* Here? Careers die, ruin people and negatively impact their families. *It's all bullshit. Say what you mean, mean what you say, do what you say you'll do and stand accountable.* But he doesn't want me to do that. He wants to run a 'cleansing' operation. He doesn't want me to come off too strong with the brass. *It's just the way it is, but it sucks, so deal with it. I have a hard time 'dealing with it'. I've always struggled with the politics of it all.*

My wife arrives and makes it all better. We're together again, where we belong. Her Mother is not doing well. She's stable for now, but she feels that she might not be around much longer. The possibility of another funeral so soon after my friends puts a dark cloud on our ride home. *I don't do well with funerals.*

We arrive home and head straight to bed. My wife's out like a light. *I'm not. I'm in Bryan, Ohio. Second funeral we've done in the last three months. I'm home from Nam and about to get out of the Corps. My last duty station will be here at the Reserve Center in Fort Wayne, Indiana. My boss, the Major in charge, couldn't convince me to reenlist, so my duties are leading the firing squad for military funerals and cleaning the building. The Reserve Staff, which I'm part of, and the Marine Reservists conduct all Marine funerals within a one hundred mile radius of Fort Wayne.*

Today's a tough one. The second son, of one family, has died in Nam in the last two months. The Major does all notifications to the families, face-to-face. He won't delegate his responsibility to anyone. I admire him for that. But I can see the toll it takes on him. He drinks a lot. He's aloof, distant, angry, a lot like me. When the Major went to notify the family this time, he found only the Mother home. Turns out, after the last son died, the Father took the $10,000 insurance money and split town. Hard to see the good in people when assholes like him take center stage. I've found military funerals are the high, and the low of war. It's pretty low here today.

My firing squad always stands off in the distance. We want to be in view, but not close. It gave me a unique vantage point to watch the misery and the charades. At every funeral, I stand at attention, watching the procession arrive, the Honor Guard lift the casket from the hearse and deliver it graveside. Then the services start. It's a tough, unnerving experience for me.

Every funeral I've attended I see the ashen face of a Marine, I'd once zipped into a body bag back in Nam. Zip 'em up and send 'em home. It became a mind game. We didn't know it at the time, but we compartmentalized tragedy into neat boxes so it wouldn't mess with our young minds. Standing off, watching all these ceremonies, opened up those old compartments. What came out, crashed down on me like an old, wet, smelly blanket, tossed over my head and tied tight. It would take more than a few beers to heal these scars. Scars that we scratched open four times a week for four months. Each new funeral would rip that scab off, leaving new, bleeding emotions, emotions that dripped over my day like a leaky faucet that keeps you up all night.

The most disturbing part of the funeral, the part that messed with my mind the most, was watching people in attendance. In the front row sat the family. Still in shock, mourning the loss of a loved one, a loss they'd never understand. Shaken to the core, they're unconsolable in their grief. They are comforted by people in the second row, and a few in the third row, people close to the family. They're people who obviously care, and were there out of love and respect for the family. After four funerals a week, I could see that every funeral was the same.

My anger erupted beyond the third row, and burned brighter the further back in the pack I watched. In this group, is the 'make an appearance' crowd. They were there for show, nothing more. They always mouthed small talk, a little laughing, and at the back of the gathering came the 'grabassing' crowd. It turned my stomach. It fueled my new found rage at a society I no longer understood, nor cared to live in.

It was our turn. Three volleys of seven. Twenty one gun salute. When our guns went silent, off in the distance, unseen, came the shattering sound of taps. The true mourners were now in tears, shoulders shaking, grasping to hold one another. The heavy sadness brought a midnight darkness over the crowd that permeated all but the assholes in the back. That same sadness shot holes in my heart, a heart I didn't know I had, and didn't want anymore. By my fifteenth funeral, I envisioned taking the back row, the grabassers, out, with a blast of my M-14, set on full auto. Thank God we only had blanks. Funerals would be a problem for me, for years, many years.

14 February, Sunday - Brookfield, CT. Home

Been busy. That's good. I'm blessed with a great family. I'm blessed with a wonderful wife. Today is Valentine's Day. Personally, I hate Valentines Day. It's just a day made up by the greeting card industry. Fortunately, my sweetheart feels the same way. We went to church and spent the day and evening together, which is perfect.

After a great day, I laid down to sleep. It wasn't long before *I was startled awake by the shrill cry of a rock ape and a Marine screaming for his life. Crutch and I both scurried to the sound of the screams. We were nine hundred meters up on a pitch black night. The Force Recon Marines with us were moving about. Gunfire erupted on the west end of the Rockpile. Chaos filled the air. When we moved about we had to be careful of falling off the ragged mountaintop we occupied.*

Confused, we took up defensive positions on the edge of the massive cliff we call home? It was difficult to assess what was happening. Could the gooks be scaling our rock walls? We couldn't imagine. The shrieks continued, only now off in a distance, on a sister peak nearby. As suddenly as it started, the night quieted down. I crawled over to the Recon communications guy. Found out the Marine who'd screamed was attacked by a rock ape. He wasn't injured, just freaked out.

When I crawled back to our position, Crutch was already asleep. He didn't deal in chaos, he left that up to me. Order, just give me order.

18 February, Thursday - Brookfield, CT. Home

Took the day off for Gloria's birthday. She's always said that's the best present she could get. I'm a lucky man. We didn't do anything special, just be together. It's special because our life together was a long shot at best. We didn't know it at the time, but we both came from what they call today, 'dysfunctional homes'. The odds weren't in our favor, but we didn't know that.

We met through a girl I was dating before Nam. After two years over there I came home, didn't know anyone and then thought of Gloria. While finishing out my funeral duty in Fort Wayne, I wondered where she was? Wrote her a letter, we got together on a weekend and nine months later, we were married by a lady Justice of the Peace in Winchester, Virginia.

From our first date, we were soul mates. I took her to a car wash to spruce up my new 396 Chevy. I had no intention of settling down. My plans were to come home, party the summer away, and then head to Brussels. Some British Marines I worked with in Nam told me where I could find mercenary work in the Congo. It was through contacts at a specific bar in Brussels. I'm not sure I would have gone, but thought I would at the time? But when I felt what I did being with Gloria, something told me she was my only chance for a normal life. That has proven to be true.

We got a sitter tonight and went out to dinner. Just being together is all I need. She's a great listener. She's never been surprised by anything I shared. There were many times she should have run like a wild animal. She's endured several of my snipers coming and going, even one who stayed for three months our first year of marriage, another who came and left a stolen car at our house and one who wanted me to run drugs on the trucks I was dispatching. She endured my drinking until the birth of our son. That's when she'd had enough and delivered her ultimatum - her, or the drinking, choose. I made the right choice at the age of twenty-eight. I quit. Our life improved dramatically.

We had a great day today. I'm thankful to have her in my life.

21 February, Sunday - Brookfield, CT. Home

Sunday evening, good day at Church. It feels like we're settling in here, finally. I called Bobbie, Greek's wife. I try to check in regularly to see how she and the boys are doing. I can't imagine how she feels. She's left with two great young boys, all alone. She's struggling, but she's an amazing woman. Such a good person.

When I laid down, I was thinking about Greek. When I drive to work, I think about him, especially when I see signs for New York. What gets to me, is after all these years, we finally lived an hour apart, and now he's gone. Tonight, I'm in bed with the love of my life, and my ghosts. *It's 1967, my C-130 ride from Da Nang has just landed in Phu Bai. I pull my aching body up from the web seat and step off the plane. The noisy hour flight from Da Nang gave me a splitting headache. Twenty-four hours ago I was drinking myself sick in Hong Kong. Five days of R & R in an amazing city. All I saw of the city were the inside of bars and my hotel room. I was sick. Felt like I had the flu. I had the Grand Canyon of hangovers.*

Gear in hand, I stepped into the steamy afternoon of Vietnam. I needed to sleep this off. Walking through the rows of olive drab tents, I wondered where I'd be heading in the morning? As I reached my tent, Gunny Dubay yelled, "Kugler!" I dropped my bag on my old cot and went to meet him.

"I've got bad news Kug. Perl's dead". He could have just slammed me in the face with a rock. "Not Perl, Gunny", I pleaded. He confirmed the obvious. Gunny was a good man. He took it hard. Agony was etched on his face like a cheap mask. Perl was my second sniper partner, really nice kid. Didn't swear much, nor drink as the rest of us. He looked like a baby faced kid, but he was tough. When several of us decided to stay in Nam for another year, we convinced Perl to sign on with us. He did. Now this. It was his first patrol after a thirty-day leave home, to Algoma, Wisconsin. Now he's gone. I loved him as a brother.

All Gunny knew was he took an inbound mortar between the legs. "Kug, you need to go over to 3rd Med and officially identify the body." I didn't see that one coming. The news was bad enough, now go ID my dead friend. "I'll go now Gunny". I walked back to the air strip, thinking of all the patrols Perl, and I ran together. I thought of the time he and I hooked it out with eight gooks, and survived. My mind drifted to tripping the booby trap, the dud, and we survived. Now, he's dead. ID the body and back to life in Nam.

I found 3rd Med in an old French hangar. Wide open spaces in this ER, it was open air. I walked inside; bodies lay everywhere in various states of disrepair, like damaged cars in an old junkyard back home. Some were hooked up to lifelines, with tubes running in and out of every orifice, bandages in unimaginable places, making sounds you never want to hear. It was hot. Like sitting in a hot fondue pot. All the beer and liquor I'd downed in the past five days was dripping out of my body, spotting the concrete floor of the hangar. Apparently, I looked out of place, being one of the few standing in an upright position. A Corpsman made a beeline straight for me. I told him I was there to ID the body of Lance Corporal Steven O. Perlewitz. Before he could respond, an older, tired looking man came towards me. He carried himself as a man with some authority, seasoned. The eyes reveal the degree of death you've experienced, and this guy was at the top of the leader board. He asked me if I knew Perlewitz. I told him I knew him well; he'd been my sniper partner. He took me by the arm and pulled me aside.

Turns out he was the Battalion Surgeon. He shared the detail of the last night of Perl's life. He'd flown out on the Medivac chopper at 0300 when the call came in. When they picked him up, he said everything below the hips was blown off. Why's he telling me this? I ask, "Nothing?" And he affirms nothing, from the belly button down.

He told me, his, was an ugly business. As Perl's friend, he wanted me to know, he'd never had a patient with the will to live, like Perl. He'd lived for four hours, but his injuries were massive, and they couldn't stop the bleeding. He said he should have died instantly, or within minutes. "I don't know how he lived for four hours?" The man was obviously bothered by what he'd seen.

He hung his head, as we stood in silence. I didn't know what to say. He turned and said, "I'll get the Corpsman to take you to the body. The Doc looked like he needed to talk, the weight of the scars he carried will bury him one day. As he walked away, I heard him mumbling, "We did all we could". I knew they did. They were amazing people, working in our medical centers under less than Third World conditions. They get a lifetime of experience in a few months over here.

The Corpsman I originally met joined me, soon after the Surgeon disappeared. We left the back of the hanger and walked through a couple of tents. We came to a row of green metal boxes. They appeared to be about ten-feet by ten-feet square and about eight feet high. They reminded me of shipping containers we knew as Conex boxes.

The Corpsman walked silently in front of me. Our walkway is a row of wooden pallets, laid out between long rows of these green boxes. Each box has a big handle that lifts up and over, similar to a commercial freezer. Then I realized; they are freezers, or coolers at least. The bodies were held in these containers until the C-130 body plane came by to pick up the next load of misery and deliver them to the embalming station somewhere here in Vietnam.

Perl was in the last box on the left. My dark humor broke the silence of a bad morning. I say to the Corpsman, "It must have been a bad night here at 3rd Med, if my man's in the last cooler". With nothing more than a bad look, he turns and opens the big metal door.

The inside looked like a meat locker to me. The Corpsman stepped in first. I followed. The only body inside was my friend, Perl, or what was left of him. The pieces of my young friend lay on a gurney. His upper body was there, clean, a sick gray color, plastic like. He was flat on his back. The bottom part of his torso looked like the ragged edge of dry, raw meat. Most of one leg was next to him, and part of the other. His left arm unattached, was neatly laid next to him.

The Corpsman looked at a tag tied to his finger, turned to me and asked, "Is this Steven O. Perlewitz?" I looked up, and said, "What's left of him". The Corpsman asked if I'd like a minute? I did. I wasn't sure what to do, but I wanted to be alone with my brother. As I stood in the coolness of the death locker, my sweaty jungle uniform made me chilly. At least that's what I hope it was? It was weird. I didn't like it. I didn't like knowing what they looked like after we zipped them into body bags.

I was determined not to feel anything, and it was now time to practice it. That's the way to survive Nam. When I became a sniper, I made the decision to have no feelings. Standing here, I was glad I did. I was an Atheist. Today, I knew why. It reinforced my belief in nothing meaningful. How would a loving, all knowing God, let this happen to a great young kid like Perl? My head was pounding. As I stared down at what was once my friend, my brother, I fought to control feelings I didn't want to have. Guilt. Anger. Rage. Sadness, overwhelming sadness, consumed me. I didn't like it. I stared at his face. I leaned closer. His baby face had wrinkles. His color was ashen, no longer tanned; he was old looking. His once sandy hair, now tinted with strands of gray. He looked like he was in his forties. My young friend had aged. His last four hours were hell, if there is one?

The Corpsman motioned it was time. I bid my brother farewell. The metal door clanked behind me, and he was gone. As we walked away, I looked at all those green boxes filled with bodies, and wondered why? I knew another load of tragedy was waiting for the ride home. Headed back to the world, to unsuspecting loved ones about to be changed forever. We walked back to the hangar. I thanked the Corpsman, who barely spoke. I saw the Battalion Surgeon standing nearby. I walked over, "Sir, what's with his face? He looks like he's aged twenty years. I swear his hair is gray." He looked up, "Sergeant, it happens sometimes." He turned; shoulders stooped, and walked away.

Death was Vietnam. McNamara and his Whiz Kids quantified our war. Body count. So the asshole could report progress to Congress. The enemy killed Perl. Perl and I killed them. All the while, McNamara and Johnson, sip wine and look concerned for their media appearances. It didn't seem to matter either way. Nothing made sense anymore. Nothing.

When I got back at the sniper area, it was nearly 1600 hours, time for the club to open. The 'club' was nothing more than a tent filled with fifty-five gallon drums of gook ice and Budweiser beer. My hangover now was lost in the misery of a long, hot afternoon, looking at a dead brother. Now it's time to bury my misery in the nightly chug-a-lug contest our Gunny required us to win. With each swig of beer, I tossed another layer of dirt on the feelings I was determined to bury. Another one, please ...

24 February, Wednesday - In the Air Over PA. US Scare

On my way to Pittsburgh for another meeting. In this part of the country, the only way to fly short distances is on a US Air

Commuter. We call it US Scare. We shake and shimmer all the way. I keep telling myself; these things are safe. I rationalize the pilots would have to be good to keep these contraptions in the air. *The shaking and noise remind me of flying in the old the UH-34 choppers we flew my first year in Nam.* We're about to land; it's been a good flight today. We're even on time. Looks like it'll be a good day.

26 February, Friday - Somers, NY. Pepsi

In the office early. It's 0600. Short night. Booked in meeting's all day. If I want to get actual work done, the time is now. Things are settling down at home. Cortney seems to have made a few friends. She's still having trouble connecting at church. Moving kids is so tough. Takes a year to get settled. Didn't help, that one year to the day from when we moved to Baltimore from Pennsylvania, we moved here. Seize the day anyway!

***

Home now. We had a terrorist attack today. Truck bomb at the World Trade Center in New York City. Reports say we're lucky. Right now they're reporting five dead, one missing and maybe a thousand injured. Lucky? *We don't have to worry, with Commander in Chief Bubba, in charge. I can't stand the guy. If his lips are moving, he's lying. And his wife, our First Lady, not worth the words. Pisses me off just thinking about it.*

28 February, Sunday - Brookfield, CT. Home

Church has been my peace. I've been losing lately. The whole terrorist attack and President Bubba wants to lob a few Tomahawks and scare the bad guys. I also read he wants to 'prosecute' them. Now that'll scare the shit out of a raghead. Last night was tough, but I've had worse. I'm always tired, run down and struggling.

As I sit here writing in the kitchen, family in bed, I can see the demise of America coming. Our morals are in the trash and being buried quickly. The military was destroyed by Jimmy Carter. Reagan brought it back and now Bubba the Draft Dodger is following in Carters footsteps. He'll almost surely allow gays in the military sometime soon. It's hard to imagine we elected another loser liberal. We're going down.

I know I have to get to bed. *But I'm soon in Lock Seventeen, sitting on the porch of our neighbor, Virgil Lindon. He was a truck driver who lived two doors down. Sitting with him was always a treat. He served on a submarine during World War II. Listening to his stories on Sunday mornings ignited the flame of my patriotism and desire to serve. One of Virgil's friends, another truck driver, Bob McMath, planted the seed that led me to the Marine Corps. He was a veteran of the Battle for Iwo Jima. He said very little but he didn't have to, even at my young age I knew.*

Before I knew it, the clock read 0100. I collapsed in bed.

"We the unwilling, led by the unqualified,
to kill the unfortunate,
for the ungrateful."

Found on a Zippo lighter from the war

MARCH

7 March, Sunday - Brookfield, CT. Home

Home from church, trying to relax. Been seriously stressed. It's many things. The debt I'm paying off, the adjustment of the family to our third home in three years and my heavy travel schedule. And *losing Greek*. Trouble connecting at church isn't helping either.

Charlie, my last Frito boss, told me I needed to handle stress better. *I told him I didn't have any stress. In my mind, I'd done Nam; I was a Marine, and I could do anything.* We lived in Pennsylvania, an hour from Penn State at the time. He paid to send me there for a stress test. He said they had the best one. I scored a 90% probability of having a major illness in the next year. *Yeah, right? Not me. Keep moving.* Then I thought about a little incident I had back in Pennsylvania at the same time. I was flying in from Philadelphia when I had chest pains. I landed and immediately called my wife. "Just got off the plane, I had chest pains, better come and get me". My wife wasn't happy with that call. She'd been telling me to slow down. After a quick trip to the emergency room I was told, "No heart attack, you have a stress problem. I decided to take a couple days off at home.

It was the end of basketball season, 1991; my son's senior year of high school. There were five more games left in the season. He was averaging twenty seven points a game and hoping to play D-II basketball in college. He and the coach were always at odds. Trevor owned most of the problem, he was immature with an attitude and not teachable. He was good because he dedicated himself to one sport and ate, slept and breathed basketball. The coach was a good young guy, but played small town politics which hurt the team and was about as mature as my son.

When I flew home it was a Wednesday. I took Thursday and Friday off. It was freezing outside, temperatures in the teens. Thursday evening my wife was out shopping and I was kicking back at home, T-shirt, Levi's, no shoes, reading a book. It was around 6 PM when I heard a knock at the door. As I walked into the kitchen I could see Chris, one of my son's teammates outside. I motioned him in.

"What's up?" I asked. It was about time for the kids to come home from practice. Chris looked at the floor, then said, "Mr. Kugler, here are Trevor's clothes. Coach asked me to bring them to you." My heart raced. "Where's Trevor?" Still looking at the floor he said, "We don't know? He was kicked off the team for swearing and took off." As he talked he reached out to hand me the pile of street clothes and shoes. When I saw the pile of clothes in his hands, I wasn't in Woolrich, Pennsylvania anymore, *I was in Vietnam in a hot musty tent packing up Perl's clothes and Greeks clothes and others to send home to their unsuspecting parents. Adrenaline replaced every ounce of blood in my body.*

I excused Chris and tossed a pair of shoes on with no socks and headed out the door T-shirt, and all. Outside I met my wife pulling in the driveway. As she opened the door, I said, "Get back in! Do you have the checkbook? You're going to have to bail me out! On the way to town, my rage rolled out like hot lava. "Take me to the Coach's house I'm kicking his ass!" My wife tried hard to change my mind. My life lens, distorted as a fun house mirror, drove my rage.

I wouldn't realize for sometime, what a blessing I was about to receive. I would later learn he and his wife intentionally left their home. No one was home, so we left to look for our son. We rode around for over an hour and couldn't locate him. We headed home, with me still on fire. Home, I called the Principal at his home. To my surprise he answered. I told him my issue and that we needed to meet in the morning. He abruptly told me he was busy. He had an inservice meeting at that time. I told him I would personally hold him accountable if something happened to my son. "Mr. Kugler, are you threatening me" I assured him it wasn't a threat it was a promise. "Sir, you have a choice. You can meet with me in your office, or you can deal with me in your meeting, but you will meet with me." He hung up. My wife drew the line on me going to his house and jack-slapping the shit out of his pompous ass.

My wife called Trev's friends to see if anyone had heard from him. It had been five hours and no one had seen or heard anything. The weather was getting colder and he was wearing his basketball uniform and no coat. We drove back in town to look for him. We didn't find him. Home again, we found him in his room. He'd been at the college playing basketball and chilling out. Someone gave him a ride home. He gave me the scoop from his end. He was wrong for what he did, telling the coach to 'F-off.' I told him so, and he knew it. Did it justify being kicked off the team? Maybe, if those are the rules. All I wanted was an explanation and equal treatment. We'd sat behind the bench during Tuesdays game when another player, an underclassmen, told the Coach that very thing to his face, during the game. Several parents were appalled he did nothing. At 1130 PM, I called the Principal back. He wasn't happy. Tough. I told him I wanted to confirm our meeting. He told me I was out of line. "The meeting?" He sighed and told me to be in his office at 0800.

After a sleepless night in Nam, it was time to head to the school. My wife insisted she go along. As I arrived at his office there stood a Police Officer. Ushered inside, I found only the Principal and the Athletic Director, no Coach. "What's up with the cop outside?" I asked. The Principal explained that I sounded quite 'unstable last night, and we thought it best. That went right up my ass, and I was sure nothing else would fit there right now. It was time to blow a few minds. "Sir, I am a Vietnam Vet and occasionally have bouts of red rage, but this is my first in awhile". He sat a little further back. I explained my position. "It's simple. My Son is wrong for cussing the coach. If that is his rules, my son will apologize. And all I ask is the rule is applied evenly". I explained what happened on Tuesday night, gave him the names of four other sets of parents who witnessed the outburst. "All I ask is if my Son is off the team for saying that in practice, the other boy should be off for doing it in a game, in public."

I knew their minds were made up. I already felt bad for my behavior. Some of my blood was returning, my flooding adrenaline receding. The two of them agreed to consider it over the weekend and get back to me on Monday. That was reasonable. Then the Principal said, "Mr. Kugler, we would like to ask you to attend no more games this year? We just think it would be best". I'd never missed one of my kids games, ever. When I was traveling, I would fly home for the night, on my own dime, to be there for every game. I wasn't missing one now, and I told him so.

The remainder of the year I showed up to support the team. And when I did, two Police Officers would meet me at the door. I'd go in and sit with the parents I'd been sitting with for the six years. The two cops would sit in the top row behind me. It took all five remaining games to settle me down. I shouldn't have acted that way, but seeing those clothes and telling me they didn't know where my son was shot me like a rocket to my bad place.

Thinking about those days, a mere two years ago, I was thankful I was a little better. My anger was better, maybe a little deeper beneath the surface. It wasn't a proud moment in my life, but the trip wires in my head are wired tight.

8 March, Monday - Somers, NY. Pepsi

In early again. Just checked my schedule. Meetings all day again today. Tomorrow, I head down to PepsiCo headquarters in Purchase, New York. Meetings all day to review the change project. My boss wants to know what's going on. Then I head to California on Wednesday. I have meetings on a new a project to better train warehouse workers in inventory management and route truck loading. Exciting shit, eh? What the heck, it pays well.

Just remembered, I have to teach a class in Valhalla, New York next week. The folks at Pepsi International invited me down to teach Stephen Covey's class on the Seven Habits of Highly Effective People. When I was at Frito, I became a trainer of the program. Taught it to four hundred truck drivers. Made an incredible difference in their lives and mine. I might be sitting in my office in Somers but I was suddenly in Utah. *I just love this place. Been coming here every six months for three years. Sundance Resort, Sundance, Utah, where Stephen Covey holds his seminars to teach his Seven Habits program. It's isolated, rustic and very special. Stephen told me that Robert Redford, who owns Sundance made an exception for him to hold his programs here. Apparently, he's not a very business friendly guy. We're always told if we see him here to leave him alone. I've seen him once. He's much smaller, and not as nice looking as I expected.*

I'm here for an advanced seminar on leadership. Yesterday was good. This morning they introduced a new instructor. A middle aged, neat freak, energizer bunny type, who wears his Ph.D. on his sleeve. That goes right up my rear end. The guy is unbelievable. The others I've worked with here have been outstanding, down to earth, 'been there done that' people. This guy is different, in a bad way.

Right after lunch, he tells the twelve of us that we have an outdoor exercise in leadership and teamwork. I don't like this guy, and I don't like grab ass, so I'm not looking forward to his charades.

Outside, he casually tells us we're going to hike up the mountain. Before we do, we should take a 'stone' with us. A stone? What kind of gimmick is this? It was a gorgeous day, so let's play along. People were laughing, picking up pebbles, and a river biscuit or two. I picked one up about the size of my hand, slim and flat. Man, do I hate bullshit.

We hiked for a quarter mile up in the pines. He found a semi-flat area with a few downed trees. We stood and watched, while he laid two logs parallel, maybe fifty feet apart. Then he called a group huddle. He explained the 'game'. We were 'in a prison camp' as POW's. To escape, we needed to use the 'stones' we'd carried up, to stand on and get us safely across the 'minefield' that stood between us and freedom. The minefield was the space between the two downed logs. He told us to 'step on the stones' to avoid the mines. If our foot slipped off the stones we 'blew up'.

About half our twelve, immediately got excited. They got together and started organizing stones, figuring how to work our way through the imaginary minefield and our escape to freedom. I was no longer present. I'd slipped into my bad place. The nerve of this little nerd to play a POW game with us. Who the hell does he think he is? What bullshit! Where are the choppers? Get me the hell out of here, now.

I was a good boy and played along, for awhile. The assignment was impossible. Our illustrious leader laid on his belly, head to the ground looking under our feet. When we stepped on our stones, the biggest was half the size of our shoes, the little nerd would go 'boom'. He'd smile and tell us to start over. Truth was; there were only two stones big enough for an adult foot to step on and not touch the ground. Life's too short for this shit.

People began to mumble, complain under their breath, and the exercise began to take the air out of what was, a fine afternoon. While the nerd lay there going boom, boom and smiling every time he did, I'd had enough. I went over, sat down on the ground, perfectly content to be in 'prison'. In a few minutes, another fellow came over, then another and soon, his exercise was going up in imaginary smoke, just like his imaginary minefield. I hadn't planned on starting an insurrection, but I could see that I did. The leader of the mess stood up, dusted himself off and walked straight for me. I hadn't said a word to him all day.

He sat next to me and asked, "Ed, why are you sitting here and not participating in the training?" I was in a very bad place by then. I said, "I'll just stay in prison. I don't want to escape. You all can do what you want." He stood up, looked around and witnessed his training disintegrate around him. First one, then two and then all but a few suck ups, dumped on him. He cancelled the rest of the afternoon, and we descended for dinner.

In all our sessions with Covey, right after dinner, we'd meet at the lodge, sit in a semi-circle and report on what we'd learned that day. It was a group sharing exercise. Tonight, fortunately, I was on the opposite end of the semi-circle from where he started. One-by-one the same people who were moaning about the exercise up on the mountain, were now espousing bogus crap, pretending they got something out of it. Maybe they did, I didn't, and wasn't going to lie about it.

Finally, it was my turn. He says, "Ed, what did you get out of the exercise this afternoon?" I thought he'd have known better than ask me. I said, "I'm sorry. I'm happy for you all. I'm glad you got something out of it. My light bulb never went off. Got nothing. Thought it was all BS." He immediately dismissed us for the night, said we'd convene at 0700 in the morning.

As I walked up to my chalet, I was troubled. The whole thing bugged me. I'd enjoyed every seminar I'd attended here. Been coming for three years. What happened? In my bad place, I was rarely able to ask myself questions. But I was truly trying to change. I needed to figure this out. Why didn't I like this guy?

Back at the chalet, I called Gloria and checked in. Everything was fine at home in Pennsylvania. I checked in with the guy running things for me at Frito. Work was surviving without me. I hung up, laid down on a big down comforter, but I couldn't sleep. My head pounded like popcorn was bursting inside. Why didn't I like this guy? I loved the Covey program, why not this one?

I stood up, walked around the room and sat down again. I took out my scriptures but couldn't read. I thought about my time in the Corps, my working life, my entire life. I walked around the room. I looked over at the clock; it was 0300. Before my answer came, I'd been to Nam and back. It was 0400. I had to be back down to breakfast in three hours.

The answer had been years in coming. It's origins were buried deep in my bad place. I realized the problem was me, not the nerd. I realized that I'd been reacting the same way to people 'like that' my whole working career. If they fit a certain mold, maybe a certain look or approach - it was a problem for me. It was a trigger. I'd found a big trigger, a 50 cal in my psyche. And that trigger was set in the jungles of Vietnam. I can't believe I figured it out.

The root of the issue was a paradigm in my head. My frozen view of young, neat looking Lieutenants, who came into our lives in Nam. Not all, but many of them would start by telling us how to do things they'd never done before. I'd seen more than one young LT who caused Marines to be killed or injured. Most were right out of OCS. They were sure they were the latest and greatest. Most, wouldn't listen. I remembered one who showed up in charge of our sniper platoon. Lieutenants weren't trained to be snipers, knew nothing about us and never went with us. But this guy immediately wanted to tell me how to run my patrols. I smile fucked him and did what I knew was right. We'd have been killed listening to this 90 Day Wonder. I saw a grunt LT who sent a squad out at night, right into an ambush, they'd predicted, and he wouldn't listen. Six of eight dead. I didn't like what I saw, and I was still playing those old tapes twenty-five years later. Maybe I could freeze my newly discovered trigger and disable my emotional 50 cal. Maybe?

I slept for an hour, showered and headed down for breakfast. Every morning we'd sit in our semi-circle and report on any 'inspiration we'd had during the night. The nerd started; I held my hand up. With more than a little hesitation, he gave me the floor. I told everyone about my night, my story and my 'aha' moment. For me, it was a breakthrough. I'd gotten in trouble many times in my career by reacting poorly to people just like this guy. What I learned meant a great deal to me.

On our first break, the instructor asked if we could have lunch? At lunch, he thanked me for working so hard to figure things out. I apologized for my actions the previous day. He shared with me that it was his first week with the company. He too was up all night, worrying about losing control of the group and getting fired.

The phone rang in my office. I was back in Somers, late for my first meeting of the day. *What had just happened?*

10 March, Wednesday - Benicia, CA. Pepsi

Just arrived in sunny Northern California. It's great to be here. I feel like winter's permanent this year. Not much snow, but tons of rain and bitter cold. The sixty degree weather here is a boost to my spirit. One of our people picked me up at San Francisco Airport. We drove to our warehouse in Benicia. It's gorgeous here.

We arrive at the distribution center, and my host says the leaders are in a meeting, so we have a few minutes. I tell him I'll stand outside and soak in the sunshine. I could see water nearby, a bay, with Navy ships. They appeared to be sitting in groups of four. I'm struck by how many there are. As far as I can see there are ships. Must be a Navy boneyard.

My mind drifts to the merchant marine ship we floated to Vietnam on. They're big on the outside, but jam packed on the inside. The sleeping quarters are close, real close. Sardine conditions. We slept in racks, seven high, so close we had to lay in one position. Face down or face up, luck of the draw, there was no turning over. We slid into our racks like a stack of cassette tapes.

We played chess every day crossing the Pacific. I was pretty good. I stood in the warm sunlight, staring at the harbor and thinking of the kid who dispatched me in three moves. First time I'd ever heard the word, 'Foolsmate'. "Ed, we're ready!" Reality reels me in when my host invites me inside. I'm back in beautiful Benecia, and that's a good thing.

15 March, Monday - Brookfield, CT. Home

Off sick today. Been sick all weekend with a sinus infection. Wish I could slow down, but that's not in the cards.

20 March, Saturday - Brookfield, CT. Home

Writing before bed. On the road all week. Our twenty-fourth wedding anniversary was this week. All I could do was call home. Marrying Gloria is the second best decision I ever made. First was joining the Marine Corps right out of high school. Both changed my life for the better.

On our anniversary, I love to think back to when we married, 1969, a year after I left Vietnam, in Winchester, Virginia. The official 'ceremony' took place in the home of Justice of the Peace, Martha Grimm. It was just before noon. Married, we went to downtown Winchester and ate at the lunch counter of the old Woolworth Department Store. We both had Johnnie Marzetti, a favorite at the time. It was fun.

Every year after that, we'd find a Woolworth's and have our 'Anniversary' lunch or dinner. We made it for seventeen years before Woolworth's bought the farm. I miss our annual Woolworth lunch. It's hard to believe it's been twenty-four years since we took that huge leap of faith. I knew I needed her the rest of my life, whatever I was going to do with it. I only went to work in a 'real job' because she wouldn't marry me if I didn't. Our 'Honeymoon' was our wedding night at the Cacapon State Park Lodge in Virginia, on our way back to Akron, Ohio, where we'd be living. I had to be back at work the next day.

As I write tonight, our ride home from getting married comes into full view. Driving home, Gloria wanted to stop and buy a few last minute things for the apartment. Fine with me. "Come in with me," she pleads. I get out, walk in the small department store. It has narrow aisles and too many people. *Anxiety crept into my world, as my grab ass meter went off; I was in trouble. I hate crowds and nonsense. I can barely tolerate most people, let alone mobs.*

Gloria's having fun, she likes to shop, and I like her. *I suck it up. My nerves are crawling towards my fingertips. In my 'minds eye', a red fog's rolling in.* "How much longer?" *I ask as nicely as I'm able under the circumstances.* She smiles and keeps on shopping. *My breathing is now coming in short bursts.* She turns to me with two towels, one in each hand and asks, "Which one should I buy, the thick ones or the thin ones?" She unknowingly *tripped a booby trap, the one always strung tight in my mind.*

I had a brain freeze. The flip cards in my mind started spinning. Get me back to Nam. My friends are still fighting. What towel should I buy? Thick or thin? My mind fractured from the two different worlds colliding in my head. I see the filthy, chocolate milk rivers of Nam while people are closing in on me, laughing, shopping and playing grab ass. People are living on crappy C-rat's while the mob around me is bitching about petty bullshit. I don't want to deal with anymore.

"Ed, what are you doing?" My new wife asks. *I didn't know.* "You're staring into space". She didn't recognize the *'thousand yard stare' frozen on my face. My rage suddenly channelled into a vision of me standing in the store. Staring, I saw myself become a big, old, giant Packard automobile. A big Mobster car. I was a big Packard about to rev my engine, put my head down, and plow through these candy ass civilians. I could see them laying everywhere when I broke through the front windows of the store.*

"Are you okay?" she asked, laying the towels down. "*No, I don't think so. You go ahead and shop. I'll wait in the car*". I walked quickly from the store to my new 396 Chevy Super Sport. I sat down, turned on the key and my 8 track cassette tape deck. I laid back, closed my eyes and tripped out to Neil Diamond. Both Sides Now. I'll be okay. Just give me space, I'll be okay. She came out and we drove to our new apartment an hour away.

"You need to come to bed". My wife was standing in the doorway to the kitchen where I was writing. *I knew tonight wouldn't be good. Restless, I tossed and turned into the early hours. I'm dead tired. I'm stepping off the plane at Cleveland Hopkins Airport. My Mom's coming to meet me. My flight from Oakland was a big disappointment. The plane was full, with six servicemen amongst the passengers onboard. They began serving meals, but ran out. The Stewardess came over the PA and said, "We are just a few meals short today. We're sure our military passengers won't mind giving up their meals for you. Let's give them a hand". People clapped. Pissed, our welcome to the land I'd left behind had begun.*

To my surprise, my Dad was standing there to greet me. He reached out his hand, and we shook. Unfortunately, that was our relationship. I knew then, that Mom, the eternal peacemaker, had orchestrated our encounter. My Dad and I, sadly, had never connected. He was a great provider, but work was his life, not his family. He never found his way to a single Little League game I played, or anything at school. It's just the way it was. We walked down the concourse to baggage claim, and I knew nothing had changed. He started right where we left off, talking about his business, complaining about this guy, or that, and the world in general. It was all he knew.

Standing in baggage claim, half listening to Dad, I noticed the hippies, the long hairs, dressed like they'd just slithered out of the gutter. The world we talked about in Nam was different from the one we left. I'd never felt quite like this before; I wanted out. I wanted to run as fast as I could back to the plane. Where's a chopper when I need one? My mind's overrun, as a tiny outpost in Nam. I wanted to run to my brothers and scream, 'Don't come home! It's a trick! No one here gives a shit!'

I tossed my sea bag over my shoulder as we headed to Dads car. I knew it would be the same, a big Buick sedan. As long as I could remember that's what he drove. It was an hour and a half drive home. Riding in a car was odd, unnerving. We drove for maybe fifteen minutes of cold silence that Dad broke with, "We're going straight to the race track". Our family had been running a go-kart race track for several years before I joined the Marines. Welcome home.

I loved racing growing up. But I'd been in the Corps three years, in Nam most of it and had no plans on racing while I was home. I realized my parents were rightly thinking this might be a big deal for me, but it wasn't. I just wanted to go home, unpack, get a hot bath, sit back and enjoy some peace and quiet. The last thing I wanted was a bunch of people around me acting like they gave a shit.

The drive was pretty painful for both of us. He didn't understand me before I left; I could tell he was nervous about me now. The small talk we used to make was more strained than before. It was a pretty spring day when we pulled into a large crowd at the race track. He parked by the concession stand which my Mom operated. She ran out of the stand and gave me a big hug. It was nice to see her. She said I looked good and ran back inside to serve customers. There were suddenly lots of other well wishers around me, some I knew, some I didn't. Life in the world wasn't what I'd envisioned laying back staring at the starry sky, wondering what people were doing here back in the world. I was here now, seeing firsthand what they were doing.

My Dad disappeared; he had things to do. I walked over to a small set of empty bleachers. I was just killing time. Sitting at a race in a Marine uniform made me stand out like a forehead zit at the senior Prom. People came and sat nearby; I got up and went to the restroom where I could be alone. I eventually wandered back over to the concession stand for one of Moms steamed hot dogs and a Mountain Dew. The bleachers were empty again; I sat down. I had about two hours to endure before I could head home. I'd rather be on a jungle hill right now with my brothers.

I drifted through the afternoon watching my brother race. He's eight years younger. He's growing up and a very good driver. That was nice to see. My Dad had become involved in the politics of kart racing. He was an official in the governing association. Therefore, lots of people were sure they knew me. They'd been bugging me all afternoon, with the usual well wishing bullshit. I was killing people five days ago, leave me the hell alone. I knew the last time most of them thought about the war was when they saw their last serviceman.

With one race to go I see a lady in her fifties, with horned rim glasses, drawing a bead on me. She'd been eye balling me for half an hour. I turned the other way to get up and there she was. She's the wife of the Big Kahuna of the karting association my Dad helped start. My head wants to give her a quarter and tell her to call somebody who gives a shit. She drones on; I smile, dying inside.

As she talked, I was desperately trying to hold the door to my red rage shut. My heart raced like a hundred gooks just came over the horizon. She'd been holding my hand as she talked, now she placed her other hand on mine. The bullshit sign that says 'we're so close'. Before I can run like hell, she says, "You poor thing. I know you're so glad to be here, home from that terrible, terrible thing going on over there."

I was now holding as tight to my core as she was my hand. My red rage was seeping around the door in my mind. Would she ever shut up? I don't want to embarrass my parents, but I'm about to deck her ass. "They just need to get all you boys home and leave that Godawful place to those awful people". I can see the red in my eyes now. She has no idea she's holding the hand of a booby trap about to go off.

I pull my hand from hers and thank her for her 'kind' words. Apparently thinking she's someone important to me, she grabs my hand again, sporting a more serious look. "You have to appreciate your parents. They are concerned about you every day. They sacrifice for you. You should be happy to be home, away from that hellhole and those people in the Marines you have to associate with".

The wire sprung and this booby trap went off. I jerked my hand from hers. "No M'am, as a matter of fact I wish I was back there right now! Not listening to your bullshit! I wish I was back there killing gooks with my friends, my fellow Marines, the best people I know". As I spoke a look *of horror covered her face, as she did a backwards shuffle and ran into my Mom.* "It's people like you that I can't stand. It's people like you that make me wonder if America's worth dying for anymore".

I looked around; there was a small gathering looking on. Mom was embarrassed. The horned rim glasses was furious, and my Dad was angry, but what else was new. The lady suggested 'I get help' before I hurt someone. That brought the second time in my life that Mom told me I should 'see someone'. The first was when I volunteered to go to Nam. It wouldn't be the last.

Mom quickly agreed to loan me her car. I got my sea bag, tossed it in her car and headed home. I swung by the Long Branch, my early life watering hole, and it was closed. I'd forgot. In Ohio, no booze sold on Sunday. Going to be a tough night.

21 March, Sunday - Brookfield, CT. Home

Back from another week on the road. West coast a week ago, southern states this week. Came home run down and tired. Sunday is family and church day. I live for my family; they make my world go round. My church is my refuge from the storms of reality.

The weather here is still bad. This week, while I was away, they had what they called the 'blizzard of the century'. Don't know if it was, but I came home to two feet of snow. We worked all day yesterday shoveling the driveway. I don't have a snowblower, so it's a hand job. The girls helped, but it was hard work and yet fun in the process. The girls and I just came in from building an igloo in the front yard. They love the snow, my wife and I not so much.

I'm a Celtic fan, so I warmed up and sat down to catch a late game. The girls are complaining about the noise. My daughter tells me she's getting me a Miracle Ear for my birthday. Of course, *I deny the problem but know better.* In my last company physical, they identified a *hearing loss in my right ear of 10-15%; the left was somewhat less.* Gloria thinks I should go to the *VA, but screw them. I know how they treated Greek, Bu, Crud and countless others. Not me.*

As I sat there, I couldn't help but *think of Scout Sniper School back in Phu Bai where we trained. From six in the morning to six at night we took turns shooting at four hundred meters to one thousand meter targets. We worked in two man teams. I would shoot for thirty minutes; my partner would shoot for thirty minutes. We'd repeat for twelve hours a day for four weeks. Ear protection? Grab a cigarette butt if you want ear plugs.*

I'm home again, Time for dinner.

22 March, Monday - Detroit, MI. - Pepsi

Here today, back home late tomorrow. Got pulled from my projects to visit a robot manufacturer here. Seems we have built a bright and shiny new Pepsi plant in Detroit, but nobody comes to work. The Plant Manager told me he assigns 125 people, to get 100 who actually report to work. Incredible. They're thinking of replacing people with robots.

I was supposed to fly from here to Toronto, but cancelled that trip, since I have too much to do right now back in Somers. Tired. Checked voice mails. A Manager in Texas wants me down there. He needs help cutting costs in his battle with Coke. A Manager in Rhode Island wants to talk to me about the new inventory program that doesn't work. Somebody else wanted me to come and do some more training. I guess it's better to be wanted than not.

24 March, Wednesday - Brookfield, CT. Home

Walked Whit out to the bus this morning and stayed with her. She's eight years old, our youngest. My wife is back in Ohio with her Mother. She's coming home from the hospital and needs help getting set up on her own. I'm Mr. Mom again for a few days.

When we walk outside, and it's pouring. *I mean a pounding rain. Monsoon morning to me. Whenever it rains like this, it's the monsoon to me. I have to fight, not to be ten-thousand miles away.* I stand, covered by a big umbrella, watching Whit and the neighbor kids are splashing in puddles. *I think of the first monsoon I spent in Nam. Rained twenty seven days and nights. Sometimes hard. Sometimes a drizzle. But rain it did. Mud to your knees. Crawling up slopes on your hands and knees so you wouldn't fall on your face and slide back down. Grey mud and muck, your world is a filthy old sponge of rotten dishwater. That's your life.*

My life now is watching my little girl have fun in the rain. *It wasn't fun twenty-five years ago. I'm fighting the black as my mind switches channels between now and then.* I look at the kids, today, and they're so young, so pure and safe, wouldn't the children of war, any war, long for a morning like this one.

The bus is running a little late but finally comes. My little pride and joy ascends the big steps, off to another day of learning, fun, and I realize, peace. I wave as she leaves, then walk back down the drive to my Bronco. I'm soaked from standing out there, but it was worth it. I'll dry on the commute, which I know will be awful this morning.

I negotiate the side streets and ease into traffic on the Interstate. A sea of cars and people, slowly making their way to what is important today. I tune the radio to my commuting fix, Imus in the Morning. I used to listen to his bizarre world back when he was in Cleveland. Away we go.

25 March, Thursday - I-287 Greenwich, CT. Driving

Had a meeting today with some Pepsi Franchisees in Greenwich. As I was driving from our headquarters in Somers to the hotel, I had a tough time. *I couldn't help but think about Greek. I drove the same route today that I'd often go when I visited him on Long Island.*

My heart is still heavy over his loss. We had some great times together. I lighten up as I drive thinking *about him and his wicked sense of humor. He looked and acted like the Actor, Gene Wilder. Funny. In Nam, he told us if we ever wanted to kill anyone, bring them to New York City and do it between 0600 and 0800. He said that's when all the cops are on break, switching shifts and don't care. We all laughed. Then he took me to Manhattan after the war and he was right.*

We were out all night. Sitting at a light on 7th Avenue, I can't recall the cross street; he made his point. The city was waking up; it was 0630. I look over, and this big dude slams a hammer into a plate glass window of an old clothing store. He steps inside and comes out with both hands wrapped around what must have been a rack of suits. He proceeds down the street, just two doors, and disappears into a doorway.

I got all excited. Greek was laughing his head off. I said, "Greek, let's find a cop and report that guy. That's bullshit". He laughs and says, "Kug, you're in the city. Nobody gives a shit." He was driving, so I told him to find a cop. Laughing out of his mind, he drove around for an hour until we spotted our first police cruiser. It had two cops in it and was about three blocks away.

Greek reminded me of our conversation in Nam. If you want to kill someone, do it between 0600 and 0800. I'm beginning to believe him. Greek stops behind the police car. He lets out a big laugh, as he motions me to the cruiser. I get out and walk up to the driver's side. They're having coffee.

The Officer doesn't even look up, although I'm sure he knows I'm there. I knock on his window. He winds it down with a gruff look over his left shoulder and says, "Ya?" I say, "Officer, I just observed a burglary". I tell him where it was, and he says, "Got it". He winds up his window while I'm standing there. I knock on his window again. He winds it back down, very irritated, and says, "What!" So I say, "Are you going to do anything?" He turns and gives me a look as deadly as a snipers bullet. "I told you I got it! Now scram!"

I turn to walk back to Greeks car, I see his head is bobbing up and down, he's slapping the steering wheel and laughing hysterically. When I get back in the car I have to admit, this is the time to kill someone here. I'm thinking, let's start with that cop.

My daydreaming made the hour drive to the Greenwich Hyatt go by fast. The meeting brought me out of the past and into the present. More corporate bullshit, but we do meet in nice places.

28 March, Sunday - Brookfield, CT. Home

It's well after midnight. The kids are asleep; I'm wide awake. Gloria is still in Ohio with her Mom. I have trouble sleeping when she's gone. I'm glad it's not anxiety, but I hate having health problems. I've got headaches and my jaw's killing me. I can't sleep. The headaches and pain started about a month ago. I've been working through it, but it's killing me tonight. Getting worse. I'm not big on modern Doctors. Go to one, and then another, get a different diagnosis. The Pepsi Clinic said it was a sinus thing. Been treating me to no avail. I went to the Doctor in nearby Danbury and ended up with a Physicians Assistant. She says it's TMJ. I ask her, since she's a 'Physicians Assistant', if I am paying less than I would have seeing the 'Physician'? She's not amused, but I'm serious. I leave with no answers.

I went to see a Chiropractor. He takes a couple of X-rays and tells me I should see a Dentist. I'll go to a Dentist tomorrow. I'm up a lot walking the floor with sharp pain and chills. I walk the house until I can't anymore. It's 0300. I lie down and finally pass out.

30 March, Tuesday - White Plains, NY. Airport

Two tough days and late nights. I'm dead, zoning out. Waiting on my wife to arrive from Ohio. Her Mother seems to be settling into her new digs. My tough time here mirrors that of Gloria in Ohio. Both of us are the Black Sheep in our families, so going home is not an easy task for either of us. Our conversations over the phone are strained. She worked hard, pulled herself out of the crap of life and is not too interested in returning. Sometimes when either of us goes home, it's hard to get 'home' back out of us. Norman Rockwell it's not.

Sitting here in this joke of an airport waiting, I'm at least thankful I don't have the headaches and pain anymore. I went to a Dentist cold turkey. Didn't know who to ask, so I just drove down the street, saw a Dentist and stopped. The problem turned out to be a wisdom tooth. A guy wanted to take them all out. I told him that's like getting one flat tire and buying four new ones. Take one out dude. He broke it off in the process, then informs me I'll have to see an Oral Surgeon. Man, this is a racket.

I went to the Oral Surgeon this morning, and of course he wants to pull them all. I felt like saying, and I want everyone to drink Pepsi, too. I tell him I've had the pitch, take just one. He does the deed and here I am. I'm not feeling any pain from the med's he gave me, not feeling bad at all.

Gloria came in on time, and we headed home. Things started out subdued and turned downright chippy by the time we pulled in our driveway. We agreed to disagree for now and get some rest. I down a couple more pain killers, I'll be out soon. No ghosts with these babies.

31 March, Wednesday - Somers, NY. Pepsi

Today wasn't the day to be late for work. Pepsi's been working with an Army of consultants to redesign the entire company. The project is called 10-X. It means we're going to improve every 'core' process ten times over, like that's going to happen. The changes were to be announced in headquarters today. And when we're done, I'll go out and start selling left over Florida swamp land, the land the Teamsters still have from Jimmy Hoffa's day. Give me a break.

I don't know what's up with all the rain; *it's another monsoon morning.* My saving grace today is the purchasing big wig lives near us and wants a ride. His company car is a Corvette. He doesn't like taking it out in this weather. Whatever, he's a nice guy, I like him and I learned a few things about this great 10-X project as we rode.

The driving was slow and the traffic heavy. I can see the senior stud was becoming agitated as I drove. I ask him what's up? He's flipping through print outs and says, "Do you know that in the two years of this project we have spent nearly a $100 million dollars on consultants". I had to admit; that's an astounding number. At the time, our sales were like $6 billion. I could only wish I was one of those consultants.

As we're pulling into Pepsi he says, "Ed, all that damned money and we have nothing on the street. Nothing." I ask him about the big announcements coming today. He shook his head and said, "Wait until you hear them. Just wait." I dropped him at the front door. Rank has its privileges, especially in corporate America. All our regular travelers were apparently grounded today for the meeting. Out of five parking lots here at headquarters, I'm in the furthest one away from the door. Oh well, I know a lot about walking in the rain. I whip out my big umbrella and brave the downpour for the quarter mile walk inside.

My mouth is one day removed from surgery, but I'm jacked up on pain med's so the meeting should be interesting. I dry off, drop my computer in the office and head for the conference center. Somehow, I didn't think this 'reorganization' would be much more than a massive butt moving exercise.

I walked in just in time for the Human Resources VP to begin his dog and pony show. Although it's hard to imagine, what I'm about to write is true. You can't possibly make this shit up. The first big, big change he announced was the National Headquarters, where we were all sitting, is now, the National Business Unit. There is total silence. The disbelief filling the room was deafening. He even announced our new acronym is … the NBU.

His charades went on for half a day. In my department, we were no longer Headquarters Operations, we were now, the National Operations Business Unit. That's heavy. That makes us the NOBU. There were four of us leading groups in the department, er, NOBU. I was previously the Director of Distribution, but with the 'New Pepsi' I was now the Director of Delivery Processes. Hang with me. My fellow compatriot, the Director of Manufacturing, would become the Director of Make Processes. And the Director of Sales became, drum roll please, the Director of Sales Processes. I got up and left. I had work to do. I don't know what our fourth guy became. That was the big announcement on our big day. Unbelievable is all I can say. Corporations and their games.

The university Professors they'd hired, and all those consultants must have worked all year to come up this shit. Imagine these bullshit announcements and ninety consultants, two hundred Pepsi people, working full time for two years, and they haven't put a new system on the street. And we get new titles but have to fight for a raise and a bonus. *It's the same bullshit as Nam, just a different venue. Where have all the leaders gone?*

Walking back to my office, *I'm sinking fast. I'm fighting, but sliding deep into my bad place. The tapes playing in my head lead to turmoil.* I reach my office and quickly shut the door. I check my voice mails; I have fifteen since I arrived this morning. I call my Secretary and tell her not to disturb me for awhile. I turn my chair and stare out the window. *The rains continue to pour down. I'm in a small village in Thua Thien Province, South Vietnam. It's October 1966. Greek and I have been drafted to ride security for a U.S. Aid mission. What the hell ever that is? We were just back from ten days with crazies from the 1st Battalion, 9th Marines. We went with them as a sniper team, just the two of us. It's going to be great having a three day break, or so we thought. Get drunk today, sober up tomorrow and get ready to go back out on day three. That was our life and life was good.*

"*Kug*", *I looked up to see Gunny Rider. "You and Devoti have to go out as security for a U.S Aid mission". My first thought is, I just got back. My second thought is, what the hell is a U.S. Aid mission? So I asked. They needed a couple of guns to ride out to a local village and distribute something. Easy enough, just a pain.*

Greek was not a happy sniper, and neither was I. But then the Marine Corps isn't in the happiness business. We grabbed some C-rats to eat on the way, our M-14's and a few magazines and headed out to meet whoever we were supposed to secure. Two 6-by's sat outside Motor T. One loaded to the brim with boxes upon boxes, all tied in with comm wire. The other one was half-full of boxes.

A raggedy looking American civilian man and a woman met us. They introduced themselves as U.S. Aid representatives. Okay. We were relegated to the back of the half full truck. A Marine was driving, and the long haired guy in civies climbed in with him. The truck behind us had a Marine driver and the woman. Off we go to where, we didn't know. We did know if Greek and I were the only Security, we hope to hell the village isn't far from here.

We bounced our way out of Phu Bai, heading south on Highway 1. The only north south highway in the country had two lanes, both full of holes from rain, traffic and bombs. Our guts were sore after a short ride. Eating C-rats on the drive was a pipe dream. We turn off the bad road onto a worse road. The area looked a little sketchy so we decided we'd best sit up and look like security.

We sat up, 14's at the ready, aiming at either side of the truck. We go about a quarter mile and stop at a small village. It was filled with Palm trees, grass huts, betel nut Momma's and people milling about, not looking all too friendly. Greek and I stood up, attempting to look 'bad'. The village surrounded by working rice paddies, and Old men peddling bicycles with no wheels, just cups where the pedals had been, moving water from one paddy to another.

I couldn't wait to see what we were delivering. I guess it was an attempt at humanitarian efforts from America. That wasn't my deal, so we stood about ten yards apart at the edge of the village and looked for trouble. The man and lady from U.S. Aid unloaded the boxes with the help of the two Marine drivers. They lined up the boxes, presumably in a way that represented the prize inside. The villagers were lined up, excited, with an obvious expectation of the surprise making their difficult lives easier.

The lady American motioned a short, dark and stocky Vietnamese villager over to the boxes she was working. She opened the first box and my eyes had to be lying to me. The sun was burning hot, maybe I was hallucinating. She reached in that box and proudly pulled out the most flowered, *frilly, laced dresses and nighties you could imagine. What the hell? The truck loaded to the gills with boxes, turned out to be a truckload of clothes, donated by American churches for the poor people of South Vietnam.*

I'd give anything for a picture of the first Vietnamese lady in line. She went from excited to a puzzled look of 'what the hell'. She graciously accepted this crap and bowed her head, turned and returned to her hooch. As did all the rest of the confused Vietnamese villagers behind them. I couldn't resist. I went over to the American lady and asked, "What on earth are you doing with this stuff?" She resignedly said, "People donate it. We deliver it." She might as well have said, "I'm just doing my job, Marine". Bullshit in living action.

I was looking for Rod Serling, we had to be in the Twilight Zone. All I could think was that she did her job. The churches back home did their part. They feel good. Somebody packed it and shipped it. They feel good. We came out to secure it, and we feel like shit. U.S. Aid delivered it. But not one damned leader had the brass to ask if it was worth doing! I was angry as hell. I walked over to Greek to bitch. He told me not to burn any brain cells on it.

Disgusted, I sat down and watched them open the boxes from the second truck. Appalled by the first truck, I lost it on the second. I was hysterical, and so was Greek. Maybe to be nice, or maybe to keep me informed, the lady came over and told me the second truck had health care items, to help people stay clean. As incredible as it sounds, they opened up the cases and handed out individual boxes of Freddie Flintstone Bubble Bath. Fucking bubble bath in a village of dirt floored huts and no running water. The villagers don't read English. How the hell would they know what to do with it if they could use it?

I thought about going over, putting my arm around her and saying, "M'am, look around. These folks don't have bathrooms, bathtubs or showers. They have dirt floors and shit in a trench, and wipe their ass with their heels". But I'm sure she was just doing her job, but I am dumbfounded how incredibly stupid this is.

Greek was having fun. He had spirited away about six boxes of bubble bath. He motioned me behind our truck. "Kug, let's take some of this bubble bath and spread it around these rice paddies. Can you imagine, they'll never figure out what the hell all those bubbles are in their paddies". I agreed it would be colossal. But I didn't want to wreak more havoc into the lives of nice people, just trying to live their lives without outside influence.

Bouncing our way back to Phu Bai, I stared into the clear blue sky of a burning, hot afternoon, reflecting on the absurdity of it all. I realized that we were all pawns in an ugly game, where some people on both sides are going to get filthy rich. It sure as hell wasn't me. I made $235 a month with combat pay.

We arrived where we started, jumped down and looked around for our familiar reality. The U.S. Aid workers got out of the trucks and walked off. The drivers drove off to Motor T and Greek, and I headed back to our mirage, a day off.

"I've been down so Goddam long it looks like up to me"
Found on a Zippo lighter from the war

APRIL

1 April, Thursday - Brookfield, CT. Home & Work

I wake up at 0445. What happened? Where's the truck that hit me. I feel awful. I made a trip to the head. Back to bed, I sit on the edge and reach for my glass of ice water. *Every night of my life, twenty-five years and counting, I go to bed with a glass of ice water. Most nights I don't even touch it. After two years in the heat of Nam, drinking piss warm water with who knows what floating in it, I need the security of a simple glass of ice water by my bed.* Just the way it is.

I lay down, glad my headache disappeared. The Chiropractor was right; it was my teeth. It's a wonder all those Doctors couldn't figure that out. I guess they don't have a command of the obvious. But right now, I need sleep. I looked at the clock and it's now 0450. Sleep dammit. But it's not to be.

Then, *silent as a cat, yet speeding like a runaway freight train, depression comes with its total blackness. It's unbelievable. Where does depression hide when it's not haunting me? I lay staring at the ceiling in utter despair. I feel like the world is crushing my chest. The weight is bearing down, pushing me deep into the bed. It's a mystery to me.*

I have a wonderful, loving family, so why be depressed? I never choose it; it chooses me. I found Jesus Christ years ago and embrace His eternal gospel. Why am I depressed? I lay flat on my back, crushed by an unseen enemy. I have it all, everything I ever wanted, yet the black buries me every time.

I look at the clock. It's now 0518 in the morning. I decide to get up and head to the office. Work will push it out of my mind. It works for awhile. The project I'm leading needs to be written in sand. Our out of touch leaders make changes every day whether they need to or not. I stayed busy all day. I needed several breaks between meetings. Just to go in the office, shut the door and be alone. *Depression is exhausting.*

When I got home tonight, things went from bad to worse. My sixteen year old is still having trouble adjusting to our move. The timing for problems was bad, *the blackness in my head had long chased away any patience I might have had. Before I knew it, I'd ruined my daughter's day; I was pretty hard on her.* She ran up to bed crying. *I walked up to my bed as depressed as when I'd left this morning. Exhausted from a few hours sleep a night, I crashed. As I lay there, I knew I'd been a jerk.* My daughter had started high school in Pennsylvania; I moved her to Maryland. She started her Sophomore year in Maryland and now she is in Connecticut. *I was a first class jerk. And a severely depressed one at that.*

2 April, Friday - Brookfield, CT. Home & Work

The early morning rain woke me from a much needed sleep. The monsoon rains of Connecticut continue. At least we're beyond snow. It's 0500. I'm wide awake. I showered and headed downstairs. I needed to apologize to Cortney, she was none too friendly with me. I told her how very sorry I was for being such a jerk the night before. She agrees with the jerk part, and we head our separate ways for the day.

At work, I present my finished project to my boss. He was cool with it. He tells me he has a new, bigger project he wants me to lead. *I peer out through the blackness of my soul, trying to psych myself up and look interested.* The project sounds pretty interesting, until I find out I'll be doing it along with my full time job. I guess it's a great deal, if you say it real fast.

My boss is a nice man, knows the political maneuvering; that's how he got so high in the organization, so fast. *As long as he gives me air cover, gets people out of my way, I can deliver anything. I'd rather work alone when I can.* We agree on the parameters of the project, then comes the timing. The Perfumed Princes of Corporate America are famous for pulling a project completion date out of their sweet smelling butts, and my boss was no different. The date he wants for the meeting was a bad wet dream for me. I told him so. Of course, it didn't change his mind, but he knows where I stand. *He, like most corporate leaders, liked to forecast heroism.* It never worked.

I had my marching orders and double the workload than when I'd walked in. Leaders in companies never cease to amaze me. They think because they dream it, and set the date, it will happen. Crazy. Frustrating, but it pays the bills and gives us a good life. The joke at PepsiCo is, they have great jobs, but no careers. That's true. I had a great job, so I went back to my office to regroup. With my new workload I've got some adjustments to make.

A couple guys I worked with stopped by, they wanted me to go down to the cafeteria with them for lunch. I declined. *I needed to shut my door and be alone in my blackness. Door closed; I sat down and was gone. I don't know what's going on, but it's big? Standing in the COC bunker at Camp Evans, we were packed in like maggots in the shitter. The Gunny sent me here to represent snipers. I was Senior Patrol Leader and would be taking six snipers on this operation. Grunt operations were always a big risk, and this one sounded like insanity at its finest.*

I look around, as a Sergeant, I must be one of the lowest ranking Marines here. The Colonel, our Regimental CO, walked in, and the room went quiet. He stood by a large map mounted on a 4 x 8 piece of plywood. The map was covered with acetate paper and had arrows and symbols drawn with red grease pencil.

He announces a major operation. We will invade the Ashau Valley. It lays to the west, near Laos, and the Ho Chi Minh trail runs right through it. He explains that one battalion, about 1,300 Marines, will be airlifted into the valley. Another battalion of similar strength will enter via convoy. It will take place tomorrow morning with a 0300 liftoff from the Phu Bai Airstrip, a few miles south of us.

I listen to the nonsense in disbelief. I know a little about Ashau, it's a very tough place to operate. I'd been in country over a year. I'd spent three months working with our Force Recon teams. Every time Force Recon tried to insert into Ashau they were either shot down, or chased away with heavy fire. The Ashau valley was not only a major infiltration route for troops coming south; it was a staging area. North Vietnamese tanks were there. We were listening; it really was insanity at its finest.

A young Lieutenant sat next to me taking copious notes. The Colonel turns the discussion over to a Major, our Operations Officer. He dives deep into the details of the upcoming massacre. When I first arrived in Nam, there was a major operation in Ashau where Marine chopper pilots rescued remnants of a Special Forces Camp recently overrun. Soviet led North Vietnamese forces did the deed. No friendlies have occupied that land since that day. But hey, we're flying in tomorrow morning, somebody's dreaming bad dreams that will give us nightmares.

The valley was remote, surrounded by mountains so steep, the contour lines on our topographic maps were black, signifying the rugged height of the land. If we were cut off in the valley, we'd be alone. I looked around; the room was somber. Heads bowed; people were shuffling, and worried looks filled the room. More people than me knew this was a bullshit proposal.

As the Major got into the details of the tragedy in waiting, it became apparent we'd underestimated the degree of bullshit being planned. The Major laid out the assault plan. We'd do an insertion with eighty choppers. We'd land in waves of twenty each, a massive operation for the Marine Corps. They must be calling in every chopper we have in Nam? The other Battalion would be driving in a large convoy, through the mountains on a little used road that had to be ambush alley. I don't need those fancy bars on my lapel to know this plan is asinine.

The attention turned to assumptions and contingency. They explained there were two probable scenarios. First, the NVA will let the first wave of twenty choppers into the LZ, and then cut off the rest while they decimate those that landed. If that happens, the Marines on the ground will have to secure the area and fight for their lives. The second scenario is, they would not let any choppers in and try to blow them all from the air as we arrived. In scenario two, they assumed that 25% of the choppers would be blown out of the air and go down.

As the briefing turned to troop specifics, I realized why the Lieutenant next to me was taking all those notes. He was a Forward Observer, and found himself on chopper number one. Ouch! He needed to get on the ground and set up supporting fire to neutralize the enemy guns. He turned to me, pointing to the map, and said, "The small hill, just above our LZ, had an anti-aircraft gun emplacement as late as yesterday". He looked like he was waiting for a response. "That sucks, Sir," is about all could muster.

The briefing progressed with assignments being made for who was on what chopper. They wanted snipers on choppers eight, sixteen and twenty-four. They wanted snipers on the ground early. I nodded with the raise of a hand; I got it. My emotions were a toxic mix of excitement, fear and resignation. I don't know what it was with me; I always wanted to do crazy shit, and this was some seriously crazy shit. I also knew my snipers weren't going to be thrilled with the news of this operation. We were small unit guys who won on stealth. We were now entering the battle of brute force.

The last contingency covered was what to do if we landed and reinforcements were cut off. We'd organize in four man teams. One Marine of the four, would carry thermite grenades. A thermite grenade burns at four thousand degrees. We'd use them to destroy any equipment that we had to leave behind. We'd then depart in groups of four, splitting for the east, up and over the black lined mountains, mountains so steep; we'd be climbing on our hands and knees. You didn't have to be able to read tea leaves to know how this was going to turn out. We'd be left to fight to the death.

The meeting droned on for another hour. It was hot; we were all sweating and scared. It was surreal. The plan was so absurd; it was hard to take seriously. Would our leaders try something this foolhardy? Apparently? My mind was numb. The meeting ended, and I walked to our sniper area to round up my guys and deliver the news of our death sentence.

Word of the operation reached the Rogues long before I did. "Kug, you dumb shit. You got us into this bullshit. But if you're going, I'm going!." My Iowa farmer was always straight up. I loved him. The six of us sat down, I reviewed what I knew. I could never ask someone to do something I wouldn't do. I took Chopper 8. Stu said he was with me. The others, two teams, would be on Choppers 16 and 24. It was as subdued as I'd ever seen my team.

All talk of drinking stopped. We began preparation for the big show. C-rats were passed out; ammo issued, canteens filled and letters written *home by some. There was a quiet today, rarely experienced before operations. We all knew about Ashau Valley, and what we knew wasn't good. Our Force Recon friends knew what was happening; they stopped by to wish us well. They weren't optimistic; they'd lost a seven man recon team the month before, trying to insert into Ashau. As the day crept on and nightfall approached, the reality of our early morning date with the grim reaper came into full view. We were ordered to keep our normal routines until nightfall. There was concern about Russian satellites picking up our activity and passing information to the NVA.*

As nightfall came, a line of trucks began to form. We piled in for the short convoy south to Phu Bai. It's dark, hot and muggy. The stars are out bright; it's a clear night. There's a silvery hue to everything the eye can see. We arrive and roll out by unit, by chopper. The choppers are lined up along the tarmac. We lie in the grass at the edge of the tarmac and drop our packs and sit down.

There was little small talk. We were just a few hours from an event that will end many of our lives. Stu laid down next to me, hat over his eyes, flat on his back. I laid back too, but sleep was missing in the vain imaginations of what was to come. Tomorrow may be my last. I laid on my back, staring at the perfect sky above, contemplating my young life and the fact it might soon be over. I often stared at the starry sky and imagined it to be my magical mirror to my life back in the world. It was reflecting tonight; I could see my life before Nam.

I saw my childhood, my friends and girlfriends, and my life to date. It was as if time stood still. I'd wanted to be a Marine since Fifth Grade. I could see that book report, my Recruiter, boot camp, Santo Domingo, and here I was, leading snipers in Nam. About to fly off into the fight of our lives, because some General, or worse, some politician, driving a big desk back in DC, thinks this foolishness is a good idea. Anger filled my brain; the possibilities freaked me out.

I sat up, looked around, Marines laying everywhere, waiting, just like me, for 0300 and the lift off to hell. A Catholic Priest walked by quietly recruiting people for 'last rights', whatever that was. I was an Atheist and glad of it. I lay back on my pack once again, staring up at the stunning night sky. I thought through my young life one more time. Then it happened.

A calm washed over me with a peace I'd never felt before. The anger I felt disappeared. The darkness lifted, and I felt good. Good? I felt outstanding! I remembered a thought I had when becoming a sniper, 'How many people in all the annals of time will ever have the opportunity to do what I'm about to do?' Everything was okay. I've had a good life, let's get it on. It's okay to die in the morning!

Energy filled my body from inside out. My heart raced. I stood up, took a deep breath and was ready to go. Stu woke up. I said, "I'm gonna' die this morning. All I want to do is go out in a blaze of glory". He stared at me through the darkness and said, "You're crazy". Maybe I was, but I was crazy excited, pumped, as I'd never been in my life. It felt like I'd crossed over some imaginary line, and everything was suddenly okay. I was walking on air.

It was 0230, just thirty minutes to lift off. The flight line was alive with activity. Dark silhouettes moved in all directions. The muffled noise of activity broke the silence of the night. I just wanted to get the show on the road. Pure adrenaline pumped through my veins and sweat ran from my pours. I was ready.

Instead of boarding the choppers as planned, we were placed on a thirty minute hold. Made no sense. Weather was great; we were ready, I was ready. Not a good thing, lots of bitching and moaning. No time for the hurry up and wait bullshit of the military.

I was pacing, then decided to lay back down against the pack on my back. Ignoring everything around me, all I think is 'today is the day', let's hit it. It's time. I'm ready. My mind had never been so focused.

0330 came and went, no word, can't be good. We continue hanging out on the tarmac. The element of surprise is gone, if we go now, we're going to be toast. Let's go, lock and load, lift off. Ashau, here we come. I've worked through this in my mind; it's okay, today I die. Our other snipers stroll up. I don't want to talk. I hear them all agree I'm out of it.

Somewhere around 0415 word comes down to muster at the hanger. I know it's over. Dammit! I'm pissed. I'm all dressed up and ready to die, and they cancel the party. Our Gunny shows up, tells us the word is DC pulled the plug on the operation. My red rage raced to max RPM's. I'm ready to die and now this shit.

In typical Marine Corps fashion, they decide we need to do a bullshit sweep south of Phu Bai. There's never any action down there. We're all dressed up, so they make busy work for us. I was so wound up I knew I couldn't do it. I couldn't go out there and bump around to stay busy. Bullshit! I knew they weren't going to find anyone to fight. I had to fight gooks, get drunk or punch somebody.

I convinced the Gunny to pull snipers from the new walk in the park. I'd take the Rogues and head back to the valley. We needed to do our own thing. We needed beer, but the Gunny made us head straight to the valley. The five click walk to our home away from home cleared my mind. The adrenaline overflow subsided by the time we got to Hill 51. It would take days before I could accept the fact we'd dodged a big bullet by not flying into Ashau. At least one leader, somewhere, had enough sense to cancel the madness. I realized we were lucky, but I was pissed.

3 April, Saturday - Brookfield, CT. Home

Still fighting the black. Preparing for Ashau made for a tough night. When I'm full of adrenaline, and the action stops, it's almost like a hangover. My depression is bad today. Gloria and I lay in bed this morning and talked. That always helps. As we got up, we realized we'd planned to drive down to Long Island and visit with Bobbie and the kids. She wanted me to help her review her finances. Greek didn't leave her in the best shape.

It's not in the cards today. I feel a little better after talking with Gloria, but going down there, with all my memories of Greek, would not be good. The black is now gray, but it wouldn't take much to bring down the blinds. I call Bobbie. We bump it a day, tomorrow, Sunday we'll go down. I gave Greek my word, on his death bed, and I'll keep it.

4 April, Sunday - Merrick, Long Island, Devoti's

We skipped church this morning and headed down to Greeks, on Long Island. We made good time; there's little New York traffic on Sunday. Our girls are happy to see the boys. They know each other from our summer vacations in Canada. When we first got together, it took Bobbie a while to warm up. Once she realized I wasn't a partier or druggie, as some of his friends, we have become close.

Bobbie is an amazing young woman, a wonderful Mother. Her life's her boys. She's struggling with Robert gone; he was Greek to me, not Robert. We had a good visit. Talked through some issues she was facing. The loss and strain showed on her face. But she was strong. Before we left, she invited us down, to be with them in June, when her youngest graduates from grade school. The previous year we were there when her oldest graduated. She's concerned having the party alone this year. We'll be there.

It was a struggle for me too. His family felt like my family. After Nam, I stayed with his parents, who lived down the street. I knew them well. I knew his older sister well, too. I stayed here at his house. I spent a long evening with him, in his bedroom, early in his cancer. As we prepared to leave for home, *the blackness was hovering around me like a swarm of flies.*

The ride home was uneventful, except the adventure of driving the freeways of New York City. The kids love counting the junked out cars sitting by the road. If you break down along here, at a minimum, your wheels will be gone when you come back. I've seen several with the doors missing. Interesting place. As we drive, Gloria and I reminisce about the old times with Greek and Bobbie.

As we drove and talked, I felt better. We made our last turn towards home when Gloria said, "Do you remember our anniversary last month? That's when we all went to Crud's funeral?" I hadn't remembered that our anniversary was the same as *Crud's suicide. Blackness smothered me with a vengeance driving my face into the ground.*

We pulled in the drive, unloaded kids and went to bed. Gloria had inadvertently handed me the weight of the world. *Sometimes the demons of war are merely an innocent comment away, hiding barely under the surface, waiting for the trip wire to spring.* Another short night was in store. I closed my eyes in Brookfield but *I was soon in Columbus, Ohio; it was March, 1970. "I'm not walking in there until 0959!" Greek laughs looking forward to the scene that may unfold when we arrive. I was driving near the funeral home where our man Crud, Thomas Carothers, was about to be planted. His Mom called to tell me he'd died. His estranged wife called to tell me he committed suicide. I wasn't surprised; he'd struggled mightily since coming home from Nam a cripple.*

He tripped a booby trap in the valley on a very dark night. Shrapnel tore through the back of his body, Stu got ripped in the front. Both severely wounded, they were evacuated together. They spent most of the next year in a VA hospital near Chicago. Both full of shrapnel that wasn't coming out for years, they made the most of it. They were lucky.

We pulled into a full parking lot; I could see his ex-wife standing by the door. She told me she'd wait; she wanted to walk in with us. She wasn't too fond of Crud's Mom; Mrs. Carothers was none too happy having her around either. In her mind, she'd caused a lot of her Tommy's heartache. Truth was; they were equal partners in the heartache department. I parked far back in the parking lot, in the last spot available.

Walking to the building, I was reminded how much I hated funerals. After Fort Wayne, I could do without another one for the rest of my life. But Crud's Mom was adamant, I needed to get as many of the Rogues here as possible. The best I could do on short notice was the Greek. He'd flown into Akron the night before from LaGuardia. Together, we called the others and broke the news about our brother's demise. None were surprised.

I walked around the side of the building and there she was, his wife, waiting proudly. She grabbed my arm on the open side; Gloria had the other arm and Greek was behind us, looking every bit the Gene Wilder look alike he was. And if you didn't know it, you'd never guess he was walking with one good leg and one fake leg, courtesy of the VA. He was amazing.

We walked inside and found that Mrs. Carothers had held up the services awaiting our arrival. I didn't want to walk up front with his ex on my arm, but I had no choice. My greatest fear was his wife grandstanding, or breaking into a wailing fit at the casket. She was known to play it up, big time. Thankfully, we reached Mrs. Carothers without incident and offered our condolences.

The room was full, overflowing into a side room we could barely see. His ex-wife went up to the casket, leaned in and kissed his cheek, as she placed her wedding ring on his chest. She left, I told Greek to reach in and hide the ring before his Mother saw it. I don't know what he did with it but it was gone when I got there.

My wife took his ex-wife and headed for the front row seats reserved for us. Mrs. Carothers grabbed Greek and I, one on each arm, standing between us she stood staring at her only son. Her husband, Crud's adopted father, had died one year ago this month. She was now all alone. She'd told me on the phone about adopting Tommy, as she called him. She told me that he was the love of her life, but was never the same after returning from Vietnam.

The three of us stood there, looking at her now dead son, until we were pretty uncomfortable. He looked better than I'd ever seen him. Pasty, but adorned in his dress blues, the finest uniform in all the world. I think back to our many discussions of his time machine. I think of the many calls I'd get in the middle of the night, when he was up studying the encyclopedia. He'd wake me up at all hours, higher than a kite on Darvon's and Whiskey. Telling me some new thing he'd learned. He was a lost soul but he was our brother.

My flashbacks of Crud vanished when Mrs. Carothers asked, "Boys, how does he look?" Greek and I were tall enough to look over her head at each other. He looked at me with raised eyebrows, and after a small pause I said, "Mrs. Carothers, he looks good". I knew in my mind; Crud was in there laughing his ass off at the two of us being put in the middle. The music playing in the background became monotonous. The little lady between *us looked up, with sad, grieving eyes and said, "I know, I know. But I want Tommy's last day to be perfect. The undertaker told me he wasn't sure how to set up a Marine uniform. Is his uniform perfect?"*

She took us each by the hand and led us one step closer to the casket together. The audience was getting a little anxious. I was too. I needed a drink. Standing there looking down on our brother, I noticed his medals and ribbons were on his right chest, not his left. Without thinking about the ramifications, I broke the pregnant silence. "Ma'm, everything is perfect, except they have his medals on the right side, not the left."

Her frail hand squeezed mine as she looked up and said, "Would one of you boys change them?" Before I could say a word, Greek put his arm around her shoulder turning her towards the seats as he said, "Ma'm I'll take you to your seat. Kug will change the medals." I was alone, standing in front of two hundred people, left with nothing but the wink Greek gave me, as he turned to walk away.

I turned, and faced the casket that held the body of my friend, and brother. He was at last, at peace. I was no longer an Atheist; I'd become an Agnostic. But I had no idea where Crud went, because he now looked like a life size plastic model in Marine dress blues. The Funeral Director came over and asked if I needed assistance. I answered in the negative.

Leaning over the casket, I reached down for the buttons on his blues. I could only imagine what Gloria was thinking. Hopefully, Greek filled her in on our 'special request'. As I looked down I swear I could see Crud's sly smile, creeping into his frozen mouth, as I unbuttoned his blues. His ribbons were fastened to his jacket with small, circular, metal clips. The clips go over the point that sticks through the clothes, as a tie tack. He had three rows of ribbons, which made for six clips to take off and reposition.

I moved the ribbons, as I did; I touched his pale, rock hard body. The music droned on. I wanted this done right now. I got the ribbons moved to the right and five of six of the clips secured under his uniform. As I placed number six, it dropped and rolled off his chest into his armpit. Shit! I couldn't reach it. I quickly buttoned up his blues, brushed him off, and straightened his uniform as best I could. I looked down, one strip of medals stuck up on one end. The missing clip was the culprit. I reached in and pushed it down.

It popped back up. I did it again with the same result. I feel like I'm about to be ambushed, screw it. I get the ribbon in place, lean down near Crud's ear and say, "Sorry Crud", as I slam my fist down hard, driving the end of the pointed pin into his clay-like chest. It stayed down! Mission accomplished.

I stand up and walk back to my seat, to the delight of the worried Funeral Director. I sat between my wife and Mrs. Carothers. The service went by without me knowing it was over. I was lost, thinking about the fighting, laughing, and living Crud and I had done. I remembered the part I played in his divorce. About a year ago, when they were still together she called me and said, "Kug, he threatened to kill me. What should I do?" Without hesitation, I told her to leave immediately and not look back. It wasn't behind Crud's back. I called and talked with him, told him what I'd said. He knew I was right. Now, he was gone.

Graveside, Mrs. Carothers, hugged all of us, and thanked us for being such good friends to her Tommy. Then she said something that was so true, and will be with me forever. "Boys. You know Tommy didn't die here in Grove City. Tommy died in Vietnam. We just buried him here today". Greek and I looked at each other, and knew she was right. Maybe we all died there? Time for a drink.

5 April, Monday - In the Air to Dallas - US Air

Up at 0 dark early for the drive to LaGuardia. Short night when you have a 0630 flight. Couldn't get Crud out of my mind. Loved that guy. Heading for a two day meeting in Big D. A few hours on US Scare, my most unfavorite airline. The black is leaving fast, chased away by the work ahead. Not nearly as depressed as I was late last week. Had a good day traveling, everything's on time. Rare.

7 April, Wednesday - LaGuardia Airport and Home

Driving home, near midnight. Just in from DFW. I'm dead tired. I don't sleep well on the road. Trying to listen to late night talk radio out of New York.

At this time of night, nothing on but trash talk, UFO's and sex shows. Reminds me of an audio version of Tijuana in the sixties, where we made weekends on the way to Nam. Nothing mattered; you were going to Nam.

Home, my wife brings me up to speed on Cortney's problems at school. One of her friends who lives next door, was accused of copying from Cort's papers. They called them both in, the friend, admitted she did it, and Cort didn't know. So the teacher says Cort's fine and tells her to leave. Yesterday, the Vice Principal issues an edict, delivered in class, she's suspended. I just love all those new titles in school administration these days. That's where they're wasting their money. What the hell is a Vice Principal?

To her credit Cort walked out of class and straight to the Vice Principal's office. I'm proud of her. We raised her right. Take no shit from bureaucrats. She's not suspended, and that does my heart good. That's great news. It's 0100. A short night awaits.

8 April, Thursday - Somers, NY. Pepsi

In early, gotta' get ready for our all day meeting with the folks from Pepsi Canada. Rained all the way in, what else is new? The drive was slow. The clouds were gray, hanging low, dark, hanging low like you could touch them. *Reminds me of Nam, every time. Adrenaline seeps into my veins, but* recedes, as I enter the lobby with Pepsi music playing pleasantly in the background. With an all day meeting, I'll have a good day. *The black has been faint, hiding in the background of my life, lurking for the next time.*

9 April, Friday - Somers, NY. Pepsi

In early again, Staff Meeting. My boss asked me to lead off, report on what I've learned in my recent travels and provide an update on my new project. My boss is interested in the scuttlebutt regarding the massive change project which is blowing up as we speak. Unfortunately, what I have to report, is not good. The last part of the project to roll out totally bombed. Word has it; they'll have to start over.

We get into a discussion regarding the perception of the field versus what I called 'headquarters'. My boss corrected me; it's now the National Business Unit; we're in the new Pepsi. After a deep breath, I continued leading the discussion. My boss didn't like what he was hearing. I was supposed to leave 'truth' home today. I should be able to tell him the truth, and being the political animal that he is, he should run interference for us.

I tried to smooth his damaged ego. I'd been telling him the products of the change effort weren't ready for implementation. He's now more concerned with how to 'position' things with the big guys. *Who cares? More deep breaths and patience for me, as the inane discussion continues.* My boss wore those half glasses and looked at me, glasses sitting halfway down his nose, and said, "That's what makes my blood boil". Then he smiled and said, "Let's go to lunch". We all went down to the Pepsi cafeteria and continued the endless debate on how to 'massage' my message.

Lunch down, I walked back to my office. I realized I was getting slightly better in dealing with nonsense. When I was first in the working world, *after Vietnam, my bullshit meter was set on zero, no tolerance* I shut the door and sat down in my office. My mind drifted. I was dispatching for a trucking company a year after Nam.

"What did you say?" The man asking the question was our number one customer. He was also the number one customer of the pipe company we served. It was early 1969. He apparently thought he could degrade people. I had taken his shit for the six months I'd been in this job, but today, my bell rang and the trip wire went flying.

"I said you should lighten the fuck up. The sun's going to come up today whether that truck gets there, or doesn't!" We exchanged expletives for about fifteen minutes, and my truck showed up just like I said it would.

We delivered clay sewer pipe to him every morning. It could be one truck load, or it could be four or five. It was winter; they were eight hours away, he was on the west side of Chicago. Predicting an on time delivery to the minute took all the stars lining up and all the chinchilla's in heat. When they didn't line up, he'd call my apartment at 0 dark early, calling me everything but a man. Screw him!

I'd sucked it up long enough. Life just isn't that serious, or shouldn't be. I still have friends dying in Nam asshole, and you're having a heart attack over a load of pipe to build drains for the shitters in Chicago. When he hung up, he promised me he'd have my job for talking to him that way. I asked him if it was okay for him to talk to me that way? He slammed the phone in my ear. People here in the world are just too uptight for me.

I went to work and within an hour I was called in and ripped a new one. Then I was informed I needed to drive to Cleveland, an hour away, and meet with the Vice President of Sales for the pipe company. I had lunch and a couple of shots on the way to my afternoon meeting. The VP was nice, professional and explained to me that Mr. Kloos was the biggest customer both of us had. We must do what he wants. I apologized. I knew better. I just didn't think he should treat everyone like second class citizens. "He treats me that way, Ed." I felt like saying 'that's your problem, you're a pussy', but I didn't.

He asked me to use the phone in his office, and call George to apologize. I knew I had to do it. I was newly married, and needed a job, whether I liked it or not. He got up and stood by the window, while I took his seat and pushed his George button. The guy apparently had a hotline on his phone. I'd yet to learn that's how business worked. It would take awhile.

"George, Ed Kugler here." He was calmer than in the morning when we had our spat. "I called to apologize for how I talked with you this morning. I was out of line, and I will see to it that the trucks arrive when you require them." The VP is nodding his head, and smiling as I talk.

On the other end George says, "I want you to know that when you hung up on me this morning, I ripped my phone out of the wall. Just got it reinstalled." I think so what, you did it. He says, "Why are you upset with me? I just want my trucks on time. We string the pipe right into the ground; it's all scheduled. I have deadlines to meet." I took a deep breath. I didn't need this petty bullshit in my life.

The VP in my room was longingly looking at me, wondering what the hesitation was. I thought for a minute and said, "George, to be honest, I do understand your demands. I need to meet them. No question. I want you to know I will do everything possible to do that. But I have to tell you. I'm less than a year out of Vietnam, where I spent two years as a Marine sniper. I have a very hard time being treated like a dirt ball. I'd just like a little respect, and I'll deliver what you want."

That wiped the smile off the VP's face and replaced it with a look of concern. George thanked me for the apology, and asked to speak to the VP. I stepped out of the office and let them talk privately. It wasn't long, and the VP invited me back into his office. "George said he was impressed with your apology and your honesty. Just deliver on what you promised".

I have to admit, I was surprised. I hate the politics of work life. I thanked him for a second chance and left the office. It was quitting time, so I called our office, told them what happened, George and I are cool, see you all in the morning. I couldn't wait to get home, have dinner, be with my wife and have a couple shots of Tequila.

11 April, Sunday - Brookfield, CT. Home Easter Sunday

Easter Sunday, Gloria makes our holidays special. She decorates for all seasons and reasons. Today was no exception. It's very springlike, except the continuing rain. Trev is away at college and working. Cortney went to DC on a church trip for the weekend. She's staying with friends in Baltimore. So it's Gloria and me, and Whit.

It's been a good day. Played some games and lots of one-on-one time playing with Whit. Early to bed, we're driving to Baltimore in the morning. A good day it's been.

12 April, Monday - Baltimore, MD. - on to Richmond, VA.

Up early this morning and off to Baltimore. Had rain and fog most of the way. Near Baltimore, it started to clear up. I drove into BWI and Gloria took over, dropping me off for my flight to Richmond. Gloria will connect with Cort, and they'll spend some time visiting friends while I'm gone.

On board my brief flight to Richmond, I read the morning paper. *An innocent article trips a trigger. There's an article about recently released Russian documents that indicate the North Vietnamese held more than seven hundred POW's in 1972. They claimed to be holding some three hundred-fifty or so after the release in 1973.*

As I read, adrenaline fills my body, head to toe. I never believed Kissinger. I never believed for a minute that all those guys came home. The numbers never added up. We had POW's in Laos, hundreds of them. We had them in South Vietnam. We knew of many in North Vietnam, who are unaccounted for even today. The POW issue is connected to one of my trip wires. The issue is plagued by half truths, lies and dirty politicians.

My plane lands in Richmond, the jolt brings me back to a better place. I had carry-on bags, so I went straight outside and hailed a cab. I was heading to the downtown Marriott. At check-in, I learn the Coliseum across the street, is the site of last week's execution style slaying of a teenager at a Rap Concert. I guess some other teenagers did it. The nearby mall remains closed. Welcome to life in 'declining' America.

In the room, I turn on the boob tube while I unpack. There's an ad for tonight's Nightline, with Ted Koppel. Be damned. It's the story of the Russian POW documents. What are the odds? *Trip my trigger twice today.* I'm tired, but I'll have to check it out. I promised my wife I'd try to get some rest. Look likes that's out.

My room service order came about the same time as Nightline. Koppel is MIA tonight, has a no-name stand-in. There's a Harvard Professor, who claims to have discovered the documents, and two Senators who are supposedly investigating the POW issue. One of the Senators is a pussy looking guy, a Vietnam Vet by the name of John Kerry. He's most famous for lying before Congress during the war. *I don't trust any of them.*

I eat while I listen. The Harvard guy is explaining how the documents are authentic. He sounds good. Long faced Kerry's trying to shoot him down big time. He's not interested in truth. The other Senator is in support of getting it on, forcing the gooks to fess up. As quick as he says something, Kerry's acting like it's no big deal. *I'd like to slap the shit out of that phony.* He wants to normalize relations with the gooks. *As I watch him talk, I see crosshairs superimposed over his ugly, privileged face. I'd like to put his ass on ice, and gently squeeze the trigger.*

Disgusted, angry and now adrenaline filled; I turn the TV off. I lay down for the night, a fat chance for sleep. I hate Kerry. I'm a conflicted Christian. I want to turn the other cheek, but when it comes to people like him, I'd like punch him in his horse face. I wanted sleep but was *soon back in Dong Ha with 3rd Force Recon.*

"Sergeant Rich, we going out with the same team tonight?" *My sniper partner and I had been working the mountains of the DMZ for two months. We worked near the Laotian border. We'd be dropped off, snoop and poop for signs of the NVA, spend ten days out and three back, then do it all again. Never knew what day it was, didn't matter.*

"No, we're one short. We lost one." I asked him who bought it? *That wasn't the case. He told me who it was, a hard nosed, tough, Corporal who'd been with Force awhile. He'd sit around on his off days, polishing his M-14 and his K-bar. All day long, he'd sit and polish them. He'd never talk. He had the eyes of Charlie Manson. We just left him alone. He was weird, but when the shit hit the fan, you wanted that sort of crazy at your side.*

The Recon team had made a night parachute jump last week. Five of them jumped, all supposed to pull right on exit. When Crazy jumped, he pulled left, not right, as they planned. When they regrouped on the ground, they couldn't locate him. There's an investigation. He had all his private things packed, and addressed for home. Sergeant Rich explained what the team thought happened. Either he flipped out, went Rogue or decided to join the gooks.

Vietnams a weird world. Never heard another word about him, ever. He was just gone. We lost your son Ma'm?

13 April, Tuesday - Petersburg, VA. Pepsi Meetings

Restless night. Early breakfast alone. I grab a USA Today, which is a habit when I travel. Always have my nose in the news. There's an article on the POW issue. Our illustrious President, Bubba the draft dodger, is going to send an Envoy to Vietnam. He wants answers. I'm sure having him in the White House puts the fear of God in the Vietnamese commies. *Give me a break. This pussy could be Kerry's brother.*

Our meetings went well. We met in Richmond yesterday afternoon and with the folks down here today. The 'good ole' boy thing' is alive and well here. When I was running this area from Baltimore last year, we had to fire several people because of racial discrimination. I grew up in rural Ohio, in my world, I didn't even have an opinion on the race issue. It's alive and well and unbelievable here in Virginia.

The local folks took me back to Richmond for my return flight to BWI. I had an hour or so to people watch. I sat there, thinking about the two young black Supervisors I had in one of my warehouses, in Danville, Virginia. What an awful thing. I went to Danville to meet with them, and they didn't want to have breakfast with me. I pushed the issue. They didn't want to put me in a bad position. Said they couldn't get served in Danville. I'm pissed. I told them to meet me at a local restaurant. They did. The waitress and staff avoided us for an hour. I finally went and had a 'chat' with the Manager. How awful is that? In 1991 no less.

My plane's here.

14 April, Wednesday - Washington, DC. A day off with the Family

I was supposed to have a breakfast meeting this morning with the Pepsi folks here, but it's been canceled, until tomorrow. Gloria and the kids suggest we take a day off. I'm hyper, so I wanted to blow off tomorrow's meeting, head home and work in New York. They remind me I've wanted to see the Vietnam Wall Memorabilia display, at the Smithsonian. It was a pretty spring day, and they convinced me to stay. I hadn't been to the Wall since my first visit in 1989. That visit was a rude awakening; *I broke down.*

We made our way to the American History Museum, through the usual DC traffic. We got lucky; there weren't any three hour waits as the last time we were here. The displays are touching. They aren't just artifacts; they're the core of war, and the lives that have been touched. I'm blessed, our two girls have an interest in the war. The materials are things left by people at the wall over the past ten years. *Reading the letters, is overwhelming, but I must.*

The displays captivate me. *I'm back in my world, Vietnam.* My family is patient. *There are boots, hats and medals. But what gets me are the letters.* When I go to the wall, I read every letter. *I can feel every word I read from a brother, a sister, a girlfriend, and parents. As I read, I realize the bullets of war continue to ricochet through the lives of loved ones, forever. They are wounds that never heal.*

The letters amaze me. I lost an older brother in a vehicle accident when I was eighteen, and he was twenty-four. I was sad and missed him, but I don't write him letters. *A typical letter at the Wall is from a woman, now in her forties or fifties. She's writing to the love of her life, telling him she has always wanted to visit the Wall, and finally made it. She tells him about her husband, her four children and how much she has missed him. Her heart is on that paper and so are my tears now.*

There's one from a soldier, still guilt ridden, writing to his friend to ask his forgiveness. Many make the trek every year, some every five or ten. But they keep coming. My heart's heavy, my nerves numb. I'm blessed to be with the three women in my life. They care, and understand. Even little Whitney seems to get it. My wife has always wanted to see the Cherry Blossom's, and they're in full bloom today. They pry me out of the museum. We walk by the Washington Monument and along the river. The trees are beautiful. We walked a long way.

I could see a crossing point, so we walked across the highway to the Reflection Pool. I knew the Wall was close. Without a word, we were pulled like a magnet to the Wall. We walked and took pictures. Whit had a little camera; she was our semi-official photographer. We pass vendors, guys my age, dressed in their old fatigues, presumably vets, selling paraphernalia, trinkets, flags and books. Still infuriated by the Russian report, and Senator Kerry's attitude, I buy a couple POW flags and window decals.

We walk by the statue of the three soldiers at the entry to the Wall. We stop; I struggle as I stare at the young faces on the statue. I'm struck by the Sculptor's ability to capture the youth, the innocence, on the faces of the young soldiers they represent. Yes, we were soldiers, sailors, airmen and Marines, and once, we were young. We leave the statue after a picture and head down into the V of the Wall. *I have to stop, every letter calls to me. I stop and read them. The first letter I read is from a sister, written for her brother. It's her five year update on her life. My mind begs me to leave, but my heart breaks for the fifty-eight thousand plus young men represented in the black granite. Many I helped zip into green plastic body bags.*

My reaction again surprised me. In Nam, I could care less. *You live you die, so what. If you're standing in the morning, you're a winner.* We walked away, *me a little slower, I was carrying a heavy heart the Wall had left me and my soul was struggling for air.* We headed to find a restaurant, and a motel. When we settled in it would be another troubled night for sure.

As I lay down, *It was 1989; we were visiting DC on a church trip. "I think its time for me to check out the wall." My wife agreed. We were in DC with a group from church to attend our temple there. We came down Friday afternoon from Pennsylvania, where we lived at the time. When the Wall was dedicated back in 1982, Greek begged me to come with him to the dedication. At the time, I didn't care. I wasn't into monuments or dedications.*

I never understood all the whining Vets did about what the government owes us. Get over it and move on. My feelings, neatly buried in a cement vault were not allowed out. By the time we found the Wall, and a parking place, it was near dark. We walked across the grass above the Reflection Pool. It was our first time in Washington at night. It was pretty, very impressive. Looking around it represented everything we fought for.

As we approached the sculpture of the three soldiers, my anxiety began to rise, along with my apprehension. I didn't know why. I'd never felt anything before. The lights gently bathed the faces of the men in the sculpture; I'd seen that sight before, in person. A bright Nam moon is bathing the faces of my brothers, as we sneaked through the jungle in the dead of night. The past twenty-one years, since I'd left Nam, to me, it was simply the adventure of a lifetime. My sniping days had caused more than a few screws to come loose in my head. But the ones that remained, I tried to keep screwed in tight. I didn't need anymore mental rattle.

We walked directly in front of the statue. I stared into the youth captured on their faces. That's when my roof came crashing down. I didn't understand what was happening to me. I'm captivated by the lifelike nature of what I'm seeing. Emotions I've never felt, welled up inside me. I mentally reach for my reserves, the place I call Nam. When things get tough, I go there. I tell myself, if I endured Nam, I can do anything. My emotions fight for air; they've been sealed up for a very long time. I can't take my eyes off the faces before me. I am them.

"Are you okay? My wife asks, as she squeezes my hand. My mind is now a kaleidoscope of emotions, images race across the screen of my life in living Technicolor. I'm staring into their eyes, but I see Dong Ha, Greek, Crud, Quang Tri, Camp Carroll, Perl, NVA running around us, the Rockpile, Con Thein, Cam Lo, Hood ... "Are you okay? I pull my hand from hers and bend down, placing my hands on my knees.

Someone walking by in a fatigue jacket says, "It's okay. Welcome home, Brother". I can't even relate, welcome home my ass. After several deep breath's, I stand and take one last look at the sculpture representing my brothers. I take my wife's hand in mine, turn, and head down the walk to the Wall. It's completely dark. The sounds of the city are alive in the background, but I might as well be alone as we walk to the black granite.

The Wall angles down into the ground, representing a war most want to forget. Yet, the Wall is impressive and inspiring. It starts small, then becomes wedge shaped in the middle, only to do the same on the other side. Over fifty-eight thousand young American lives are represented here. All lost. For what Mr. Johnson? Mr. McNamara? Mr. Westmoreland? For what?

I stopped to read a letter left by a girlfriend. My wife had a small flashlight in her purse that I used to see. She professed her love she once felt for the fallen soldier and the life she lost. Tears welled up in my eyes; a lump in my throat the size of a hand grenade.

We found a few names of those I knew, I wondered how many others were there, names of wounded I loaded on choppers, or zipped into body bags? They were just dead Marines with no names. I found Perl, Steven O. Perlewitz, my second sniper partner, blown to bits by an incoming mortar. There he was, a name on a black granite wall in the nation's capital, and a painful memory to loved ones back home.

I touched his name, rubbing each letter, as if touching my brother one more time. I bowed my head and knelt on one knee. I saw his body on a gurney at 3rd Med in Phu Bai, laying there in pieces. Now a follower of Jesus Christ, I said a prayer for my partner. Gloria wanted to keep moving, so we did. As I walked to the other end, I scanned every inch of the misery engraved on that dark wall. I would later tell my son, the value of that Wall, is that, in your generation, it must never happen again.

We walked silently across the grass and to our car. I was on patrol. My mind was ten-thousand miles away, in a land far, far away. I assured Gloria I was fine. That was a lie. Walking, I saw the funerals I'd helped conduct in Fort Wayne. I saw a rib cage in a tree. I saw everything, but where I was. It was chilly as we reached the car. We'd been there over an hour. My plan was to get in, take off and drive my feelings away. I helped my wife into the car and walked around to my side. I took several deep breath's on the way. As I sat down, I was sure I was back in control of my world. The doors in my mind were shut.

Inside the car, I put both hands on the wheel and stared into the night. I looked over at my wife, who knew me better than I knew myself. "It's okay. Let it out," she said. An F-5 tornado tore through my mind. I began sobbing uncontrollably. Why? I didn't know. I've never felt guilt. I've never felt sorrow. I've never felt anything, until right now. The damn broke and the flood waters gushed out, and Sgt. Kug was overwhelmed.

My wife slid over and put her arm around me. There were no words. I cried for an hour, she held me tight. We didn't talk. There was nothing to say. There was a crack in my core, the compartments I had neatly sealed, were cracked open. The feelings I never wanted, never allowed, now had air. What would I do with them now? Only time would tell.

We held each other for a long time, then, it was okay. I had my love with me, my therapist and my best friend. We drove back to our motel and went to bed. We had an early meeting with our church friends at the temple. It was the only place for me to be, after what I'd just been through.

16 April, Friday - Somers, NY. Pepsi

Back to work in Somers today. The girls and I had a nice day off. The drive home was nice; it was dry for a change. I entered my first meeting of the day and sit down. One of the Pepsi visitors from out of town looks at me with a strange little smile on his face. I say, " What's up?" He says, " Ed, is it true you were a Marine Sniper?"

I hardly know this dude. I say, "Who've you been talking to?" He avoids my question. "So, were you a real sniper?" I say, "What is a 'real' sniper?" He looks at me, then at the guy next to me, then back at me. "I mean a sniper that killed people?" My boss walks in and says, "Hey, what's up guys? You solving all our problems?" The questioner says, "Was he a Marine sniper in Vietnam?" My boss smiles and says, "He sure was!"

Fortunately, my boss started the meeting, and the guy disappeared into the audience before he could ask the proverbial 'how many people did you kill'. I never answer that question. That's not what it's all about. I'm not in the mood today. Too many meetings. I don't need to take the lid off my bad place. Not today.

17 April, Saturday - Brookfield, CT. Home

I had a great day at home with the family. We have sunshine. We worked outside. The blue skies reminded me of so many blue skies in Nam. That rattled around in my mind most of the afternoon. We had fun. We got cleaned up and went out for pizza. I went in to drop off a movie Cort had rented. When I went in, I was a still a little funky from my blue sky adventure.

I was looking around and saw the movie, Article 99. It was an offbeat movie about the problems of veterans. Gloria is a good barometer of what makes me weird. I asked her if she minded if I rented it. She gave me the green light. I wish Greek were still around; he'd appreciate the humor. But he's gone. Crud's gone. Demo Dean is too weird. He still lives with his Mother and runs his own patrols on the family farm. The rest are on radio silence for awhile. I pick up the movie, and we head home.

We get Whit to bed, and Gloria heads there, as well. She's given up on watching my weird movies. The movie was interesting, but admittedly, on the strange side. I have a hobby of studying organizations. Article 99 could be a study on the idiosyncrasies of bureaucracies. It was sad, the state of affairs of our veterans in this country. It seems far fetched, but it's true. Greek was in Philadelphia Naval Hospital and the Long Island VA hospital. Crud and Stu were in Chicago. Meatball was in Philly with Greek. All the stories were bad. I made it through the movie and didn't lose too much sleep.

18 April, Sunday - Newtown, CT. Church

Okay day at Church. I've been troubled about paying off the debt from our failed business. I seemed to sleep okay last night, but my anxiety has been going up all morning. Church has always been my haven from the storms of life. Lately, the storms have been invading my peaceful space. I scheduled an hour with the Bishop today. He's a good man. I just need a little counseling. It went okay. He doesn't understand my sleeping issues, but he's a good listener.

19 April, Monday - Danbury, CT. Shopping

I took a day off today, lots of travel on the horizon. Gloria and I went shopping. We needed a day together. I'm about to roll out my latest project, it has lots of different sites across the US and Canada. We have some housekeeping items to handle. Car license, driver's license and more moving items on the punch list.

We had lunch at our favorite Chinese restaurant. Got some tires on the car. I stopped by an auto supply store to pick up a bulb for the Bronco. I was standing by the car putting the bulb in when right behind me, *BANG!* It was loud. *Sounded like a rifle shot. I whirled around and went down on one knee. Eyes scanning the horizon in all directions. Where did it come from? Adrenaline flooded my veins; I was ready to fight.*

Fight? *I scan the immediate area in full Nam mode. Then I spot it. An old red Datsun with a blown out tire.* A friggin' blow out. *I nearly sprawled on the pavement. Goodness. I traveled from an outstanding day to war, in a split second. Twenty-five years, ten thousand miles and the demons are with me in a split second.* Oh well.

20 April, Tuesday - Toronto, Ontario, CN. Hilton Inn

Flew in this morning for an afternoon meeting. Had dinner with the folks and am catching up. Our family cottage is four hours north of here, near Sudbury, on the gorgeous French River. Can't wait for August, when we head north for our annual vacation. Greek loved the place. It is the only wilderness where I've been at peace since Vietnam.

As I write, I'm watching Canadian TV, the news. It's always interesting to see the difference in cultures, as close as we are. Tonight though, I can't believe what I'm hearing. The Canadian

Forces have troops in Somalia, on a Peacekeeping mission for the UN. Two Canadian Airborne soldiers are being accused of 'murdering' two Somali's in cold blood. They're playing the same crap up here in Parliament, accusing the military of covering up the truth. *The door to my bad place is pushing itself open. I saw the same shit in Nam. For every Lt. Calley rightly charged, there are a hundred poor guys who are fodder for the turncoat media and attention grabbing politicians. I'd like to jack slap those holier than thou bastards. The new ruling elite, our phony politicians. We're screwed.*

Another short night. Sleep is nowhere to be found. *"Sir, there were no water buffaloes." I was sitting front and center before our sniper Lieutenant in the 4th Marine headquarters tent. The Colonel's chopper had just picked me up in the Co Bi Than Tan Valley. I had to leave my Rogue patrol with Hood in charge. A couple Vietnamese civilians, I'd called a Medivac chopper for, came back to 3rd Med and reported we shot them off their water buffaloes. The Lieutenant was our 'administrative' leader. When he first came in three months ago, he thought we snipers were out of control. He wasn't a fan. So this could be interesting.*

When he first came to the platoon he ordered me to shave my mustache. He was on a power trip. I went to the bush and stayed six weeks, just to avoid him. When I returned for a day, he happened by my tent. When he saw me he was furious. I'd anticipated this day. I recited a specific Marine Corps order that permitted Sergeant E-5's or above, to have neatly trimmed mustaches. He wasn't impressed.

He shot right back with a Marine Corps order that said I would obey my commanding officer. He was serious. "You will shave that off by morning Sergeant!" I stood and thought for a minute. "With all due respect Sir, I request mast to see the Colonel." Every person in the Naval Service has the right to request mast, that is a request to see the next highest in command. The Lieutenant stormed off, only to return about five minutes later.

"Sergeant Kugler, the Colonel will see you at 0700 hours. You will shave that mustache tonight, or I will Court Martial you in the morning." He turned and left me to smoke that message. I led a team that did the Colonel's bidding in the bush. I had bought his wife items he requested

when I went on R & R to Hong Kong. But this Lieutenant didn't like me. I'd grown that mustache on the way to Nam aboard ship. But I shaved it and waited for morning.

I walked into the command tent at 0655. The Colonel and Lieutenant were already there. The Lieutenant went first, explaining his case. The Colonel turned to me and said, "Sergeant Kugler, what's this about?" I told him it was simple. I was a Sergeant E-5, had been in country over eighteen months, and felt that a neatly trimmed mustache was little to ask for my service.

The Colonel smiled, turned to the Lieutenant and said, "Lieutenant, quit screwing with him. He can have his damned mustache. We have more things to worry about than this shit." Chalk one up for the Kug. He dismissed us both, and we went our separate ways. Now, I'm sitting before this same Lieutenant three months later, with charges my team shot innocent civilians. It wasn't starting out to be my best day.

The Lieutenant wanted to know the details, no bullshit he said, before he took me in before the Colonel. It was pretty simple. I'd had my Rogues working the valley for nearly six months. Business was good. The valley was what they called a Free Fire Zone. Shoot any living thing that moves. It was, as they say, a target rich environment. Before we inserted, the Marine grunts went on a sweep of the entire valley, removing all non-combatants. Then the Seabees built them new metal roof huts, down by the sea. The South Vietnamese government told them they couldn't return. The valley was a major infiltration route south, from the mountains, into Hue.

The issue we faced was driven by our illustrious allies, the ARVN's, the Army of the Republic of Vietnam. Thanks to them, the bad guys knew the exact boundary of the Free Fire Zone. They would dress like local villagers, pretending to pick berries, right at the edge of the Zone on the east side. Then they'd call mortars on our heads. Made our lives pretty miserable. They also brought women and kids along, to make them look like a normal bunch of berry pickers. The LT listened intently, looking very irritated, as I continued.

Tired of the harassment, we decided two could play the game. We crept into the tall grass at the edge of the Free Fire Zone during the night. At first *light, out came three tough looking dudes in black pajamas, surrounded by four young women, with a couple kids tagging along, one on a water buffalo. We stayed hidden, watching, as they worked their way to the top of the hill in front of us. They were about two hundred feet away.*

The women and children were picking berries and putting them into the bags they carried. The three guys, stared into the valley, looking for us. They would occasionally bend down, as though there were picking berries, most of the time, they were eyeballing the valley. An hour into the stake out, one of the dudes reached into his bag, knelt down and pulled out a pair of binoculars. He is now a combatant.

We wait. In a few minutes, another guy reaches in and pulls out a radio handset. We could see the cord reaching back into his bag. That's where the radio had to be. We knew they were spotters, about to call mortars on grunts in the valley. He was a combatant. The third guy stood scanning the countryside around them. The women and kids were all around the bad guys.

No one would fire until I fired, it was my decision. We had also counted off, with me being one, then two, and on through our six. If there were only three targets, then only three would fire. We set in position, about five yards apart. There was no communicating now, except with hand signals, we were too close. I motioned to Hood, closest to me, it was game time.

Two hundred feet was a chip shot for us. I cranked off the first round, and the radioman dropped where he stood. The others took off running. We fired a total of five shots, hitting two of the three. The survivor made an Olympian dash over the top of the hill to safety. We leaped to our feet and ran to the scene.

The women and children stood frozen in fear, as we descended on them. We found two of the women with minor graze wounds, both on their lower legs. They weren't life threatening, nor were they bleeding badly. But I knew the right thing to do was to evacuate them to 3rd Med. I also knew if I called a Marine Medivac and told them it was for 'indigenous personnel,' as they were so eloquently called; I'd sit there all day waiting.

So I called a Medivac for a Marine casualty. The birds came zooming in looking for a fight. The Medivac chopper was an old UH-34, a *gas job, accompanied by two Huey gunships. The Huey's were swooping over us on both sides. I was on the radio. I knew these pilots were pissed. We popped our yellow smoke; the Medivac lined up for approach. The gunships kept circling, I told them the direction the bad guy ran. As the Medivac chopper neared the ground, the pilot saw the two women and started cussing at me over the radio. All I could do at that point was turn my back on him. They loaded the women on the chopper and headed back in the air.*

Within half an hour, I received a call from the combat operations center telling me the Colonel wanted to see me. He sent his Huey out to get me. I knew what it was about. I left Hood in charge, hopped my personal escort back to Camp Evans, and prepared for the worst. That's what got me here, sitting before the LT who didn't like me much. After the mustache incident, I figured this was his opportunity for payback. He told me the women said there were no men, and we'd just shot them off their water buffaloes. That's when I said, "Sir, there were no water buffaloes." He finally broke his stare and smiled. He said, "Kugler, you Marines do a helluva job out there. I'll talk to the Colonel. Get the hell back out there with your men." The truth had never failed me, and it didn't fail me here.

21 April, Wednesday - Toronto, Ontario, CN. Hilton Inn

Good day today at Pepsi Canada. Good people. Wish I could get transferred here. I'd be within four hours of our cottage. Snowed here today, so spring hasn't sprung just yet. Same routine as last night. Watching the evening news. I see an Admiral Vessey, in Hanoi. He's with a couple Generals from the distinguished Vietnamese Government. The report says he's on a mission, from President Billy Bob himself. The draft dodging President will solve the problem. Sure he will.

The Admiral is letting the Vietnamese attest to the fact that the Russian documents on the POW's is a fake. Vessey asserts that the Vietnamese are telling the truth. The Russians are lying. I'm certain he's going to say the moon's made of cheese too.

In the few seconds I've spent watching this political bullshit, my red rage is rising. It gets worse. I see this smiling little gook, a General, offering Vessey some 'newly' discovered hospital records what will clear up some more names. And of course the pussy, Vessey, says how important today is. My ass!

I turned off the TV and tossed the remote across the room. Going to be a tough night. *I've got gooks dancing in my head; they're holding AK's, not fake documents. "The American government are killers. They killed on our main campus last week; they've been killing for years in Vietnam. They must be stopped, now. They are the problem".* Since the killings by the Ohio National Guard, my Sociology class has been nothing but an anti-war, anti-government and anti-American propaganda machine. Our woman Professor has always walked with a left bent, but since the tragedy during the protests on the main campus in Kent, it's been ridiculous.

My wife talked me in to trying college. It was a Branch Campus of Kent State University; it was May, 1970. I've been working full time and attending here full time. I've been playing charades with these people, teaching us things they've never done, for two years now. Today, it's just too much.

She turns every class into a platform to rail against America. I hold up my hand, "What happened up there is a tragedy. But none of it would have happened, were it not for the students burning down the ROTC building." She smiled, obviously amused at what I'd said. Then she says, "Well, it was an old building. We don't need those people on our campus." With that epitaph, the long hairs in the class clapped, some cheered and others just sat there.

I stood and said, "You don't need me on your campus either." I turned, walked out, and vowed whatever I accomplished in this world, it wouldn't be because of a college education. I would never attend college again. Screw it!

23 April, Friday - Brookfield, CT. Home

Home again, worked late tonight, after a week on the road. Got home after 7 PM. I have three weeks of solid travel coming up. I feel disjointed. Tired. Need this weekend.

24 April, Saturday - Brookfield, CT. Home

I woke up, and *my world is black. Depression. Or the black bastard as I call it. It rained last night, poured actually. I lay awake listening.* But I did fall asleep, no demons in the night. It's about 10 AM. I don't feel like getting up. Feels like a big ass elephant is sitting on my chest. Trevor and his girlfriend are driving up today from Pennsylvania.

Greek's wife Bobbie wanted me to have his boat It's a Boston Whaler he used in Long Island Sound. Trevor is interested but doesn't have any money. I shouldn't spend the money with what I owe on my failed business. Wasn't sure where we'd go with it. When Gloria and I were there last week, Bobbie insisted I bring it home. She didn't want it sitting at her house. I understood. Now it's in our driveway.

I got myself together by the time Trevor arrived. We all went to lunch. His girlfriend is nice. I struggled all day. Couldn't shake whatever crept into my head overnight. Spent the rest of the day at home. Trevor loves Greek's boat. Greek wanted him to have it. I'll have to cut a deal with Bobbie, and work out the money.

Time for bed, it's dark outside, and inside as well.

25 April, Sunday - in the air to Atlanta, US Air

Hate when I have to leave on Sunday. *The black will have to be pushed aside, I have a mission.* In the air to Atlanta, doing training tomorrow and Tuesday. Tuesday evening I fly to Cleveland to do it all again Wednesday. From there, to Boston for two days of the same thing. I'll be sick of hearing myself speak by Friday night.

As I write today, *it's just one more corporate patrol. In Nam, with Force Recon, it was ten days out, three back, repeat for three months in a row. Never knew what day it was, and didn't care. With the Rogues, we lived in the valley for six months of patrols. Put your head down, and do what needs doing. That's how I cope here.*

Time to go over my material for the morning.

27 April, Tuesday - Cleveland, OH. Stouffer's Towers, Downtown

At the hotel. It's midnight. I had breakfast before the meeting at 0700. I slept most of the way in from Atlanta last night. The cab ride to the hotel cleared my head. It wasn't a cab; it was a dilapidated van. The driver looked as bad as his ride. He even had a computer in his piece of junk. Told me he needed it for messages. I didn't wave the green flag, but this guy was clearly in a race. We burned up the freeway, passed everything in sight and a few that weren't. He weaved in and out of traffic while trying to read messages on his computer. It was good therapy on a late night.

Almost made me forget my walk out of Cleveland Hopkins Airport. It's where I flew to Parris Island from when I joined the Corps. I flew to California on my way to Vietnam from there too. I knew Hopkins well. *I remembered my Dad shaking my hand when I left, and again when I came home. There were no 'hugs' in our house.* As I write tonight one trip home sticks out, it won't go away. *Easter weekend, 1967. That was a real trip. A twenty-seven year old girl started writing me while I was in Nam. I thought it was cool; she was older than me. She was living in San Francisco. I agreed to pick her up at the airport when I was home on leave between Nam tours.*

I showed up early and stopped in one of the airport bars. While sitting there sipping a Manhattan, I met a United Airlines pilot. We talked; he bought me a drink, thanked me for being a Marine, and serving in Vietnam. He couldn't believe I was heading right back. Turns out he was meeting two Stewardesses there in a few minutes and offered me a night on the town. Told me I could have my pick of the two. I told him I appreciated it, but had a date. When I told him it was a 'blind' date, he soundly encouraged me to blow it off, spend the night with him and his friends and assured me I wouldn't regret it. Something told me he was right, but I couldn't do it, even in my Nam state of mind I didn't want to leave whoever she was, standing with no ride home.

The pilot and I split when I went to meet my surprise girl. It didn't take long to see her letters were the best part of our short relationship. I stood at parade rest, dressed in my best Hong Kong suit. I held her gift behind my back. Many cute young women walked off that plane, but my date walked off last. She looked every bit like Mama Cass, wearing an Easter bonnet the size of Texas. She walked straight over to me and said, "You must be Ed?" I dropped the gift I'd bought her behind me. Unfortunately, her personality matched her outfit and the night went downhill from there. I drove her home and split. The Rogues predicted my demise, so they got a kick out of it when I got back to Nam.

Time for bed.

28 April, Wednesday - Boston, MA. Westin Hotel

Just arrived, late. I'm tired. *My corporate patrol, this week, is on its last leg. At least they don't shoot bullets at me on a stateside patrol.* Just caught the late news, it's disgusting. *Our great draft dodger President is talking about sending troops to Bosnia, wherever the hell that is?* I remember taking my son to the Wall, and telling him, "Trevor, remember Vietnam, make sure the lives represented by the names on that wall are never forgotten. They are young people like you. It's not for nothing, if, IF, you and your generation see to it, that this never, EVER, happens again!"

I sit here tonight, getting more pissed off by the minute listening to this clueless, so called Commander in Chief, supporting the United Nations in another ill-fated intervention, that will do nothing more than make somebody, somewhere, rich. Our military leaders say we shouldn't put troops in Bosnia. Sounds like Vietnam when Lyndon Johnson and McNamara, ignored the military's advice. How can these bastards sleep at night? I give up; I gotta' get to bed.

29 April, Thursday - Boston, MA. Westin Hotel

I skipped dinner with everyone tonight. Needed some space, time to wind down from the week. Flying home tomorrow night. I'll go by the office on the way home. As I look back on this week,

I'm grateful Nam taught me that preparation is survival. That knowledge gives me an edge in business. I learned so much there that serves me well today.

I learned to stay close to my people, the boots on the ground. It pays off here in the world, big time. Another big learning is how organizations work. There are two organizations. One is on paper, represented by the organization chart. That's the one most leaders think makes things happen. The other, the informal organization, makes everything happen.

Talked with my boss tonight. The feedback on my training is great. He's already getting calls. He said one field manager called and said, "This guy gets it. His training is real." Glad to hear it. That makes all the work worthwhile.

As I've been writing, I've also been channel surfing. Normal for me. I just hit CNN, a network I can't stand. They have a Special Report on, called, the 'Vietnamese Syndrome'. A news piece on veterans and why Nam won't go away. I guess if I knew, I'd make mine go away. I watch it for awhile, then turn it off. I don't want to get wired heading home for a much needed weekend.

***

I quit writing, and my phone rang. It was a guy I worked with for a decade at Frito. Great guy. He was calling to catch up, and tell me about his new job. He got fired in a unique way on Black Monday at Frito. That's when I got fired. Their strategy was to dump guys in their forties, at the same time they were dumping other people, thus, no issues with age discrimination. In my friend's case, he was out of work having gall bladder surgery. He got a letter in the mail, telling him he no longer worked at Frito Lay. Had a three month severance check attached. That's the thanks he got after twelve years with the company, and nothing but Superior reviews. It was the PepsiCo way. Great jobs, few careers.

It's past midnight. I'm having trouble lying down. Been getting four and five hours sleep a night this week. Not good.

30 April, Friday - US Air, Boston Logan to LaGuardia

Logan Airport on a Friday is not the best of ideas. But we're finally in the air, running late, but airborne. *Bad night. That's three in a row. Spooked by noises, and lights in the window. Went on all night. You'd think a forty-six year old man could figure out there wasn't any real threat. I'm sleeping on the third floor, is Spiderman coming in? Who knows? The ghosts keep coming.* I head to Denver Sunday night. Lovely.

Just looked at my planner, and realized today is the thirtieth of April. It was twenty-eight years ago today, I'd been wounded fighting in Santo Domingo. It was a blur then, *clear today. I woke up the next morning in Womack Army Hospital, Fort Bragg, North Carolina. I came via evacuation to the USS Wasp. We transferred to a plane in Puerto Rico. A lot of that day is still a blur.*

I remembered my poor Mom. She's no longer with us now; she passed away at age fifty-three, in 1984, from cancer. Santo Domingo was tough on her. I'll never forget my call to her that first morning. I was back in Womack Army Hospital, in Ft. Bragg. That's where all Dominican casualties were evacuated. "Mom, this is Ed". *The nurses told us to call home. I was standing in the hallway off the ward where the wounded were being treated. There was silence on the other end.* "Mom, I'm in the hospital. I'm in North Carolina. I'm fine. It's minor stuff. *I could hear her quietly crying. I waited.* "I'm okay Mom". *I waited. Then I hear her broken voice,* "Eddie, it's okay. I've prepared myself. Tell me the truth!" *The truth? It baffled me why she didn't believe me.*

"Tell me the truth! I know you can't walk!" *Can't walk? I walked out here to the pay phone.* "Mom, I walked out here to call you. I'm standing here. I'm okay. What are you talking about?" *Mom rarely raised her voice, but she was upset and didn't want to hear the 'fine' treatment from me. I got a nurse who explained to her I was fine.*

When we sorted it all out, it was a terrible snafu. For starters, she had seen me on the front page of the only Sunday paper in our area, the Akron Beacon Journal. I was lying on a stretcher at the Polo Grounds, with the other wounded, waiting to be evacuated. That was her first clue. When the telegram arrives via the local Sheriffs department, the real pain hit home. She read me the telegraph. It described wounds I'd received to my neck area. It went on to say 'possible paralysis from the neck down'. I realized the injuries were to the New Jersey kid who took two machine gun rounds to the throat. Had to be him. We didn't think he would live.

Mom was ecstatic when she realized it was a mistake. I went back to the Ward, got back in bed, and realized somewhere in New Jersey, my Mother's happiness was about to turn into tragedy for another Marine Mother. Until now, she was probably feeling pretty good. When the Marine Corps got it all straightened out, she'd be wondering the same thing I was, how do you make a mistake like that?

MAY

1 May, Saturday - Brookfield, CT. Home

Slept in with the love of my life this morning. We were up late talking. Cortney is still having problems adjusting at school. We got up and had brunch with the girls. Then, we headed out, to checkout a couple of used Yamaha jet skis. We've wanted some for a few years now, but with my business debts, still can't afford them.

Tonight we drove to Milford, Connecticut, an hour away, to attend a performance of the Folk Dancers, a BYU performing group. The kids took friends, and it was a great evening. The group was incredible. It was a great break from life on the road. We stopped on the way home for ice cream. Everything feels right for a change. Jesus Christ and His Gospel are my saving my life. The gospel and spending time at our cottage on the French are what bring peace to my soul.

Gloria asked me today if I saw the POW report on TV. I didn't. She said it detailed sightings of POW's that are certified as real, by an Intelligence Officer in our government. She said the guy saw a pilot code, in an aerial photo dated in 1992. Apparently, it was written on the ground, to be seen from the air. They reported that the number in the aerial photo tracked with an actual pilot's code, the type used during the Vietnam War.

If that's not bad enough, the report will say that the Navy, Marine Corps and the Air Force have destroyed the list of codes. The Codes tied directly to every pilot who flew in Vietnam. Is that bullshit or what? How the hell long can the government lie to us about this stuff? *It's infuriating.*

The drive home was in the moonlight. The silvery nights I remember so well. We arrived home a little while ago, just past midnight. Got the kids off to bed, and laid down for my last night at home for another week. The moon was still *bright, glistening through the blinds in our bedroom.*

Gloria fell asleep quickly. I opened the blinds so I could see the full moon. *I smiled to myself, thinking about that same moon in Nam. I wondered what Vietnam was like today? What do the killing fields of the DMZ look like now? I smiled again, as I thought about the rock apes who accosted us on top of the Rockpile. I wondered about it all peacefully for a change. Tonight was a good night; even Nam couldn't ruin that.* Somehow, *I still find it all perversely, romantic.*

2 May, Sunday - Brookfield, CT.

Sometime after midnight Gloria woke up. When she lay down, she asked me why the blinds were open? She knew about my mirror, when I told her; she just leaned over, gave me a kiss and a sigh. I got up and closed the blinds.

The bright light of the moon streaked through our room in slivers, *reminding me of nights in the jungle. The hundreds of angles of light shooting like lasers through the eerie night was freaky.* I stood up, opened the blinds, allowing one big blast of light back into our room.

I drifted off. In a deep sleep, *I heard running outside the house. I tensed up, but tell myself it's a dream.* I close my eyes again. *I hear laughter outside.* I sit up. The clock reads 0130. Gloria is up, she heard someone talking. *I'm in a fog. I'd finally been sleeping, now I don't know if it's gooks or I'm dreaming?*

I hear running again. We didn't have street lights close, but *I was used to seeing in a full moon. Adrenaline surged, as I got up and went to the window.* I hear kids talking that I can't see, one running up my driveway and a couple on our trampoline. I thought about two older boys who came to the door, asking to use the trampoline. When I said no, they weren't very happy. I guess they decided to use it in spite of my refusal.

The trampoline was in a wide spot of our driveway. I was looking out our second story bedroom window. *My first thought was; one grenade will gettem' all. But I was in Brookfield, not Con Thein.* My wife joined me at the window. We watched for awhile, then I reached over and flipped on the flood lights. As I did I yelled out the window. They scattered like cockroaches. They were just kids. Doesn't say much for their parents, who should have their butts kicked for not knowing where they're kids were.

The excitement over, we got back to bed about 0200. Another short night. Church in a few hours, and a flight to Denver this evening.

Later Sunday: In the air - Denver, CO. US Airway

Short night. Long day. Changed planes in Pittsburgh. One more corporate patrol. Five out and two back, reminiscent of days gone-by. Just woke up from a short nap. Got in late, Denver time. My body is on Eastern time, I think? Will spend tomorrow at the plant. We just bought it from a franchisee. Teach classes for a couple days.

03 May, Monday - Denver, CO. Stouffer's Concourse Hotel

Got up this morning, and opened the drapes to the snow covered Rocky Mountains. Gorgeous. God's beauty in the form of a mountain. Did my heart good.

The plant was interesting. Very nice facility downtown. They were removing a plexiglass walkway through the plant while I was there. They used it for school kids to come and take tours. Why remove it? Seems Pepsi Corporate, where I work, has ordered them to take it out. I guess they'd rather pay Michael Jackson millions of dollars, than get the kids hooked on the product while they're young. Makes no sense. The old owners told me they 'owned' the market in Denver.

But, headquarters never listens. *Just like Nam, they never listened, sure they knew better. They'd sit back in the rear, commanding those big desks and send young people to their deaths.*

04 May, Tuesday - Denver, CO. Stouffer's Concourse Hotel

Getting ready for bed. Long day, then dinner. Good folks out here. Training went well. Talked with Gloria. My travel is hard on her. She has to deal with everything and the kids alone. I'm not watching the evening news this week. Too hard.

05 May, Wednesday - Denver, CO. Stouffer's Concourse Hotel

Heading home tomorrow, taking Friday off. Need a break from Pepsi. Just packed up, ready for my ride to the airport in the morning. Had some Pepsi Pretty types show up for the training today. They are the chosen ones, dark suit, red or yellow tie, suspenders are a plus, wire glasses and a few strategic questions on queue. *Politics to most, bullshit to realists like me.*

I have several years under my belt now. I learned to deliver results in the Marine Corps. These college types, who wear their MBA's on their sleeves, know only how to deliver a 'performance', not results. Don't talk to them about the real world, just the one they play games with other peoples money. I struggle big time with where our world is heading. It's no longer what is - it's only what it appears to be.

06 May, Thursday - In the air heading home - US Air

A rare night. I slept until morning. Feel pretty good, for being on the road all week. At least being on the road keeps me out of the headquarters culture of 'meetings r us'. It's amazing. One of these days, we'll be having a meeting to decide how many meetings to have. Incredible.

07 May, Friday - Brookfield, CT. Home (at last)

Home late yesterday afternoon. Almost made dinner. Got up to see the girls before school. Gloria and I spent the day together.

We all went out to eat tonight, which was great. It must be spring, the trees in the neighborhood are green again.

08 May, Saturday - Brookfield, CT. Home

We rode to Hartford today, for a little shopping. As we were driving to Hartford, Gloria and the kids kept asking me if I could hear the squeak in our brakes. I didn't hear a thing. They teased me about getting old. My last Pepsi physical showed I had about twenty percent hearing loss in one ear. *Probably came from sniper training. We shot for thirty minutes, half hour on, half hour off, twelve hours a day. Did that for four weeks in a row, seven days a week. Doubt if that can be good for the ears. All we had for ear plugs was used cigarette butts.*

Came home and worked in the yard, doing some landscaping. Gorgeous day outside, finally. It was supposed to rain today, looks like it might yet tonight. Planted some shrubs, and made an island of sorts in the yard with wood chips. It was a fun break, to work together outside, and do something physical for a change.

We discovered a screen was removed from a downstairs window in the back of our house. We could see marks, where someone used a tool, maybe a screwdriver, to tear the screen. Not good with me traveling. Hope it's the local kids and not a pro. I do not own a gun for a reason, I'd use it.

As I was cleaning up the front yard, *I heard the unmistakable whomp, whomp, whomp of chopper blades. I didn't even need to look up. It was a Chinook. I always get a good feeling; it's a resupply, or an extraction or a rescue. For some reason, in the midst of a wonderful family day, I could still feel the pull from my bad place.* I don't know if it was the torn screen on our window, who knows? I don't. *But my bad place was creaking open, I hoped it wouldn't swallow me whole.*

We lay down for bed around eleven, rare for me. I dozed off quickly only to wake up half an hour later. It was raining. *I felt anxious.* It was a steady, but gentle rain. *It unnerved me.* I thought about the kids on the trampoline last Saturday, the window screen today and the mailboxes. *I jumped up, quickly going downstairs to check the house. Adrenaline was my friend at times like tonight. I checked the house.* No security issues, I returned to bed.

Back in bed, I listened to the rain and drifted off ... *"Sergeant Kugler. Get your snipers. Help us gather the dead." It was one tough night, in the Street Without Joy. Morning light raised its ugly head. We had six snipers, with two Marine company's. A total of about three hundred Marine grunts. We'd been fighting all night, been overrun at one point, but fought back and retook the ground we lost. It was brutal.*

"Yes Sir!" I rounded up our snipers and did a head count. We'd all survived the night. The first choppers were on their way. They'd pick up the wounded, who were lined up in triage order, awaiting the help they so desperately needed. We had half an hour or so, to gather the dead from the battlefield, zip them in body bags, and line them up for the next choppers.

The carnage we witnessed came straight from Washington. Assholes! Yesterday, which seems like a lifetime ago, the commanders called the grunts together, made them hand in their trusty, proven M-14's and then issued them the brand spanking new, McNamara supported M-16's. To say that the decision was 'unimaginable' wouldn't do it justice.

Marines loved their reliable M-14's. Every Marine regularly tested out on their 14's, field stripping them while blindfolded, in sixty seconds or less. That means; they'd take it apart and put it back together, blindfolded. They did this so they could fix it in combat, day or night.

The higher-ups, the Bastards, ordered the change of weapons. The grunts got exactly two hours training on the shiny new M-16. Then they wished them well and sent us all on our way to one of the nastiest areas of Nam. Nonsense disguised as leadership. Craziness. All to meet some asshole in Washington's deadline for the roll out of the new weapon. A deadline they pulled out of their ass.

We wandered the battlefield, picking up thirty-five dead Marines, half of which had their new M-16's apart in their dead hands. Their new rifles had jammed, misfired at the wrong time. These brave young Marines, our brothers, died trying to fix an ill conceived, rushed out, new weapon. Wish

McNamara and his Whiz Kids were here with us today. After they zipped up a few body bags we could stick their college degrees up their asses, sideways.

Everyone dealt with death differently. Some became angry. Some became quiet and sullen. Others filled the time with black humor. Me? I had a switch in my head. I just turned it off and kept going. Better you than me brother. Zip. Done and gone. Where are the choppers? Take me with you.

09 May, Sunday - White Plains, NY. Airport

Heading to Detroit. What else is new? Good day with the family. Church, home, and an afternoon together. *Very tired, after a tough night in Nam.* Feeling better now, than when I got up this morning. Gorgeous day. A beautiful day to be alive.

10 May, Monday - Detroit, MI. - Marriott Downtown

One day down, another here tomorrow. Then back to New York for a meeting, then to Chicago Thursday and Friday. The group here is an interesting one. Experienced in years, but not learning. Michigan, the Union state. Unions limit a person's growth. The gross entitlement mentality will one day destroy the place. Learned that truth when we lived here, when I ran logistics operations for Frito Lay. If it's easy anywhere else, it will be hard in Detroit. If it's hard anywhere else, it will be impossible here.

They got up in arms because the new process is too 'directive', it won't work here. They're suffering from the 'we're different syndrome'. My mission is simple in the 'New Pepsi'. We're improving processes, and whether I waltz them, charm them, or drag them, this is the way we're doing it. Corporate claims they've driven a stake in the ground, their way or the highway. We'll see if I have air cover when the shit hits the fan here?

By lunch, the discussion turns to how disempowering it is to be told what to do. I told them I was most empowered in the Marine Corps. They looked surprised; some laughed, many in disbelief. I explain my rationale. In Detroit, the reaction is expected. I told them every single location thought it was the right thing to do, but in Detroit, you guys don't like it. They're unimpressed, so am I.

At lunch, one of the local leaders who's assisting me, tells me his dad was in the Army. Turns out, he just got out. Discharged from Fort Benning, an Army Ranger. Nice young guy. Each subsequent break in the afternoon, he'd come over and talk sniping. Others came by; the fascination started. Glad breaks had time limits.

Dinner tonight was okay; things warmed up between me and most of the participants. No news tonight, trying to keep the black from taking over my mind.

11 May, Tuesday - US Air - Circling, White Plains, NY. Airport

Woke up dead tired this morning. Slept all night, still worn out. Trouble sleeping in hotels unless Gloria's with me. Training finished well. At least as well as it can in Detroit. Now the problem belongs to local management. I see why they want robots here now.

Been quite a trip home. Right now I'm five hours late coming in from Detroit. Flew to Pittsburgh and ran into US Scare cost savings again. "We're so sorry ladies and gentlemen, due to 'mechanical difficulty', we have to cancel your flight to White Plains. We will re-route you through LaGuardia". The third time this month they've cancelled a commuter flight through Pittsburg. You'd think they would use an excuse other than 'mechanical difficulties' in the airline industry. Truth is they always cancel if the flight is less than half full, as it was again today.

I refused to go to LaGuardia, since my car is in White Plains. The bus they promise from LaGuardia is usually nothing more than a mirage. I had to connect through Syracuse. Syracuse Airport was a real trip. I stand corrected. It's Syracuse International Airport. International? They must have flights to Canada? It looks like they just chased the cows off the runway.

Finally got my flight to White Plains, and now we're circling. Why would we have to circle an airport with eight flights a day? It'll be after midnight when I get home.

12 May, Wednesday - White Plains, NY. Airport

Seems like I was just here. Oh yes, I was. Waiting for my flight to Chicago. Meetings in headquarters weren't worth the flight back. But, mine is not to question, but to do. Great, but short night at home. Got to see the girls this morning. Need to sleep on the way to Chicago.

13 May, Thursday - Schaumburg, IL. Marriott Hotel

Meetings all day. With Pepsi's largest bottler, General Bottlers. Great people. They run better operations than we do at corporate Pepsi. It's been a good day. More meetings in the morning, then home again. Looking forward to the weekend.

14 May, Friday - US Air, heading to White Plains, NY. Airport

Enjoyed working with these folks here in Chicago, class act. It'll be good to be home. At least I wasn't cancelled out of Pittsburg tonight. Should be home by seven, maybe eight. Tired this morning again. *Sometimes I think I wear myself down, so I know I'll sleep. Maybe it works; the demons have been silent.*

15 May, Saturday - Brookfield, CT. Home at last

We had a beautiful day today. We finished working on our landscape project out front. Lots of digging, planting trees, shrubs and flowers. Then came the wood chips. As I carried forty pound bags of wood chips from the garage to the front yard, *I was in Nam. We were filling sand bags in Camp Carroll, to build the Taj Mahal of bunkers for the COC, our regimental Combat Operations Center. We spent a week, sun up to sun down, building a fortress thick enough to withstand a direct hit from NVA rockets. Each bag I carried brought new memories.* But my family brought me back to Brookfield.

We cleaned up, and drove to Southbury, Connecticut to do some shopping. Gloria's great with a dollar and saw some sales down that way. She was on a mission to get me to wear sandals, which I've never been able to wear. *They remind me too much of the gooks. She's used to my quirks from Nam. She doesn't ask anymore, when I take my glass of ice water to bed every night. I never want warm water to drink again, ever.*

16 May, Sunday - Brookfield, CT. Home and Church

Church and home. First time in several Sundays I don't have to leave tonight. Cortney's been fighting a sore throat. After dinner, she comes in to complain that I don't give her any sympathy. She's right. *I can still hear my DI at Parris Island. "If you want sympathy, you'll find it in the dictionary between shit and syphilis." I'm day dreaming* when she says, "It doesn't pay to get sick in this family with you around".

I tell her that's a little harsh. She says, "Hardly, you always tell us to suck it up. Think about how you were with Trevor." On that one, she's right. He was a basketball player. In Middle School, he came home early one day. Walked into the house holding his wrist. Said the Coach told him to go to the Doctor.

I'd just came home from work. My wife started for the door, I asked him a few questions, checked it out, and pronounced it sprained, not broken. I told my wife to put some ice on it, he was good to go. He complained, and I did remember saying, *"suck it up."* He wasn't feeling any better in the morning but went to school. I tell him to tough it out. He comes home; the Coach can't believe he hasn't been to the Doctor. We piled in the car heading to the ER.

The Doctor walked in the door, looked across the room at my son and said, "How'd you break your arm?" I looked up, without thinking and said, "How do you know it's broken?" He smiled and quietly explained 'that's what I do'. He asks Trevor, "What have you been doing for it?" Trevor says, "Putting ice on it". He turns, looks at me, and asks my son, "Who told you to do that?" According to him, you never put ice on a break.

My problem was reaching for sympathy and finding none. There's nothing there but a void. I try to be aware of it, be in tune to what is happening, but it rarely works. Stuck now, I was without feelings. Suck it up, no whining, just get it done. I've always had trouble separating my life in the here and now, and the life deeply imprinted deep inside my mind.

We all laughed but knew there was a big ass elephant standing in the kitchen that we didn't talk about enough. The elephant was me. We came home in a silent car. Once in bed, *I was on Dong Ha Mountain with 3rd Force Recon. It was late summer, 1966. It's been hot, tiring and nasty. We're finally out of the jungle canopy, at least enough to see the Rockpile looming above us. Crutch and I spent three weeks up there during Operation Hastings. Now we've just finished Operation Prairie. We've been with Force Recon just like in Hastings. Now we're linking up with elements of the 3rd Battalion, 4th Marines. We'd been trading blood with North Vietnam's 324th B Division. Racking up body counts that'll make the arrogant McNamara proud. That was his way of keeping score, not ours.*

We came down from Dong Ha mountain opposite Mutters Ridge and in front of the Razorback. The bulk of the fighting had taken place on what became known as Mutters Ridge. The 2nd Battalion, 4th Marines, fought there too. Hill 400 and 484 were bloody battles where many, many Marines died. 2nd Battalion's Echo Company's Captain Harold Lee won the Congressional Medal of Honor in the fighting. The intense fighting lasted over two weeks.

Once we linked with 3rd Battalion we waited for choppers to arrive. The Commanding Officer of the 3rd Battalion was a Marine's Marine. He was Lieutenant Colonel William Masterpool. He was tough. He was our leader. The Colonel led us in battle and would lead us back to Dong Ha. We'd been out here nearly three weeks. Everyone was hurting in one way, or another. I was hurting before I came out here. I was much worse now. I'd been fighting infections on both ankles, now they were swollen out of my boots. I had my boots unlaced halfway down, my ankles were bleeding. The infections had gone on for nearly six months. They came from a couple dozen nasty leech bites I got on my first patrol. My ankles were swollen tight, filled with bright yellow green pus. I'd be glad when the choppers came and flew us back to base.

I was squeezing pus from my inflamed legs when a Corpsman happened by. He invited me to a staging area for the walking wounded. I told him I was walking, but I wasn't wounded. He said the Colonel called for choppers to pick up those that couldn't march. "Doc, those that couldn't march where?" I asked. He told me there weren't going to be any choppers; we were marching back to Dong Ha, about ten miles east of our current location.

When push came to shove, one chopper showed up for a handful of Marines, who simply couldn't walk. The Corpsman had to force them onto the chopper. Everyone wanted to walk in under their own power. No one wanted to let the Colonel down. He was a real leader. The kind we'd readily die for. He promised everyone steaks in the mess hall; it didn't matter what time we arrived. We didn't believe it, but we'd finish together. It was time we all sucked it up.

We trudged our way through hills, shuffled across rice paddies and eventually into our base at Dong Ha. Colonel Masterpool never stopped. He would pass us in the column going one way, pretty soon he'd be coming back the other way. He was a dynamo. He was always chewing an unlit cigar. He didn't wear a combat helmet, just an old Marine softcover on his head. He never stopped moving, encouraging his troops.

We arrived at the security perimeter of the base at around 0200. My ankles were tight, bulging out of the tops of my jungle boots and the skin seemed about to break open. The pain was excruciating. The Colonel marched us straight to the mess tent. The tent was dark, no one there. He told us to hold tight, he'd be right back. We heard yelling, and it wasn't long until several sleepy looking Marines showed up and brought the mess tent to life. Our angry Colonel returned behind them, encouraging them to *get it in gear. He'd promised us steaks; they cooked them, and we ate good. He was 'the man'.*

With full belly's, we made it to our tents around 0330. It was a relief to sit down and get my boots off. It would be three weeks before I could get them on again. Lots of shots for infection. But I sucked it up and got back to the field early.

17 May, Monday - Somers, NY. Pepsi

I don't know how to act. I'm in the office, not on a plane. Amazing. What will I do with myself? Feeling pretty good this morning. Looking forward to a week of going home at night. Family is what it's all about for me. I get asked all the time, why I don't play golf. My answer is always the same. It's not that I don't like golf; it's that I like my family more than I like golf. There are twenty-four hours in a day. That doesn't leave time for golf. A simple question of priorities.

18 May, Tuesday - New Haven, CT. Church Meeting

Gloria rode with me to my church meeting tonight. The calling I have required I be there. I'm always comforted when she's with me. The meetings lasted three hours. She went shopping. Driving home we talked about the odds of me being here tonight.

I was raised with no religion, started drinking when I was the ripe young age of fourteen. I went to Vietnam an Atheist, came back an Agnostic. Became a Christian seventeen years ago. Became sober, thanks to my great wife, twenty years ago. The journey has been slow, the changes, when the happened, were sudden. It was a long shot for both of us.

As we drove home, holding hands, I couldn't help but think how lucky I am to have her. She saw me through my first five years home, the toughest of all. She listened. She's been my therapist for twenty-four years now. She makes it all better.

20 May, Thursday - Brookfield, CT.

One more day and I make it to the weekend. Being home at night with the family is great. Things are still hard, paying off our business debts and coping with two moves in two years. In Baltimore, we had a nephew living with us, a problem kid. Trying to give him a chance. We'd had him with us before in Pennsylvania, for a year. Got him on the honor roll, then he leaves. This time we had the same experience, but he's older and bigger. Got him on the honor roll again, but the fighting with Cortney is off the charts. Threatened to kill her. Not in my house. Called his father in Ohio to come get him. We're out of the rotation. It all added up to more stress and family drama. Life's been quite a trip these last couple years. The wheels have been wobbling, but they didn't come off. Things have been pretty good lately, but I can feel the black, it's hovering near the surface. Time for bed.

23 May, Sunday - Ashford, CT. - Church

What a day, Spent it traveling to eastern Connecticut. Went to Ashford for church. I served there as a lay minister eleven years ago; we lived out there when I worked at Frito Lay. We'd left there for Dallas, then two years later moved to Pennsylvania where we stayed for six years, then Baltimore and now in Connecticut again.

Great people in Ashford. When we first moved there from Detroit, we met for church in a Grange Hall. We worked together cutting and selling firewood to raise money. We built a small church building. Today they're having an Open House for the expanded building, complete with a basketball court. It's gorgeous. The membership is growing, which is nice.

It's nice to see old friends. The guy who visited us on New Years picks up where he left off. Talking hunting, shooting and sniping. Tells me that he fired an AK. An AK? He's a special ed teacher and one of his students sells them. "He sells them?" I ask. He affirms that he does. He's thinking of getting one. I must be living under a rock.

24 May, Monday - Dallas, TX. Embassy Suites - Pepsi

Flew down today for another training session. Here tomorrow, then fly over to Atlanta on Wednesday. At least I had a week home. Great family time. The office was just meeting after meeting. I'm still thinking about my friend and the AK. Can't imagine why you need an AK? *I almost had one to bring home from Nam. My Lieutenant took it.* Time for bed. *But sleep doesn't come. It's November 17, 1967. A day imprinted forever in the recesses of my mind.*

"There he is. Take the shot Gunny," I whispered in his ear. We were in position south of Johan's, by ourselves, no cover from the grunts on Hill 51. It was our furthest penetration into the valley. We were ten clicks from back up. Our Gunny, who was our sniper platoon armorer, never went to the bush with us. He was due to rotate home soon, and asked me if he could come on a Rogue patrol. He explained that he was on the Marine Rifle Team and didn't want to have been in snipers and go home without recording a kill. So we took him on patrol.

I motioned one more time for the Gunny to take the shot. The team was spread out in four foot high grass, hiding about three yards apart. The Gunny and I were kneeling together. The gook in front of us, a uniformed NVA soldier who looked younger than my twenty-one years, was just fifty or sixty feet away. He popped up over the little knoll in front of us. I knew he wouldn't be alone.

The Gunny was shut down by what my Dad always called, 'Deer Fever'. He was aiming, but shaking as he aimed. Boom! He finally fired; the target went down, but he started yelling for help. I knew that any minute, we might be smothered in gooks. I yelled to Hood and Raid, "Cover me!"

I jumped up, running to the downed soldier. As I approached, he was laying on his back, looking up at me. Our eyes met. I could see his AK-47 laying at his right side, his hand next to it. He was bleeding in his right upper thigh, where his camouflage uniform had a large black spot. He quit yelling for help as I approached, with my M-14 on full auto.

When I was three feet away, he grabbed his AK. In one motion, he lifted and pushed it towards my stomach. I took him out with one blast. I grabbed his pack, rifle and ammunition, and ran back up the hill to our team. We gathered our things and pulled back to a safer area in the foothills.

Hood sat down admiring the AK I'd brought back. Then he excitedly says, "Kug, check this out". The NVA soldiers rifle had a round in the chamber. When he ejected it, we could see the primer in the round was busted. That meant, when he'd pulled the trigger, his rifle misfired. When I took the bullet from the casing, the powder was wet. Advantage Kug. I could hear Greek telling me God was saving me for something. Sure, to fight another day.

We returned our Gunny safely to his rightful place, in the Armory, not sniping. I prepared to send my booty home. Especially the AK. After reading our after action report, our Lieutenant, who never went to the bush, came by and threw regulations at me. He took the AK. I got to keep the bullet. Rank has its privileges. I'm sure he shipped it home as his bounty.

26 May, Wednesday - In the air heading to Atlanta, Delta Airlines

Training went well. Good people at Pepsi Dallas. It's like going home to be there. Lived there two years with Frito. Commuted sixteen miles to the headquarters. At the time, our headquarters was next to Love Field. Took me an hour on a good day. Didn't enjoy that much. When we first moved there I didn't have a car with air conditioning. You had to go to work very early, and shower when you got home. Be in Atlanta tomorrow, heading back to White Plains and home on Friday morning.

Tired. Same problem, sleeping. *Tripping out, going back to Nam doesn't help the matter either. Things have been going pretty well, but the black hangs around like a burglar on the prowl.*

27 May, Thursday - Atlanta, GA. Sheraton Inn

Finished training the franchise side today. Went well. So far, Detroit is the only place 'it won't work here'. I've got fifteen years with this outfit, in the room today, people had thirty and forty years with Pepsi. Amazing group of people.

Just tried calling home. I can't get an outside line. Guess there's a computer convention in town, sixty-five thousand people. That explains it. I haven't watched the nightly news in awhile, so decided to take a chance. Big news here, murders, rapes, and gay and lesbian issues. Lovely. I'm afraid I've lived too long. If that's not bad enough, our piece of crap President comes on, trying to explain away his latest charades. In the last seven days, he fired the White House travel staff, that's been there for thirty years, accused them of stealing, used the FBI to put the heat on them. Then he brings in a new travel agency from Arkansas. Wonderful guy.

According to the news, the agency from Arkansas is headed by his cousin, and owned by his friend. He backs off when the media puts the heat on. Looks like he's bringing in American Express Travel. Says it was all a mistake. Then I hear a report the President will be the keynote speaker at the Vietnam Veterans Memorial in Washington on Memorial Day. Unbelievable. A draft dodger President at the Wall. What the hell would he say?

It's 0130. The short nights are a killer on my forty seven year old body.

28 May, Friday - In the air heading to White Plains, NY. Airport

Another week on the road down. I hate being away; the irony, I like it better on the road, than working in Headquarters. People in HQ are nice, fun to work with, but nothing gets done. All show and no go. Over the years, people with PepsiCo are 'talking more, and doing less'. Looking forward to the long weekend. Taking the family to Boston. Going to see some sites and visit Quincy Market. More than anything, good to get away with the family. Cashed in some of my travel points. We're staying at the Marriott Wharf downtown. The kids are excited about getting away for the weekend.

29 May, Saturday - Boston, MA. Marriott Wharf

Everyone's asleep. I decided I better write now. It was a little cool today, otherwise, just beautiful. We went to Quincy Market, which is fun and amazing. The old warehouses redone are really cool. We took a tour on the Olde Towne Trolley. It was interesting to learn the history around here. We went to the Science Museum. That's where we found the Omni Theater.

We hadn't been to one like it before. It had a wrap around screen, and what seemed like thousands of speakers. We saw an Imax film called, The Rainforest. It started out with a wild helicopter ride around Boston. We weaved in and out of Sky Scrapers, then around the city. *It felt like we were in a real chopper.*

Just when I was wondering what this had to do with the rainforest, we streaked over the horizon and into South America. We flew up and over the mountains, swooping down into the rainforest. *Instantly, the sights and sounds of the jungle came alive. The screen crawled with insects of all kinds. They were up close and personal. Then, the rains came, pouring onto the jungle floor. As sudden as it came, it gave way to the sun. Steam climbed from the jungle floor. I could smell the must, the stench, and feel the filth and dirt of the jungle. Leaves dripped on the screen, while leaches crawled on my skin.*

I was no longer in the Omni; I *was with Crutch, on a hill looking into Laos.*

"See anything?" Crutch is scanning the target area. We're sitting on a finger overlooking a river junction near the Laotian border. We've been out here for ten days. Five Force Recon Marines are about twenty yards behind us in the jungle. We're waiting for our chopper out of here. We might get a shot before we go.

Crutch puts the 7 x 50 binoculars down and shakes his head in the negative. I continue my hobby while he keeps watch. To pass the time, I count the number of different bugs that walk by my spot in the jungle. Once I counted just over a hundred. When I get bored with bug counting, I turn my attention to leaves. I take big, moist, green jungle leaves, and carefully tear them apart, vein by vein. It passes the time. We can't talk. We use little notepads to write words back and forth.

It's late afternoon, and smothering hot. It's always hot here in Nam. In the mountains, the rains come every afternoon. It's a welcome relief, while it's happening. Then comes the smothering humidity. Steam slowly rises from the jungle floor like an old sauna. You feel like your whole body, head and all is sitting inside a steam bath.

We hear a Recon Marine coming our way. Our eyes meet, he motions it's time to go. Will we get a ride out of here today? Chopper blades break the jungle silence; we make a hat to our LZ, about a hundred meters away. Our team leader pops a yellow smoke. Our ride, a Huey, is descending as a spotter plane circles overhead. Gunships buzz on either side of our LZ as a precaution.

The radio crackles as we run through the six-foot elephant grass. As we near the chopper, the grass in now horizontal, pushed to the ground by the prop wash from the chopper blades. The door gunner's yelling, "hot extraction"! We dive headfirst, grasping to hold on to the bare insides of our rescue bird.

As we lift off, AK rounds fill the air. The chopper gains altitude, is tree top level, making evasive moves, ramping left, then right. We bang into one another inside. The door gunners on either side are emptying their M-60's into the jungle canopy, as we rise to safety. A wild ride it was.

"Dad! Dad! Are you asleep?", Cortney, who'd been laying back in the seat next to me, was shaking my arm. As she did, the screen came into focus. I could see the credits scrolling down the screen. "Why are you so tense," Gloria asks. I sat up and returned to the Omni in Boston. What a great day it's been. *It's always great to go on R & R.* That's still how I think about trips like this one, R & R. We went to Quincy Market and pigged out tonight after the Omni. Give me one of everything. Time for bed. I'm exhausted. That's good. Maybe I can sleep.

30 May, Sunday - Kittery. ME. Day trip to the seashore

Back at the Marriott after a long day. Everyone's in bed again. Time to write. What a great day! We drove north, up the Maine Coast. We haven't been up that way since we lived in Brooklyn, Connecticut in 1980 and 81. Great outlet centers up there. They're real outlets. We all love it.

Great day, weather was nice, the temperatures were mild. We drove back to Boston on highway A1A. It runs along the coast. The views of the Atlantic Ocean were so peaceful. Whitney wanted to stop and walk the shoreline. It's chilly walking the rocky shore. Whit's looking for sea shells with her sister. She wants to take back to school. The shoreline is rugged. Gloria and I try to sit on a black outcropping of rock. It's sharp, jagged and uncomfortable. As I sit, *my mind slips to the Rockpile, where I spent three weeks years ago. Nine hundred meters straight up in the sky. There wasn't a flat spot to be found. We had to find a hole in the pointed rock where we could sit, curl up or force ourselves into. Move the wrong way, cut your jungle pants or your skin to shreds.* Much like I did to my Levi's today.

Gloria joined the girls while I listened to the ocean and stared at the waves crashing to shore. *My mind wrestled with my two worlds. Two worlds, crashing as the waves in front of me, converging in my mind.*

I realize I have a choice. I can sit here and trip out, or I can join my precious girls. *Still trying to learn how to live in this world every day.* To live for Christ, and become a better person. *I need to choose to keep my bad place locked,* and enjoy the beautiful family who shares my life. I am blessed.

The girls got cold, so we loaded up and headed back to Boston. We made it in time to go to the concessions at Quincy Market one more time.

31 May, Monday - Brookfield, CT. Traveling home from Boston

Great weekend. As usual, I'm writing, and everyone's in bed. Our drive home was full of rain and traffic. At least the rain waited until today. Everyone slept most of the way home, so I turned on the radio. My first touch with the real world in three days. *I love dropping out.*

The news was on. President Bubba was speaking from the Vietnam Memorial. I turned it off as fast as I could. I can't stand to hear the Oxford creep talk about war. *The draft dodger shouldn't even be in the White House. It's an insult to everyone that served. My mind slipped into the dreariness of a rainy day. The black hadn't won yet, but it was trying.* By the time we got home, I was still holding my own. Not sure what tonight will bring. Just know it will be short. I have a 0600 flight from LaGuardia in the morning.

"Live by chance. Love by choice, kill by profession"
Found on a Zippo lighter in Vietnam

JUNE

01 June, Tuesday - American Airlines, in the air from Chicago to New York LaGuardia Airport, Pepsi

Not writing very long tonight. Up at 0400 and off to LaGuardia. Been in Chicago again, meeting with our largest bottler. Meetings all day, flying home tonight. O'Hare was a zoo, which is normal. We left nearly on time. That means I get back home around midnight. Turns like this are tough, but worth it to be with the family.

Need to get some sleep. Heading for LaGuardia always makes me think of Greek. He used to pick me up there when I came for a visit. Too late to dwell on it tonight.

02 June, Wednesday - Somers, NY. Pepsi

Found out this morning, I have to go to Jacksonville next week. I'm speaking at our annual franchise bottler convention. The only flight I can get is again at 0600. It's on US Scare. I spent most of the day working on my speech. The rest of the time, getting ready for my trip to St. Louis tomorrow. Out in the morning back on Thursday. One night out's better than a week.

04 June, Friday - In the air returning to LaGuardia from St. Louis, MO. Pepsi

Jetting back from a quick trip to St. Louis. Kind of a waste, but that's often corporate life. Most people in corporations, today, are just playing with funny money. They've never had to make payroll, or fight for cash. It's all a game on paper. Tired. Two turns in a week are tough on the body.

Looking forward to another weekend off with the family. I'll be leaving 0 dark early on Monday morning for Jacksonville. Reveille at 0330. We'll see. My blackness lurks around every corner. Happens when I get tired, and when I have to deal with dip shits. Been one of those weeks. I have to finish, then practice my speech. Later.

05 June, Saturday - Brookfield, CT. Home

Quite a day. Woke up, the kids wanted to cook breakfast together. Gloria cooked the scrambled eggs with Whit. Cortney wants to help me make *'rocket fuel'*. She learned from Greek and I. She gets a kick out of it. *It started in Nam. We ate C-rations ninety-nine percent of the time. That got old. We'd get our hands on hot sauce, combine different C-rats and shazaam. We called it 'rocket fuel'.*

Here in the world I can no longer get C-rats, so we use Hormel Corned Beef Hash, dice a few onions, throw in some cheddar cheese and load it with hot sauce. It'll light a fire under you for a few days. Cort loves it, so she does most of the work. We have a fun breakfast. I went in and sat down in the living room and crashed.

"Kug, did you get the C-rat burgers?" It was a quarter to midnight. We were due to leave the Camp Evans perimeter in fifteen minutes. We had a nine click hike to Hill 51, our home away from home.

"I'll get them now," I tell Raid. I tossed my giant rucksack on my back. It stretched from the top of my shoulders to my ass. It was mostly empty right now. I'd staked out the supply tent this afternoon. The mess hall occasionally served canned C-rat hamburgers. We got the word from one of the cooks that they were in the supply tent. They wouldn't give snipers anything, they thought we were crazy, so I decided to steal a case.

I took my trusty M1-A1 government issue flashlight and carefully made my way to the back of the supply tent. It was quiet. No one in sight. I didn't turn the light on for fear of being seen. Just had it in case I needed it inside. When I walked through earlier with our friend, the cook, I'd counted the exact steps to my burgers. Inside, I quietly counted off my steps, found the row and felt for the case. I heard someone walking outside, so I knelt down. The steps continued by the supply tent; I got back up. I dare not use a light, I'd be seen and have to put up with some administrative bullshit. I felt the size of the box, it felt right; I grabbed one from the top. Man was it heavy. I slid it inside my ruck and quietly went out the back door. I met the rest of the team at our sniper tent.

We donned our ammunition harnesses, painted our faces black, grabbed our weapons and saddled up for our hike. We cleared the perimeter about ten minutes late and headed out to Co Bi Than Tan. We had a half moon to work with. Raid was on point, leading the way. I was sucking some serious wind. My ruck was killing me. It was heavier than my usual load.

It took us four hours to reach the river below Hill 51. I bitched all the way, making Raid slow down. Hoss called the grunts and told them our position. We arranged to come through the north perimeter at first light. We took a much needed break. I didn't take the ruck off, because I didn't want to go through the agony of putting it back on. I sat down, leaned back, and rested.

As dawn began to break, we headed up Hill 51. We laughed about having burgers in the bush for breakfast. Hill 51 was a steep, ball busting climb without these C-rat burgers, with them it was hell. Through the perimeter, I couldn't wait to take off my ruck. We crossed the hilltop to our sniper area. Five small hooch's we built ourselves. Each is just big enough for one person. I dropped my ruck, laid down my rifle, took off my harness and sat down. I was hot and tired. I took off my jungle jacket, and Hoss started laughing. My shoulders had bruises where the ruck straps had been. It's not funny.

Raid wanted the burgers. Hoss grabbed my ruck, opened the top and started laughing hysterically. "What's so funny?" He couldn't talk; Raid walked over, looked and said, "Do you know what you humped out here?" I said, "What do you mean do I know what I humped out here. I humped a dozen cans of C-rat hamburgers!" I go over and yank the top of my rucksack open. To my dismay, I'm staring at a label that says, 72 Bottles of Louisiana Red Hot Sauce'. I can't friggin' believe it. I just stole 72 bottles of hot sauce and humped them all night. Damn it!

"Dad! Dad! The phone's for you". Cortney called me out of my stupor. It's the new Pepsi President, Brenda Barnes, the first woman President of Pepsi. She's very nice, sharp, she earned it.

She apologized for bothering me on a weekend, she wanted to know if I wanted a ride down to Jacksonville on the Corporate Jet. "Wow, sure, I'd love to". We agreed on the time, and I was elated. No La Guardia!

Turns out she saw me on the agenda, so she called and invited me along. Dang, I'll be uptown on this trip. I have to be at the Pepsi hangar in White Plains at 1000 AM on Monday. Now that's an hour I could get to love. I can get up, see the kids off to school, then go to the airport. That's downright civilized.

We had a great rest of the day, although it was forty-five degrees, and it's the first week of June. To bed.

06 June, Sunday - Brookfield, CT. Home

As I sit here writing tonight, I'm so glad I'm flying down on the Corporate jet in the morning. I hate flying through LaGuardia. That is a relief. We went to our church in Newtown this morning. This afternoon we went down to Southfield for a regional meeting we have once a quarter. Overall a nice peaceful day. I feel refreshed after today. I needed that.

Early to bed tonight. I need to be fresh to speak in Jacksonville tomorrow.

07 June, Monday - In the air, Corporate jet to Jacksonville, FL.

I'm on board a slick Gulfstream II with the President of Pepsi, and the head of our franchise operations. Three of us. They're having a pre-convention meeting, so I'm alone. My flight here will be a mere two hours, instead of the five hours I'd have had out of La Guardia. The twenty million dollars I'm riding in, sure beats cramming on to a US Scare plane.

The Gulfstream we're in belongs to another company, Pepsi's two jets were busy today. I was talking with the pilot before departure, he told me we rented it for three days, at a mere six thousand dollars a day. Pretty pricey per passenger, but hey, we do get there fast.

As I write this morning, the on board TV intermittently flashes a US map, displaying an airplane representing ours. It maps our progress down the coast, along the Atlantic Ocean. The Flight Attendant just finished serving breakfast. She's now relaxing with a book. We have an hour to go.

I'm grateful I'm not sitting on US Air, after enduring LaGuardia. But I find that I'm not happy. When you fly around the country in luxury, I can see why leaders are so out of touch with their workers. Do this long enough, and you'd have no idea how the grunts live. You'd forget about the hideous New York traffic or being packed like sardines in airline seats. We leave the house at 0400, they have no idea. Maybe at one time they did, but once you started living large, you'd be out of touch and never want to go back.

My bad place started opening up. The black descends, I think back to the Prima Donna, General Westmoreland, visiting staged sites in Vietnam. Just like we have staged plant tours for the President of Pepsi, when she comes for a visit. I think of that arrogant, ass, McNamara, who ignored the military leaders and ran his own war, the one we paid for with our blood while Lyndon Johnson flew around the country in luxury, touting his Great Society.

I was far adrift when we touched down in Jacksonville, just in time for lunch. The plane stopped; we stepped off to a waiting limo. No rental car lines for us. We were driven straight to the Marriott Sawgrass Resort & Spa. With Pepsi, we do travel in style.

After lunch, they went golfing, and I came to my room. I need to work on my speech, do some reading, and go for a walk around these gorgeous grounds.

08 June, Tuesday - Jacksonville, FL. Marriott Sawgrass Resort

My speech went well today. Always good when it does. I slept well last night, woke up feeling like a human being for a change.

Maybe it was the ease of the trip down. Went out to eat with some of the franchise folks tonight. One of them had a rental car, so we went offsite to eat. On the way back, we passed a long haired guy, standing with a scantily clad girl, hitchhiking. *I laughed to myself, thinking back when I returned home from Nam. I was back home, in Ohio, fresh from two years in the war. It was a different world than the one I'd left behind. My little town of Lock Seventeen hadn't changed much, but the world at large was full of long haired hippies and girls with few clothes, and fewer morals. Not that I minded the girls, but the guys were, as they said back then, 'far out'.*

I hopped into my brand new, red, 396, four-on-the-floor Chevy Impala. I was home for the weekend from Fort Wayne, Indiana, where I was finishing out my Marine Corps career planting dead Marines every of couple days. At the end of Lock, where my parents lived, I crossed the railroad and hung a right onto US 36. I burned rubber going through the gears, and hit about eighty miles per hour in a blink. Then I saw a flash of legs that ran to the sun, standing on the right side of the road. She was a gorgeous blur. I slammed on the brakes, and laid about a hundred feet of rubber before I could stop. I jammed the transmission in reverse and raced backwards in search of the legs. I found the legs attached to a great looking brunette, with a mop of hair standing next to her. I didn't see him when I flew by. Guess they were both hitchhiking, I told them to hop in.

The girl was about my age, the guy, skinny and dirty looking, looked a tad younger. The girl was wearing, what I would quickly learn, was a mini-skirt. I hadn't seen one of those before. She climbed in, sat up on my middle console. The dude got in the bucket seat. He was looking nervous. I hit the gears, as I copped a look at the long legs sitting next to me.

As we sped up the highway, the girl asked me where I got such a great tan so early in the year. After two years in Nam, I was seriously dark. "I'm in the Marine Corps. Just returned from two years in Vietnam". I couldn't resist; it was worth the shock value. The girl smiled, unfazed. The long hair looked like a puppy who just shit on the floor, and knew it. He stared out the window, not wanting to look at me.

As we approached Uhrichsville, she smiled as she explained they were heading to DC, for a protest on the war. I wasn't sure if she was high, or was born that way. She was out to lunch and not coming back anytime soon. I thought of our time in Nam blowing minds. As Rogues and snipers, we were treated like crap, like we were weird and crazy. Weiner decided we should live up to the billing. He bit the heads off toads, ate a praying mantis or two, and we'd all lay hand grenades on booby traps and run, rather than set a charge and blow it. Blowing minds was fun.

I decided to blow a couple of minds right here in the world. "What are you doing?" She asked, as I pulled into the local bus station. "I'll be right back. Just need to run in here a minute". Inside, I found out the next bus heading to DC was in two hours. I bought two tickets to DC. As I turned to go back outside, I could see my two travelers staring at me through the window.

Back in the car I handed the girl the tickets and said, "Enjoy". She looked puzzled. "Are you against the war?" I smiled and said, "Oh no, I love it. But we fight so you two can go and do that bullshit." She smiled again, gave me a peck on the cheek and got out. I honked the horn, and she came back. I handed her ten bucks for lunch. "Oh, you're so nice. Peace". I smiled and said, "War". I backed out, waved, she blew me a kiss as her mate looked the other way. I burned rubber and sped off. I needed a drink.

The Tonight Show was on when I drifted back to Jacksonville. I don't even remember walking back to my room. Need some sleep. Meetings tomorrow. Meetings Thursday morning, lunch, then the good jet back north.

10 June, Thursday - In the air heading to White Plains, NY.

Jetting home on the Corporate jet. If I were traveling on US Scare, I'd get home around midnight. As it is, I'll be home by five. Pretty sweet. Slept good this trip. Feel good. Work in Headquarters tomorrow. Morning meetings. Then I'm picking up the family, we're heading to Bloomsburg, Pennsylvania. Trevor's girlfriend is graduating from high school tomorrow. We'll go to the graduation, and then head home on Saturday evening. It's a four, maybe five hour ride.

Looking forward to our trip west later this month. Taking the family on a trip to Colorado, Utah and Arizona. Mixing business with a little pleasure.

Need another R & R.

11 June, Friday - Bloomsburg, PA. - Holiday Inn

Everyone's in bed, I'm writing. Only time to do it. Work was uneventful. Got out at noon, drove home, then here to Bloomsburg. Had a late dinner with Trevor and Amy. Graduation's in the morning. We'll have lunch, then head back to Brookfield. Tired, from all the travel and driving here. Weather is supposed to turn ugly tomorrow. Storms are headed our way. Hope it holds off for her graduation in the morning.

13 June, Sunday - Brookfield, CT. Home

We came home yesterday as planned. What we hadn't planned for were the storms. As we got closer to Connecticut, things were bad. Around White Plains, which is an hour from home on a good day, the traffic started backing up. When we hit I-684, it got dark, dark like it was midnight. Winds picked up, and torrential rains came down. Cars were everywhere, lining the sides of the road, and packed like cows hiding below an underpass. We didn't get home until about 8 PM.

Our neighborhood was eerily dark. Once home, we found out the power was out. Gloria's always prepared; she quickly handed out flashlights. The girls walked to a neighbor's house and came back with the news that it had been out since early Saturday morning. A major windstorm had gone through two blocks from our house.

We're into preparedness, so it's a non-event. I got out our survival radio and tuned in to the local news. Trees ripped apart; wires down, on the ground, and some roads blocked. The kids got their sleeping bags and slept in our room. It was a fun night actually. We all lay down, the candle on our dresser was still burning. No one wanted to get up and blow it out. I got up and took care of it. *When I did, I leaned over, cupped my hand, and sucked in the candle smoke. I was briefly back in Nam. In the monsoon, on base, we'd use candles to read. The distinct smell of candles always holds a special place in my mind.* I slept well.

The power came on about noon. We couldn't take showers or get cleaned up, so we stayed home from church. We lay around, talked and read. I was studying the scriptures. In Psalms, I happened to read, "Yea, though I walk through the valley of the shadow of death, I will fear no evil: for thou art with me; thy rod and thy staff they comfort me". *I never read that scripture without hearing my first sniper partner, Crutch, saying, "Yea, though I walk through the shadow of death, I will fear no evil because I am the meanest Mother in the Valley". And we did live in the valley of death. "Hey Marines! We need your help. Incoming choppers". Crutch and I were sitting at the Dong Ha airstrip waiting for a ride to Phu Bai. Two Corpsman pulled up with a mule, a flat bed vehicle about two feet off the ground, about the size of a four-by-eight sheet of plywood.*

We heard the blades of an incoming Sea Knight chopper, the twin blades making their familiar sound. Elements of the Fifth Marines had been fighting in the mountains of the DMZ. There had been no evacuations for three days. The Corpsman yelled for our help.

It was getting dark fast. The chopper landed, spun around and dropped its rear door. Inside the chopper, dim red lights burned, revealing a packed cargo of misery. We were on the receiving end of a meat grinder. Bodies lay three feet deep on the floor of the CH-47. The Crew Chief started yelling, "Get them off! Get them off! We have to go back now!" It was macabre at best.

Body's. Body's on top of body's. We couldn't tell who was dead and who was alive, until you moved them. Moans came from the living, odd noises from the dead. Filthy, dirty, bandaged carnage, in living Technicolor. I helped a Corpsman carry a few dead off and onto the mule. We held them by their hands and feet. I looked over as Crutch pulled a Marine off the chopper by his feet, his head bouncing on the cargo rollers built into the floor. Our eyes met, he knew I was upset. He shrugged, "He's dead."

We stacked dead on the mule, one on top of the other. Some bloated from the heat, some not, some broke apart when we moved them. We stacked Marines so high; we couldn't see over the bodies. It was dark when we emptied the chopper. I stood with Crutch looking at the scene. I saw movement on one side of the Chopper. I ran over and found a severely wounded Marine, barely standing. He was sliding his way down the skin of the chopper towards a waiting field ambulance; that looked like the Korean War had put it to good use.

"Let me help you Marine", I said, grabbing his arm. He jerked his good arm away. He had bandages around his head, his other arm in a sling, and bandages on one leg, where his pants had been cut away. His face was black, as a coal miner, his eyes broadcast the thousand yard stare. He was mumbling to himself. I reached out to help again, he jerked his arm away a second time. He reached the end of the chopper and fell onto the ground.

I grabbed one arm, Crutch the other. We lifted him onto an old gurney. The whole time he kept mumbling, "Fuck it man. Just fuck it". That said it all.

I was lost for awhile today, but I'm back.

16 June, Wednesday - Brookfield, CT. Home

Got home in time for some yard work today. Summer is finally here. Most of the storm damage is cleaned up. Lost lots of trees in the area. Mowed the lawn and finished most of the landscaping. When it's hot, I crave cold water. Never want to be without cold water.

18 June, Friday - Brookfield, CT. Home

Home early. Pepsi summer hours. We get off after lunch. Nice perk. Did some shopping, and more outside work. Feels good to get outside and do something physical. Living on airplane's messes you up. I need to get in shape, before it's too late. Not getting any younger. Kids are excited about our trip west next week. I'm excited. No black lately, that's good. Hope it continues.

19 June, Saturday - Merrick, Long Island, NY. Greeks Place.

Girls are pumped for our trip. They're staying home alone today, while Gloria and I ride to Long Island to help Bobbie. She has another graduation. Their youngest son, Jimmy, is graduating from Catholic school, the eighth grade. Last year this time we came up from Baltimore for John's graduation from the same school. Greek was two months into his cancer this time last year. Now he's been dead for six months. Life is fragile, precious for sure.

It was an easy drive down this morning. We wanted to support Bobbie, but it's hard on me. My black cloud hovered closer and closer, as we approached the church for the graduation. *It was the same church where I'd delivered my friends eulogy. My old wounds tore open as we walked inside.*

Bobbie, Greeks wife, has always been a trooper. Her face betrays her today; she's having trouble. His sister Pat, comes up and greets us. She gave me a big hug, then burst into tears. She apologized, disappeared, and I didn't see her again. Her memories of Greek and me were too painful. I love Bobbie and the kids, and his Sister. Throughout the day, *I waded through a mix of adrenaline, elation and depression. My emotions were as jagged as the top of the Rockpile.* The ceremony was quick and efficient. Jimmy did his thing with style. His Dad would be proud.

We left as soon as the ceremony finished. We went to the house to prepare things for the party. I was concerned about being at the party. *I don't like groups, and today, people will be coming up, reminiscing about our mutual friend.* **I knew that would be tough.** As people arrived, the phone rang. Bobbie called me over. It was our daughter, Cortney. She had tennis practice and her ride crapped out. The babysitter for Whitney also cancelled. I took the opportunity and excused ourselves. *I hated to leave, but needed to. I was struggling.*

Bobbie was gracious, and fine with us leaving. I took the Hutchinson Parkway, made good time and got home for the kids. Good thing, I was going down fast. The blackness that started in Long Island, followed me home. I know tonight is going to be a tough one.

20 June, Sunday - New Haven, CT. Church

Tough night, tough day and I have to get up for work in the morning. I've had some bad nights, but last night took ugly to a new level. The black that followed me home kept me on red alert most of the night. It was nothing special, just couldn't sleep. I'd get to sleep, chase gooks, wake up, and do it all over again. *Greek and I had quite a time lining up the crosshairs last night.* No sleep and I had to speak for forty-five minutes today at a regional church conference. I enjoy speaking, but not without sleep. But it went fine. Time for bed.

21 June, Monday - Somers, NY. Pepsi

Tough day at work. *Woke up fighting off the demons. Depression.* Meetings all day today. On issues that should be simple, but aren't. *Make a damned decision. Stop all the Kumbaya bullshit. Lead.* If we stopped all these 'important' meetings tomorrow, no one would know. *It's like Nam. Our leaders are so out of touch with the real world. It so pisses me off.*

Where have all the leaders gone? There's a growing leadership gap in this country. It's in government; it's in business, it's everywhere. Companies are downsizing, cutting middle management and outsourcing jobs overseas. They're attacking the wrong problem. In another ten years, we'll be leaderless, and that will be frightening. Most leaders today, have no idea how work gets done in their organizations. It's a damned shame. It's all about the money and the stock options. It's getting worse by the day.

Time for the drive home. Never know how long it'll take. Time to chill.

23 June, Wednesday - Brookfield, CT. Home

I lay down, chasing my elusive sleep. It didn't come, so I'm up writing. Had the windows open when *I heard the whomp, whomp of chopper blades. I was flush full of adrenaline for a short trip. The black still lurks in the jungle cobwebs of my mind.* I'm hoping our upcoming trip will shake the cobwebs loose.

We leave tomorrow for Denver. A little business, and hopefully, a lot of much needed pleasure. My boss and Pepsi are good that way. Makes up for all the travel, and time away from family. Trevor is still away at college so he won't be joining us. He spent a year after high school working in Alaska, so now he's trying to make up for his time away.

It's midnight. Time for bed and the chase for sleep.

24 June, Thursday - Denver, CO. Marriott Hotel

Long day. Up early, down to White Plains for our flight. After a plane change in Pittsburg, we got into Denver at 9 PM tonight. All day travel. It's near midnight, mountain time. Everyone's asleep, except me. Seems like a common problem. Need to get to bed.

In the morning, I have meetings at our Denver plant. Then we'll have lunch, and be on vacation for a few days. We've had a dream for years of driving from Denver to Salt Lake City, through the Rockies. At Frito Lay, we used to have winter meetings in Keystone, Colorado. I always wanted the family to see what I got to see. Tomorrow afternoon, we'll start fulfilling one dream. It's a start.

I cashed in my travel points to make the trip happen. That's one side benefit of a heavy travel schedule. Later.

25 June, Friday - Estes Park, CO. Rocky Mountain National Park

Meetings yesterday morning were uneventful. In the afternoon, we rode out to Golden, Colorado. It's a very cool town. We had dinner at Casa Bonita in Denver. I knew the girls would love that place. Unique place.

We got up today and headed north to Estes Park, and the Rocky Mountain National Park. It was like nothing we'd ever seen. Massive mountains, gorgeous peaks, and God's majesty everywhere. We drove up Pikes Peak. It was cold up there, even this time of year.

We're back at the Marriott. Tomorrow we're driving through the mountains on I-70 to Grand Junction, where we'll spend Saturday night. Holding my own with the black that's still hovering close like a thunderstorm about to let loose.

26 June, Saturday - Glenwood Springs, CO.

We didn't make it to Grand Junction. We stopped to check out Glenwood Springs along the way. Super place. We spent the night at a place called Glenwood Hot Springs. We went in the hot spring pool, did some shopping and ate at a unique restaurant. Great day. The drive through the mountains had the girls enthralled the size and beauty of the mountains. Nothing like this back east.

It's great to be alive. The mountains are soothing to my psyche. I love being in and around them. It's healing to my soul.

27 June, Sunday - Park City, UT. Stein Erickson Lodge

Glenwood Springs was great. Up early, breakfast and drove here to Park City. It's just beautiful here. I'm starting to relax, beginning to feel like I used to feel. Most of the black is gone, the door to my bad place nearly shut. I'm enjoying the downtime. Always enjoy the family.

We cruised through the rest of Colorado and into Utah. We went through Vernal, Utah and stopped at the Dinosaur National Park. The kids loved it. It's been a serendipitous day. The kids wanted to drive through yet another state, we headed north to Wyoming. We drove through the Flaming Gorge, and it was breathtaking, therapy for me. My head began to feel clean and free, for the first time in a long time.

We ended the trip by going to Fort Bridger, in Wyoming. We picked up I-80 west, and drove down into Park City, where we are now. The Lodge here is outstanding. I'm here for a week of training with Stephen Covey. The family will spend the days visiting friends. Time for sleep. It's getting easier.

"If you think sex is exciting ... try incoming"
Found on a Zippo lighter from the War

JULY

01 July, Thursday - Park City, UT. Stein Erickson Lodge

Do I have to leave? Everything's great. It's day four of five days of training. Covey's book has been a hit; his once small consulting firm is growing. It's now known as the Covey Leadership Center. My training, this week, is on Principle Centered Leadership and Quality. My boss was all over this one. I'm grateful. PepsiCo is good about training.

It's after dinner; I'm alone in the room. Gloria and the girls are shopping and visiting friends. I'm writing early for a change. This morning I was out on the deck overlooking the mountains; we have breakfast there. The Lodge is in the tree tops. We're at the 8,500 foot level. Being here does something for my soul. It's healing. As I sat there at breakfast this morning, I couldn't help but think, 'this ain't bad for a D student, college drop out, half crazy Marine'.

02 July, Friday - Salt Lake City, UT. Marriott Downtown

The training's over. It was excellent. Love Covey's work. It feels good to be here. The people who come to his training want to be here. They care. They want to make a difference. I've learned a ton from Covey. He's not here as much as in the beginning. He just spends a day with us now. Love the man.

I'm now officially on vacation. I got a voice mail today from my boss. Headquarters is undergoing a reorganization. I've been away a week. Incredible. Another butt moving exercise. Or maybe we'll get more new titles. Leaders. Hacking at the leaves of change, not the roots.

I'm doing well right now; I'll deal with the reorg' when I get back next week. Tomorrow we're moving down to Provo. Cortney wants to visit the BYU campus and see if she likes it. Early next week we'll head south, to Arizona. She wants to check out Arizona State, as well. We'll stop at the Grand Canyon on the way down.

We moved here to Salt Lake this evening. Walked to the Mall downtown, ate at the food court. Good time.

03 July, Saturday - Provo, UT. Marriott Hotel

Night again, writing again. Very busy today, I'm bushed, in a good way. We visited friends in the Sugarhouse area of Salt Lake on the way down here. We visited Temple Square too. Very impressive. When we got here, we visited the BYU campus. It is beautiful. Very clean and well manicured. The kids, the people on campus, are well dressed, no long hair. Refreshing. The campus sits under the watchful eye of Mount Timpanogas, and gorgeous mountains run along the east side of campus. Timp, as they call it, is around 11,000 feet.

We drove up Provo Canyon, behind Timp, to the Sundance Resort. We ate there and attended the outdoor summer production of Guys and Dolls. Robert Redford's involved in its production. The girls loved it. I enjoyed being with them, sitting amidst the gorgeous mountains. I didn't like the play, but I did love the company.

When we drove down the mountain, and out of the canyon, we could see fireworks. BYU's football stadium was in front of us. They were having their annual tribute to America ceremony. It ends with a massive fireworks display. We found out it's called the Stadium of Fire. It was late, but the kids wanted to see it. No tickets available, sixty thousand people. We found a place in the foothills to park and watch.

Everyone loved it. "It was awesome", I said. Whitney was surprised. Said she'd never heard me use that word before. We watched from outside the car. The air was so clean, clear, open skies. We could smell the fireworks and hear people cheering. Gloria worried the noise and explosions would bother me. The fireworks show was awesome; I never gave it a thought. I did get a big lump in my throat when the band started playing the Marine Corps Hymn. They followed that with America the Beautiful, and tears started streaming down my cheeks. I was glad it was dark. The band finished with the National Anthem. My cheeks were wet, chilly from the cool air and tears.

For a brief moment, *I saw funerals in Fort Wayne, even began to smell the stench of dead bodies sprawled in worn out choppers.* The music stopped; I left it all behind and got back in the car with my family. It was a special moment. We leave tomorrow for Arizona right after church.

05 July, Monday - St. George, UT. Holiday Inn

We didn't get out of Provo yesterday. We got in so late on Saturday night; we needed a break. We got up and went to church with our friends from Vineyard. He and his wife operate a dairy farm. I met him seventeen years ago when he was on his church mission in Ohio. He and another young Elder baptized my wife and I. My wife was already a good person, it dramatically changed me. I'm still working on the 'good person' thing. We've remained friends since that time.

We left this morning. Everyone is still tired. Driving the Utah desert got real boring. We came by a place called, Cove Fort. Everyone was sleeping, so I made an executive decision and stopped. It was an old, restored fort. The kids weren't impressed, and my wife said she could have done without it, but it floated my boat on a hot afternoon. *I climbed up on the catwalks, looked out through the apertures and walked up front where the flag pole stood. I tried to imagine what it would have been like back then. Those pioneers must have been tough people. I looked out across the rolling hills and tried to imagine Indians lined up, ready to attack.*

Gloria pulled me out of the old fort, told me I was 'born' in the wrong era. Maybe I was. Time for bed, we're heading further south tomorrow morning. Long drive to Phoenix.

06 July, Tuesday - Flagstaff, AZ. Marriott Hotel

We didn't make it to Phoenix, a little over planning on my part. We left in good time and drove through the desert to the northern edge of the Grand Canyon. I had no desire to see it, but the girls wanted to. It was out of the way fifty miles or more. I figure if we're this close why not. Incredible blue skies and *it was hot, at least Nam hot. Walking around the top of the canyon rim brought me back to my days trudging through the sand dunes of the Street Without Joy in Vietnam.*

07 July, Wednesday - Phoenix, AZ. Saddleback Inn

We had a nice drive down from Flagstaff. The hotel here is nice. I stayed here before, with Frito, always wanted to bring the family back. The pools here are fantastic. We decided to relax today, and do nothing. Got a tan and relaxed. We're here until Friday. We leave near midnight and fly all night. Used my free tickets, that's the price you pay.

We're going to check out Phoenix tomorrow. I want to take the girls to eat at Rustlers Roost, a restaurant in Tempe. Went there when I was working for Frito, when we opened their Case Grande plant. Friday we're going to check out of here and head east to Canyon Lake. See if we can rent a little house boat, and spend the day on the water. We'll leave there and head straight to the airport. Still feeling great, no demons chasing me for quite some time.

09 July, Friday - In the air Phoenix to Philadelphia

I'll be glad when we get home, and I can chill. I've had a great time. Relaxed. Went to Canyon Lake, east of Phoenix, about noon today. Rented a pontoon. It was nice, relaxing, and boy was it hot. The water looked like Nam, chocolate milk. It was warm as bath water. The thermometer on the pontoon said it was 112 degrees. It was Nam. The heat took it out of us. We were beat by the time we got to the airport.

We arrived three hours before our flight. We didn't have seats together when I checked in. We needed at least two together; Whitney was only eight. Since I was a Gold Member in the US Scare Frequent Flyer program, I didn't think it would be a problem.

I'd called the 800 number last night to get our seats, but within twenty-four hours, the gate owns them. They told me not to worry, the midnight flight had plenty of open seats. They said it wouldn't be a problem. So as I walked up to the check-in, I wasn't prepared for the ambush I got.

Whitney worried she wouldn't get a seat with one of us, stood next to me. I was sun drenched and tired, but respectful. The lady behind the counter was very nice. I explained the situation; Whitney was just eight years old and could we get at least two seats together. She assured me it wouldn't be a problem. I noticed a guy working the stall next to me, who was looking on, not saying a word.

Then he walked over to the lady helping me, whispered something and she left. He took over the computer, printed the boarding passes, handed them to me, asking for my bags. I asked about the seats. He said nothing, reaching for my bags. I look at the boarding passes; none of my four seats were together. I pointed it out to the guy, who looked me in the eye for the first time, and said, "Sorry, couldn't help you out".

Since he stepped in late, I thought he didn't understand the problem. I explained my problem again. Whitney left with a quivering lip, in search of her Mother. He told me he understood, but couldn't help. I stayed calm, and told him there must be a way to work this out. He said, "No". Then told me our gate, an obvious hint to leave him alone. *That wasn't going to happen.*

Whitney came back with Gloria and Cortney. Whit was fighting back tears. I leaned down, and assured her that I'd work it out. I stand back up, look at this guy, all five feet five of him, hiding behind a big beard, and he says, "You can't work it out. There are no more seats". Whitney burst into tears. My wife tells the turd he's a jerk, *and adrenaline shot through me like a volcano erupting. Red rage was center stage, as I stared at little Napoleon.*

I told the girls to go have a seat. *I turned to Napoleon and said, "Understand something. I'm sitting with my eight year old daughter. Now, are you going to help me, or am I going over you?"* He was indignant. Told me there were no seats, and I should go to the gate. *I took a very, very, deep breath. I didn't want to deal with the fallout of me reaching across the counter, grabbing him by that scraggly beard and jerking his pathetic ass over the counter.*

I said, "What's your name?" He told me Gary. *"Do you have a last name Gary?" I made him give me a pen and paper.* He wrote it down, along with his employee number. He handed it back. I asked him, *"Gary, do I need to wear a sign that says, I AM THE CUSTOMER?"* He just looked at me. *I told him I wanted to talk to the highest ranking US Air person at the airport, right now. With a grunt and a shrug of the shoulders, he says that he is the highest ranking one there. We argue for a minute, but he sticks to his guns.*

There was no way this little twit was the highest ranking guy there. And there was no way he was going to screw with me. I told Gary, as I pointed to a pay phone nearby, that I was walking over there, calling headquarters and that I would get two seats together. He said, "No seats", as he turned to walk away. "Gary", I yelled. He stopped and turned back towards me. "I'll be back, don't you go anywhere".

My mind spun, a kaleidoscope of emotions flooded my mind. My heart raced. I wanted to tell that little prick how lucky he was I'd found Christ and become civilized. I wanted to go slap the shit out of him, and stuff his little ass in a shit can. People like him got other people killed in Nam. I can't stand little tin soldiers. I might hurt this little man if I'm not careful.

Napoleon walked away, and the original lady I talked with came back. She apologized for what had just happened. She said he was in charge tonight, and she could do nothing. I thanked her and walked to a pay phone nearby. I was a million mile flyer and a Gold Card member. I called the hotline. I asked for a Supervisor right out of the blocks. A classy lady came on the phone, she knew what a customer was. I explained what had happened. She apologized profusely. She explained she couldn't technically give me the seats, but she could tell me which seats were open, so I could go back and demand them. Excellent idea. I was thankful I got a problem solver.

As we worked on the problem, she asked for the employee name. I shared it. She looked it up on her computer. She told me, "It's not an excuse, but he's a Union Steward and a trouble maker". I told her I could confirm; he was indeed a trouble maker. It took her about fifteen minutes, and she had two sets of seats, together and available. In fact, she shared with me that there were over fifteen empty seats available. *I wanted to seriously hurt this guy. I was deep in my bad place. Nam was nearby.*

Armed with my two sets of seat numbers, I walked back to the counter to wait for Gary. He was standing at a computer, ignoring me. *I stand and stare.* A lady comes up; he waits on her. She leaves, and he leaves to work on a bag nearby. *I'm a sniper. I've got patience.* It's now within the hour of our departure time. I wait. He ignores me. The lady who first helped me came up and smiled. I walked up to her. She says she'll help me. I tell her I want seats 21E and 21D for my daughter and I. I also give her the numbers for Cortney and Gloria. She smiles and says, "They're all open, no problem".

Gary, who is helping a lady next to me, turns and starts over my way. He says, "No! You cannot give those to him. One is a handicapped seat". *I was about to levitate.* I turned to the lady next to me and said, "Ma'm, please excuse me for a minute". Gary is standing next to the lady helping me. *I said, reaching my arm over the counter, and putting my finger in his face,* "Gary, you had your chance. Those are my seats. *I don't see any wheelchairs around here, and they're not reserved. They are mine. Now, you get over there and help this nice lady right now, or you and I are going to have some real serious problems".* Gary turned, angrily, and went back to work where he was.

The nice lady waiting on me, smiled, handed me all four tickets and boarding passes, and told me to have a nice flight. *I went over to Gary, excused myself to his customer, again, held my four tickets in his face, and said,* "Gary I told you I would get these; it didn't have to be so hard." I handed him the note he'd written his information on. I said, "Write your boss's name on there. I guarantee you the President of US Air will know your name late next week. You should not be anywhere near a customer". He grunted didn't seem to care and wrote down his boss's name.

We needed to get to the Gate. I gathered the family, went to the gate and boarded the plane. I needed to settle down. I'd had such a great trip, *no flashbacks, few sleepless nights, and then I end it with this dirt bag.* Whitney and I settled in as the remainder of the passengers came on board. A steady stream, but not a full plane.

One of the final passengers to board is a young Oriental guy on crutches. *I saw this guy and my bees were buzzing again. In my mind, I was sure Gary had struck again. He found some handicapped guy and gave him my seat. If he did I'll miss my flight, I'll beat the shit out of Gary. As I was punching Gary in my mind,* the Oriental guy hobbled by me, to his seat in the back. Gary dodged a bullet. I laid back, closed my eyes, just wanting to get airborne.

"Would Mr. Kugler come to the front of the cabin, please?" The Flight Attendant was calling for me, front and center. Whit got scared. I told her to chill; *I wasn't going anywhere. I was on here; I wasn't leaving.* The Flight Attendant explained the problem. My tickets showed a connection through Pittsburg, but this plane is heading to Philadelphia. I explained to her I'd changed my flight yesterday. I'd opted for the later Philly flight, rather than Pittsburg. I saw her glance towards the doorway. She looks at me and back to the walkway, still attached to the plane. In all his glory, stood Gary.

I looked at him; he disappeared backwards in the hatchway. The Flight Attendant sensed an issue.

"Ma'am, it's been a long, and very bad day. That little guy in the beard out there screwed with me for the last time. I'm on here; my family's on here, and we're not leaving. I changed my flight. The paperwork is your problem, not mine". She said she'd handle it. I turned and went back to my seat with Whit. I told her everything was fine.

They finally closed the cabin door, and we were off. As I write this, we're about an hour out of Philly. I fell asleep on takeoff. When I woke up; *I was still pretty wired about Gary.* Whit wanted to play a game, her little spirit flushed *the Adrenaline right out of my system.* We've had a great time on this trip. *After Gary tripped my wire, and I didn't kill him, that's surely progress.*

11 July, Sunday - Brookfield, CT. Home

Recovering from our trip. I think it's true, you come home from a vacation to rest. We went to church this morning. Came home, ate, then unpacked. Everyone went to bed early tonight, but me. Always need to write.

I'll turn forty-seven next month. Seems like yesterday I was seventeen in Parris Island. I'm tired. Back to work in the morning. *Gary keeps jumping in my head. I can't stand people like him. I can't stand people who use their position to screw with others. I can't stand it.* I lay down, but sleep's again elusive. *"This is bullshit!", a Marine grunt yells. His platoon Sergeant is a new Staff Sergeant, who just reported in from stateside. He just told them when we sweep the village there will be no shooting. That is of course unless we're shot at first. The grunt was right; that's bullshit.*

We're in the Street Without Joy. A deadly place. Famous for all the French wiped out here. Searching villages and hooches is dangerous work. We'd been doing it for days. Your interpreter orders people out, then you search as best you can. Entering the hooch sucks. Simple process, when in doubt, empty the magazine. It's very effective and saves lives.

Now we have this FNG pulling rank, changing rules he obviously doesn't understand. He's also being an ass about it; The grunts are pissed, and so are we. He's going to get somebody killed. We carefully enter the village in line, right to left, about five feet apart. We stepped into a cluster of hooch's, with several wary villagers standing around.

The interpreter questioned them; they assured us there were no bad guys there. But the place didn't feel right. Through an interpreter, we ordered all the villagers to one area. The grunts formed a small perimeter, with a few Marines assigned to keep an eye on them. The grunts split into four man teams, and began searching each hooch. We're looking for weapons, ammunition and bad guys.

It's no place for snipers, but we're here. I was standing with my partner in the center of the cluster, when a blast from an AK erupted to our left. We turned as a Marine grunt flew backwards, landing spread eagle in the dirt. Two other grunts ripped the hooch with M-14 fire. The mortally wounded Marine lay on his back, bleeding everywhere. The gook inside stitched him right up the middle, from stomach to chest. His face was blood splattered..

The Marine in the dirt died. He'd walked up to the first hooch; and stood four feet in front, staring at the beads hanging down from the hooch as a door. The interpreter spoke, ordering everyone out, but no one came. The new Staff Sergeant then ordered the Marine to enter. He should have let loose with a left to right blast first, about waste high. But he stepped up, followed orders and took an AK hit to the chest. If you didn't shoot first, you die!

The Gunny came running, and assessed the situation. The grunts were pissed. One of their own bought the farm, for what? He got them together, calmed them down and kept them busy. The Lieutenant came by and took the new Staff Sergeant with him. We never saw him again. After that rookie nonsense, we shot first, and let the bullshit fall where it may.

12 July, Monday - Somers, NY. Pepsi

Time to head home. Wanted to write first, so I'm not up late. *Holding my own, considering how the vacation ended with Gary, and all. Still want to rip his face off. Wrote my letter to the President of US Air today. I'll send it off on the way home.* In spite of Gary, I do feel rejuvenated, refocused.

I brought my lunch today, had a small can of fruit cocktail. *Eating it with a plastic spoon sent me back to Nam.* But I kept things in balance and am feeling pretty good. Time to tackle the commute home.

13 July, Tuesday - Somers, NY. Pepsi

End of day. Meaningless meetings morning to night. Unbelievable. People are happy operating in a state of mental masturbation. Politics makes cowards of us all. People hesitate, they don't want to make decisions, for fear of how it might impact their careers. What ever happened to 'do what's right?' Gooks are charging on all sides, let's have a meeting to talk about it.

Politics is not my thing. If they want something done, they know I'll deliver it. But these bullshit meetings are killing Pepsi and me. I saw this start happening in the late eighties. It's warp speed here. Hard to tell what it'll be like in the next decade. I have a feeling it's not going to be pretty.

We're dying a slow death in this country. Between the growing demand for political correctness and special interest groups, we're heading for deep trouble. Sad. Time to head home. Got an early flight tomorrow.

14 July, Wednesday - In the air to Charleston, WV. Pepsi

Just woke up. We're descending through the clouds. Mountains are jutting up, as we drop in to the airport. Left the house at 0500 this morning. *Another corporate patrol.* I'm tired, groggy even. Coming here to teach a workshop. The rest of today I'll be touring operations and meeting people I teach tomorrow. The airport doesn't look much different than it did years ago. I flew through here heading to *Camp LeJuene one time. The mountains in the fog remind me of Con Thein.* Not time for that today.

16 July, Friday - Lock Haven, PA. A Friends House

Got home from West by God Virginia at midnight last night. Midnight tonight we're in our old stomping grounds, Lock Haven, Pennsylvania. That was two moves ago. Made lots of good friends when we lived here. The girls are excited to visit. We're here to baptize Whit, who turned eight in February.

She was a baby when we moved here in 1985. We left in 1991, so the bulk of her life has been here. The Susquehanna River runs through Lock Haven and has a big place in our church's history. I'm grateful for the gospel of Jesus Christ. I struggle to live it as I should. If we all did, the world would be a much nicer place. Whit wanted to be baptized here with her friends.

The drive down was nice, relaxing. Driving through southern New York State and eastern Pennsylvania is pretty. But not this year. As I drove, I thought things have been going well. The blackness, which sometimes smothers me, has been leaving me alone. I think the family time chases even my most persistent ghosts away. With everyone asleep, I cruised along with no radio, no tapes or CD's, and no noise. A nice drive.

I cleared a rise in the highway thinking about how blessed my life has been. A great, patient wife, who understands me. Three beautiful kids. Life is good. Looking ahead, I see a car parked on the right berm of I-80 about a quarter mile ahead. I cruised over to the left lane to pass safely. *That's when I saw two figures running from the car towards a clump of trees.*

It's crazy; *I was in Nam. My mind jumped into action. Instantly, I flip football fields in my mind, and see targets at three hundred yards. I do a quick check of the wind, scanning the tree tops and tall grass. Calm. No windage needed. Adrenaline warmed my body; my heart rate increased, as my breathing slowed down. Step it up, I tell myself, they're almost to the tree line. Drop your pack, lay it in front, drop to the prone position, rifle resting on your pack. Twist your rifle into your shoulder, cheek on your spot weld of the stock, pick up the target in your scope, lay the cross hairs on their upper body, deep breath ... I whiz past them at fifty-eight miles per hour. My spell is broken; I'm back in the world.*

Happens every, single time I see someone walking in a field. Could be one, could be two or three, but I immediately hone in on the target. Using the technique Staff Sergeant Rider taught us long ago, I flip football fields without thinking. Even driving along, enjoying time with my family, the past overwhelmed me for a few seconds. It's been a good day. I came back to the world, the one I enjoy now.

Big day tomorrow. Time for sleep.

18 July, Sunday - Brookfield, CT. Home

Home again, after a wonderful weekend in Pennsylvania. Everyone's in bed. Baptism went well. The weather was outstanding. It was nice to be among friends. I was their lay minister for six years. Good people, striving to be better. They asked me to speak in church today. It was fun and went well. When we left for home, we drove by our old house in Woolrich. We loved living there. A true 'My Three Sons' house. We missed that place. The drive home was nice; traffic was light and we made good time. Back to work tomorrow, more travel.

20 July, Tuesday - White Plains, NY. Airport

Sitting in White Plains Nairobi Airport. It's third world all the way. I had to get up at 0430 to get here. You can't have breakfast, and there's no place to sit. Amazing. The airport is in one of the wealthiest counties in America, Westchester county. *Phu Bai in 1966 may have been a step up.*

I'm off to Chicago today, Thursday I'll be in Minneapolis. I'm supposed to fly home on the corporate jet Friday night. I hate traveling so much. I look forward to our annual Canadian vacation in two weeks. Thinking about it will get me through this week.

21 July, Wednesday - Chicago, IL. Hyatt Regency O'Hare

Good meetings today, with real people from the franchise side. Teaching again. When I finished, I caught a shuttle to O'Hare. I had a meeting at the United Airlines Red Carpet Club. Met a headhunter for an interview. The Borden Company in Columbus, Ohio, is looking for a VP of Logistics. The interview went well. Interesting job, not sure about Borden though. They're trying to put a chip company together by buying Wise Potato Chips. They want to take on Frito Lay. The money's there, not sure they have a chance of competing with Frito.

He told me the job is mine if I want it. We've been talking for a month. I'll have to talk with Gloria. I have my doubts. I work for a first class outfit now, not sure Borden is in that class. The lifespan of Wise chips is questionable. To bed, early flight in the morning. Heading to Minneapolis.

22 July, Thursday - Minneapolis, MN. Hyatt Regency Downtown

Tough day. Should be in bed. Flew up this morning. Pepsi franchise bottlers' convention here. Did two workshops this morning, five back-to-back after lunch. We didn't finish until six tonight, so I skipped dinner. Went downstairs and used the lap pool. It's my feeble attempt to get back in shape. I was swimming along, enjoying myself, came up for air *into the muddy waters surrounding Don O O, the old French Fort, near the Laotian mountains on the west side of Co Bi Than Tan Valley. "Kug, I was here last week with the grunts, you can walk this river". A young sniper was talking. I was walking point, not leading the Rogues. A new Lieutenant, who was back at Camp Evans, had ordered us to run twelve man sniper patrols. He also placed a new Staff Sergeant in charge. He asked me to walk point.*

The Staff Sergeant was a good guy, but inexperienced in Nam. I was pissed. I'd just led the group about ten clicks in the middle of the night. We negotiated a heavy fog; that lay on the ground about four feet high. The fog made us appear as half persons, as we walked in the moonlight. It was right out of an Alfred Hitchcock mystery.

The Fort at Don O O had us over extended. We were near the mountains and lots of bad guys. The plan was to sneak into the fort before dawn. That would give us an advantage. The fort sat about three hundred feet above the valley floor. The vantage point it gave us was perfect for sniping, but getting there wasn't for the faint of heart.

With the sun about to usher in a new day, walking across the river would save time. The jungle hung thick around the river's edge, making crossing the river ominous, for the point man. I look at Tomo. "Kug, don't trust that FNG". The alternative was blowing up our rubber ladies, rubber air mattresses we carried for floating across deep rivers. The FNG assures me it's only about four feet deep. Screw it. I'll take my chances.

I unbuckle my ammo harness, feeling the weight of my fifty pound pack. I scanned the bank on the other side. It was time. I flipped the safety off my M-14, holding it above my chest, as I stepped into the water. I sank like a thousand pound anchor. Blub, blub, blub. I'm over my head, holding my breath, trying to kick off the bottom. My first kick I stuck in the mud. Lungs about to burst, I feel myself shooting to the surface. Tomo grabbed my pack and was pulling me to the surface. The water was filthy and cold. It was the end of the monsoon; we'd been living in the muck for months, and the river banks were mush.

I treaded water as best I could, while Tomo held me up by my pack. I tossed my water logged rifle on the river bank. Red grabbed one arm, Tomo the other. They slid me up on the bank like a beached whale. The new guy stood off in the distance, which was good. I'd had my swim for the day, blow up the rubber ladies.

I came back to reality, and realized I was standing in four feet of water at the Hyatt. I didn't need to ford the moat around Don O O, a particularly unforgiving place, anymore. I dried off, returned to the room and ordered room service. I watched TV, and thought of the last time I was in Minneapolis. *I was with Greek. It was 1972. He and I were at the Convention Center downtown, staying in a cheap hotel, trying to get my business off the ground. I had a small company called Nitro Joes Racing Oils and Fuels. We were attending a big snowmobile convention, hawking our wares. We had fun selling my synthetic racing oils and jazzed up fuels. Tears flowed down my cheeks thinking about my lost brother.*

As I thought about those days, I'd been looking out the window, staring at the city. I closed the drapes and knelt for prayer. I needed strength. *I could feel my blackness roll into my mind, like storm clouds on a hot summer night.* After my prayer, I got up and decided to write. It's now midnight. I hope I can sleep.

Six workshops tomorrow, then a long flight home. To bed.

23 July - Friday - In the air to White Plains, NY. Corporate Jet

I made it through six more workshops, even had fun in the process. I love working with the franchisees. They're business people who know how to make payroll and get work done. I struggle with the 'fraternity brother set' we've been overrun with in Pepsi. I have to say, I'm grateful for the corporate jet this evening. We'll be to White Plains in two and a half hours. If I was going home commercial it would be Minneapolis, Chicago, Pittsburg and White Plains. It would also be midnight.

It'll be wonderful to be home again.

24 July, Saturday - Brookfield, CT. Home

Gloria and I were in the kitchen, having a late snack, when she asked for her herbal tea from the microwave. When I opened the microwave door, *I got a blast of the strong, musty smell of tea. For a brief moment, I was sitting cross legged next to Demo Dean, on the dirt floor of the Village Chiefs hooch. We were trying to do our civic duty. We sat down with the old man to discuss his village. Demo Dean taught himself*

Vietnamese in about three months. He acted as our interpreter. Gloria said, "Not again?" *The tea tripped my trigger.* Need some sleep. Hope it comes.

27 July, Tuesday - Somers, NY. Pepsi

Long day. Meetings, meetings and more meetings. So much for work. Wanted to write while I am at the office, before heading home. Trevor finished his summer semester at college and stopped by last night on his way to our cottage in Canada. He loves it there. Always has. He did summer school this year, to make up for his time in Alaska last year. He's doing well.

We woke up early today to a big thunderstorm. That brought the kids running to our room. It sounded like it was on our front step. I realized I'd left some tools outside last night. The TV weatherman said there was zero chance of rain. I rushed outside and brought the tools in, getting drenched in the process.

It's been pouring all day. It'll make the commute slower, but it's always slow. Time to head home.

28 July, Wednesday - Somers, NY. Pepsi

Writing before the drive home again. More meetings. These days we talk more and work less. In Staff meeting today we talked about how private label soda is kicking our butts. The leading edge of the trend is in Canada, where Cott Beverages is coming on strong making private label soda on the cheap. We discussed ways to combat Cott. They don't get it. Soda is a commodity today. It's about price.

Our leaders have all the answers, but what was the question? They just want you to validate the answer they propose, right or not. It gets worse every day. Tell me what I want to hear. *That was Nam. McNamara, Westmoreland, Johnson, all a bunch of 'tell me what I want to hear leaders'.* I can't dwell here, or I won't be sleeping

tonight. *Thinking their names, hearing their names or seeing their faces, is a big trigger of mine. Sends me off the charts.*
Out of here.

29 July, Thursday - Brookfield, CT. Pepsi

It's bedtime. Tough day. Woke up this morning at 0400 to another loud thunderstorm. Rain pouring down in buckets. My window was open, drapes too. The lightening continued for some time. The night comes to life under the flickering, incessant lightning. Then comes the home shaking thunder.
I couldn't sleep. I sat up and looked out the window. The silvery night, when lit up with lightning, reminded me of looking through our Starlight scopes, the early version of night vision. They magnified available light seventy thousand times. The scopes were so bright, a silvery hue; you couldn't see when you took your eye away. It blinded you.
I lay down in search of sleep. I last saw 0500. The alarm went off at 0600. Need sleep right now. To bed.

30 July, Friday - Somers, NY Pepsi

Had another staff meeting this morning. Not sure why, just because I guess. My boss led the meeting. He drew some graphs on the board with a grease pencil. He turns and asks if we know what he drew? *I said, "Looks like crosshairs to me".* He shakes his head and smiles. *I can't help but think; there's something abnormal in how I view the world.*
Spent the rest of the day doing work in preparation of vacation. Time to head north to our cottage. The whole family plans for this time every year. No Pepsi, no world intervening,, just us and the gorgeous French River.

31 July, Saturday - Brookfield, CT. Home

We went shopping today, getting ready for vacation. I love books, so I had to stop by Walden Books and stock up. I always pack a half dozen books for vacation. I bought a new POW book, "The Men We Left Behind". I've been fascinated with that topic forever. I don't believe we brought them all home in 1973. *It wasn't politically expedient to fight about it.*

I couldn't wait until vacation to start reading it. I got half way through it tonight. *Now I'm wired. How in the hell can people sleep at night, knowing they didn't account for all our men?* As I sit here, writing, *I wish I could be face-to-face with Nixon, Kissinger, Carter and Clinton. They royally piss me off.*

It's going to be a restless night.

"Home is where you dig it"
Found on a Zippo lighter in the War

AUGUST

1 August, Sunday - Brookfield, CT. Home

House full tonight. We always take our kids friends with us to the cottage. A family came in today, from Baltimore. Brought their daughter up for the trip. They're spending the night, returning in the morning. He works for the DIA in Maryland. Former Air Force guy. Very quiet. You could probably pull his fingernails out, and he wouldn't say anything.

Reading my POW book, I couldn't help but ask him, if he'd worked on any POW issues, in his two decades at the Defense Intelligence Agency. He gave me the standard, can't talk about that' response. I get it. I reword the question. "In your opinion, based on your experience, did we leave any live POW's behind?" He said, "I can't imagine under the circumstances, we didn't leave some behind. But I don't believe there are any alive today". Fair enough.

Everyone in the house seems to have settled down for bed. It's after 11 PM. *The POW issues really bug me. I've always been weird. I enjoyed my time in Nam. But I'm still furious at our leaders. They tied our hands. They played games with our lives. They left some of our men behind. I'm struggling. I've always struggled with the conduct of the war and the conduct of our people back home. Conflicted would be a better word.*

War brings death and destruction. War destroys lives and changes people, and makes a few people rich? But as a young person, it was the adventure of a lifetime, the ultimate adrenaline rush. It forms an unbreakable brotherhood. Vietnam was a wild and crazy place. I'm often asked what movie best depicts Vietnam. No one movie depicts Vietnam. It all depends on what branch of service you were in, what you did in the war, where you were in Vietnam and what time frame you served there. It's different for everyone. But for me personally, that's easy. It was Apocalypse Now.

Take out the bizarre ending with Brando flipping out, but the mentality portrayed in that movie, that was my Vietnam. It was an out of body experience. The wild west. The dark humor, the brotherhood, the stupendous adventure of it all. It was awful and amazing at the same time. Conflicted by war and life, you bet.

Time for bed. It may be a tough night. As I lay down, *I can feel the blackness surround me. Been sitting here, staking out a trail junction since 0 dark early. Not our usual sniper gig. We liked to change it up. We liked to be where they'd never believe we'd be. Today we are. Three of us. We're camouflaged into four foot elephant grass, about ten feet off the trail. We were on an eight foot rise above the trail that gave us visibility. We were in a free fire zone; anyone is fair game.*

It was pushing noon; our action usually comes just after daylight or just before dark. We were baking in the sun, sitting, frozen in place. "Wouldn't it be cool if a gook came down that trail," Crud whispered, smiling. Stu and Crud sat with me. Hood was on R & R; Greek stepped on a mine and was on his way home. Stu's scoping out the two tree lines to our front with the 7 x 50's. There's one trail leading straight at us, running from between the two tree lines.

The tree lines are a hundred yards to our front, a chip shot for us. Rice paddies cover the space in between, on either side of the trail leading our way. Dry, dead, not used in forever, rice paddies. The trail junction sits about twenty feet in front of our position. There's a small foot bridge over a dry creek bed, to the right of the trail junction.

Stu put down the binoculars, disgusted. No action. I saw movement out of the corner of my eye. A gook was walking right at us from between the two tree lines. He didn't have a care in the world. Stu grabbed the binoculars for a closer look. The guy was heading straight at us. He had a carbine rifle slung over one shoulder, and a big cloth bag over the other.

I whispered to Crud, "Be ready; it's your shot". He was the kid in the candy store, smiling ear-to-ear. The gook kept coming. He had no idea we were there. I told Crud to hold fire until I told him to shoot. He got closer. One hundred meters. Seventy-five meters. Fifty meters. Twenty-five meters. Hold. Ten Meters. Shoot! He looked straight at us the split second Crud fired. He went down but was on his feet running in a heartbeat, headed down the dry creek bed.

He hobbled as he ran, Crud hit him in the upper thigh. Without a word from me, Stu ran after him. Crud's firing across the paddies at three gooks who were heading our way. I joined Crud, firing across the paddy, dropping one. Crud dropped another and the third disappeared into the trees. I turned back my gaze to Stu, just as he hit the running VC in the middle of the back with the butt of his M-14. The gook went sprawling, face first on the ground.

The tree line came alive with more gunfire. I ran to Stu, as he shot the VC soldier. The guy had his carbine and a bag full of booby trap materials. I said, "Stu, if we captured him, you'd have five days R & R". Sweat dripping from his face, breathing heavy from his run, he looked at me and said, "Kug, you gotta tell me that shit before I run him down". Disgustedly, he turned and walked back with Crud. "Let's get out of here".

2 August, Monday - Brookfield, CT. Home

We went out for dinner tonight. Celebrating my birthday. Turned 47 today. Hard to believe. Never thought I'd live this long. For many years, I couldn't see past 40. Guess we'll see how long I make it. Love my kids and family. Blessed indeed.

4 August, Wednesday - Cranston, RI. Pepsi

Sitting in the parking lot of a diner. Finished an all day meeting. Another new project my boss is taking over and giving to me. Another black hole. He asked me to come over and take a look. It's a new inventory system that's about to be rolled out. It's been 'reengineered'. That's the latest corporate buzzword for 'boondoggle'. Today was the report from a pilot test. The plant here has been running the test for four months. My boss told me to be honest.

I learned in Nam surprises are bad. I came here early this morning and talked with the Plant Manager privately. He explained they'd been using the 'new' inventory system, and it didn't make any difference, no change. He said the computer print outs were in a different format, but the bottom line was, it wasn't worth the money, nothing new and improved. I thought of my old idol, Alfred E. Newman of Mad Magazine fame. He once said, 'Just because everything's different doesn't mean anything's changed'. A true classic.

My meeting this morning was the first since the changing of the guard. When the system team reported out, I asked the presenter one simple question. "What is the payback on this project?" Being a corporate animal, the guy started with the all too usual double speak. He explained the project proposal, then the methodology. I was about to short circuit and burn my own trip wire. It's like watching paint dry listening to this drivel.

I remind him, I asked him for the payback on the project. Undaunted, he rolled right into another rant. He told me how many FTE's the program will eliminate. "I'm sorry, but what exactly is an FTE?" I asked. He looks at me incredulously, like you don't know that? He says, "An FTE means a full time equivalent". I looked at him, then asked, "That would be a person? An employee?' He wasn't appreciating my line of questioning, but agreed; that's what it meant. I knew that came directly from the last HR Staff meeting. Give me a break.

A few people in the room were snickering. *I thought back to my days in Vietnam when the CIA used to call killing a contact, 'to eliminate with extreme prejudice'.* Strange how we play word games to justify our actions. Maybe if you eliminate an FTE, you go home believing you didn't lay off a real person? You quickly learn, *the corporate world dehumanizes just like McNamara and Johnson did in Vietnam.*

The Project Manager moved on, trying to ignore my honesty assault. He explained that each plant rollout would save 2.5 FTE's. "Those savings will justify the $400,000 cost", he proudly proclaimed. I was going to question him what .5 of a person was, but decided it would be pointless. I looked at the Project Manager, then the Plant Manager. I then asked the Plant Manager, "Please give me the names of the 2.5 people who are leaving when you roll out this new inventory program?"

He looked at me, smiled and said, "Guys, there's no money here. I have not, and will, not be laying anyone off. The system doesn't work. I've been telling you that for a month now". Honesty has a way of bringing the high fliers down for a crash landing. From that point on, the meeting got real. I cancelled the roll out. I begged off dinner. I'm looking forward to a vacation.

05 August, Thursday - Somers, NY. Pepsi

Heading home from the office shortly. Heading for Canada in the morning. We have half days on Friday, so my boss told me to take off and get out of here. That's because I'm now on point when I get back, to turn around the whole mess they call, 'reengineering'. I'll worry about that when I come back.

Interesting day. Woke up to my eye acting up. Meetings all morning. Last year in Canada I stuck something in it while hiking. Came home, to Baltimore then, and had a serious infection. Turned out it was a staph infection, an ulcerated cornea. Ended up at Johns Hopkins. They fixed it.

At lunch, I went downstairs, to the in-house Doctor. He told me I couldn't leave the country without seeing an eye specialist. I told him we needed to find one fast, because I'm leaving for Canada in the morning. He made some calls and got me into one, about a half hour away, in Katonah, New York. I ran down there; they got me right in. The Doctor impressed upon me the magnitude of the problem, gave me some ointment and here I am. Crisis averted.

Time to get home. Lots of work to do. Packing, putting roof top carriers on and preparing for liftoff. Excited, *but fighting the blackness once again.* But, we're leaving on R & R tomorrow, and that's good.

06 August, Friday - Welland, Ontario, Canada. Journey's End

Everyone's in bed. Short night. Long day. But we crossed the border, we're in Canada! Tomorrow night I'll be a world away. Peace at last. Everyone in the car has been telling me I'm irritable. Every mile I travel away from the world, I relax a little more. Same thing every year.

The cars been full of life. Whitney, Cortney and two of her girlfriends liven things up. The drive to the cottage from Connecticut is fourteen to sixteen hours. From here, it should only be about seven hours tomorrow. *Met Greek and his family here last year. We'd drive up from here together. Not happening anymore. His wife doesn't feel comfortable coming right now. I understand, but the kids would have loved coming.*

We'll be meeting another family from Pennsylvania tomorrow. They have three kids, so we'll have a cottage full, just like every summer. Winding down tonight. Getting tired. To bed. Early start tomorrow.

07 August, Saturday - Near Noelville, Ontario, Canada. Our Cottage on the French River

We made it to the cottage around dinner time. We stopped in Noelville, fifteen miles away, to hit the grocery store and stock up. We made good time, stopped at Harvey's, a great restaurant chain up here, for our annual poutine. Fries, cheese curds and hot gravy. We made it through Toronto in good time. Traffic there can be horrendous. Weather is gorgeous.

Sitting at our bar here, writing on my laptop, is so different from doing it in any other place. No one understands that, until they come here with us. It's unbelievable beauty, peace and tranquility. It's why Greek loved to get out of the rat race of New York every summer, and come here. I've always said, life on the French, is life is as it should be.

The cottage is in great shape. You'd never know it was built in the mid-fifties, by a Canadian guide, and friend of my father. It was originally his fishing camp. Still has the sixties motif my Mom decorated. My kids love it. To my wife's dismay, they won't allow a single change. We've moved so much, this is their only stable place. It's their 'home'. No changes allowed. Our rule for furniture is, nothing can match. Time for bed. I love mornings here.

**09 August, Monday - Near Noelville, Ontario, Canada.
Our Cottage on the French River**

Great day on the French. The cottage has one room for the living and dining area, with four bunk rooms along the back. Being here feels so good. The stress I usually feel is nearly gone. Our friends arrived yesterday. Fun is in the air.

I haven't thought of Pepsi, or life back in the world at all. I do spend more time than I'd like, *thinking about Greek, and what was. Thinking about his family not being here this summer.* We love the folks with us. He is a great guy. He just isn't a Rogue, and it's not the same.

The routine here is play hard, work a little. We're putting a roof on the garage. Jim is a shop teacher back in Pennsylvania so he can do about anything. People get up anywhere from daylight to noon. We have lunch, then hit the water. The kids tube and wakeboard until sunset. Then everyone cleans up, eats and it's movie time.

We don't have TV at the cottage. And I forbid Game Boys and the like. So every evening, we watch movies the kids go in town and rent. Trevor went in today and brought one home. If I don't like it, I just sit at the bar and read, or write. I finished my first book last night. The one on the POW's left behind. Pissed me off, but there's healing here. Being here is therapy.

The movie Trevor picked up is, 'A Few Good Men'. He was sure I'd like it. I like Jack Nicholson, but can't stand the sight of that little twit, Tom Cruise. I'm up here to get away from the bullshit; I don't need the aggravation. I sat at the bar, writing, hearing the movie from time to time. It's one room, so I can't get too far from it. Can't go on the deck, mosquitoes own the night, just like Nam.

"You can't handle the truth", I hear Nicholson screaming at Cruise. Time for bed, don't need that stuff right now. We're now living in a world that 'can't handle the truth'. Sweet dreams?

Mid-August, - Near Noelville, Ontario, Canada.
Our Cottage on the French River

I don't even know what the date is, and I don't care. It's a week night, I know that. That's the beauty of being on the French River. It's very special. The water looks black; I love it. Rock shorelines, tall pine trees that cling to the huge rocks. Pristine wilderness. And very few people, perfect. Hiking here's dirty, and difficult. Very little solid ground, all rock. Everything is up, down, and around. The smell of the pines, the clean, fresh air, is invigorating.

Several of us get up in the morning and swim the bay. It's one hundred-fifty meters across the bay. Over and back gives us a three-hundred meter swim. The water's cold, but we get used to it. *When I'm here, there's usually no room for the blackness I live with back the world.* I love paddling our rubber kayak across the bay, to one of the many islands nearby.

I miss Greek a lot.

Mid-August - Near Noelville, Ontario, Canada.
Our Cottage on the French River

Time's flying by, as it always does here. We have the annual events to do. Floating the rapids at Five Fingers, with a picnic there. Jumping the cliffs, knee boarding, wake boarding, water skiing for some, shore lunches for all. My son is a big fisherman, as his grandpa, my Dad. We look to him to provide the fish for a shore lunch. And before we go, we always abuse ourselves hiking Eighteen Mile Island. It's rough, rugged terrain, filled with walls of mosquitoes. Hiking there is climbing up and down rocks, and crossing bogs. But everyone wants to do it, so we do.

I spend evenings and sometimes early mornings thinking about when I can retire and come here all summer. When I came home from Nam, this was the only place I felt relaxed and at peace. I love the people here. I love the culture. And I love their land. It is God's beauty. It gives me peace in my heart.

Mid-August - Near Noelville, Ontario, Canada.
Our Cottage on the French River

We went up to Sudbury today, an annual ritual. We love Sudbury. It's eighty miles north. Has a small Mall and about a hundred thousand people. We've been coming long enough to see the city grow. The kids always do their school shopping at the Mall. By the time we return to the cottage, the kids tell me my 'bad side' is showing. They're right, too many people after none at the cottage. At least we've made it to the point the kids can tell me when I'm being an ass.

19 August, Thursday - Near Noelville, Ontario, Canada.
Our Cottage on the French River

Morning, sitting outside. Most are still asleep. Can't believe our two weeks is about over. Nobody wants to leave. We decide to see what's possible. Jim's a teacher, he's good for a couple more days. I call my boss, and he's cool if I'm back for my trip west this week. I have to be in Omaha next Thursday. Even one more day here is worth it. We have two. Hooray!

**20 August, Friday - Near Noelville, Ontario, Canada.
Our Cottage on the French River**

I have to capture this while I can. It's late, but it's important. Our long time friends from here in Canada, Elma and Irmand Daoust, stopped by this evening. They are the nicest people. He's a few years older than me, but we hit it off years ago. A couple years ago Irmand suffered an unbelievable tragedy. He lost his only son, and one of his two daughters, in separate accidents, six months apart. Then my Mother, who was close to his family, died shortly thereafter. She used to bring his kids to the states and take them to amusement parks.

He and I grew close through religion. We belonged to different churches but were both committed to Christ. We were both converts, too. We always spend time each year talking about life. He made some profound statements that I have to write down.

First, as I 'talked' with him about our church, for the fourth consecutive year, he put his big arm around me, he stands about six-foot five, and said, "Eddie, we can never let our differences, get in the way of the fact we love each other". My lightbulb went off. That was profound. It was a weight lifted from my shoulders He's right; I finally get it.

Second, we were talking about how life is getting in the way of living. Things are moving too fast; none of us has enough time. He said, "Eddie, we all have the same twenty-four hours each day. It's what we choose to trade it for that matters. He said the things getting in our way are as Mother Teresa said, 'Distractions'. He may be a lumberjack, spent his life in the 'bush', as they call it, but he is a wise, wise man.

The third thing is equally as important to write down. He said that all of the 'distractions' we're experiencing are getting worse. He realized that distractions are the designs of Satan. That's how he pulls us away from Christ. That's why we often don't do what we know to be important. Man, I love this guy. Wish I could spend more time with him. I cherish the moments we have together. I'm going to bed on a high tonight.

21 August, Saturday - Near Noelville, Ontario, Canada. Our Cottage on the French River

Nice evening after severe storms this afternoon. Took down lots of trees around us, but none on our property. We're isolated here. We have only one neighbor, about thirty yards through the trees. Great people. They're from Newmarket, Ontario. Other than them, we're alone with our own wilderness. I can take the kids midnight tubing, and not worry. No one is here. They love it.

As we wind down, it's been a great trip. Trevor left yesterday. Jim and I were up on the roof, finishing the garage. We heard a car; Trevor comes back down the driveway, couldn't do it. Staying until Monday. His girlfriend isn't happy.

He took the little kids fishing today. They love going with him. Especially Whitney, she loves being with her big brother. He's been very nice and loving, since enduring a year in Alaska, squeezing out a living in the fish canneries.

Hate to think about leaving. When I'm here, my heart feels like it did as a kid, full of fun and possibilities. After I'm here awhile, the emotions, I so long ago buried, slowly come to the surface. I begin to feel again. I can feel the love everyone has for each other. I feel excitement for the future. I feel grateful for being blessed with this place. I feel the love of Christ.

Today we took our last trip on the river, a long one. We made our annual excursion to Chauddiere Dam. It's about ten miles upstream. *I remembered when I was there with Greek. He had an artificial leg but was quite active with it. He never wanted help. It was a foggy, cold morning. The water was high, unusual for that time of year. The rapids before the dam were pretty rough. I didn't want to take a boat around the corner of the river without seeing the other side first. The rapids wrapped around the corner.*

I pulled the boat over about twenty yards before the river bend and rapids. I wanted to pull the boat near the rocks, climb over the rise, and take a look. Greek insisted he'd go ashore. I didn't think that was a great idea, but he was Greek, and he was positive he could do it. He stood up on the bow of the boat, as I eased it to the rock edge.

I told him to be careful on the rocks, they'd be slippery. That pissed him off. I knew if they were jet black; they were wet and slick. He assured me he was fine. I held the boat tight against the rock by idling the engine forward. When Greek stepped off, he led with his artificial leg, not his good one. When his foot hit those black rocks, he went head over heels, under the boat, and into the cold morning water. I helped him up and into the boat. He was not a happy camper, especially with me laughing. Good times on the French.

We stayed on the water today until after dark. No one wanted to go to bed. Just before midnight, we loaded into the boat. I took everyone to the main channel of the river, under a perfect and clear sky, to our own private planetarium. It's an amazing site. More amazing because we saw the Northern Lights, which are always a treat.

To bed. Big day tomorrow.

22 August, Sunday - Near Noelville, Ontario, Canada. Our Cottage on the French River

Loading the car all day. Cleaning the cottage. Putting away all the water toys. Winterizing everything. The hardest work was dealing with seventeen tons of sand we'd delivered on the shoreline. It was a small mountain of sand. We did it for the kids to play in, and to spread it out and make a beach. An annual quest we have yet to accomplish.

We set up a bucket brigade today, to distribute the sand around the beach. It was fun, and a whole lot of work. *Reminded me of filling sandbags around the clock, back at Camp Evans and Camp Carroll.* But my thoughts went nowhere, as I stood looking over our gorgeous bay, surrounded by fresh smelling pines. It made it all okay.

Leaving early tomorrow on our trip back to the world. R & R is over.

23 August, Monday - Fort Erie, Ontario, Canada. Journey's End

Today was the day. We couldn't put it off any longer. I had to leave my favorite place on earth behind. I do have to earn a living. We're at the Journeys End in Fort Erie. Last night in Canada. Cross over to the States in the morning. It's been a long day. Started at 0500 when the kids decided, finally, that they wanted to see the sun rise on the French. The awesome place to see it is at Chauddiere, where we were yesterday. It's a forty-five minute boat ride. It was dark. But I got up and off we went. I navigate by memory, watching tree tops, to keep in the middle of the river. We made it, and it was beautiful. Orange flames came out from behind the silhouette of the pines, bringing a new day to life. It was magnificent.

Back to the cottage, load up the boat, get it in the garage, shower and off we go. We had to stop at Harvey's again for our last poutine of the year. We got to the Journey's End about 7 PM. The kids went swimming in the pool. Everyone's settled down, relaxing and facing reality. Back to school for the kids, back to the grind for Gloria, and me, back to work for another year before returning.

24 August, Tuesday - Brookfield, CT. Home

It's been a great vacation. We took our time getting home. Made some stops to shop. Anything to delay the end of our R & R as long as possible. Got in about nine tonight. We unpacked. All the kids helped. When the Suburban was empty, I sat on the tailgate, taking in the moment. I felt renewed, refreshed, and ready for another round of life in the world.

I stood up, closed the tailgate, and stood, staring into the woods behind my house. *I felt a little unnerved. I stepped around the car when I heard a sound in the woods. Staring into the dark, Connecticut woods, I was laying in a tight circle, on a mountain near Laos. We'd holed up for the night, after being ambushed by a small band of gooks. Of the seven of us, two were critical with wounds.*

After the ambush when we broke contact, we got on the ground and did the low crawl into the thickest part of the jungle we could find. We placed the two wounded in the middle. The five of us were pointing out, away from the middle like a bicycle spoke. We'd remain like that, awake, all night, staring into the darkness, on edge, wired at every sound.

"Ed, where are you?" Gloria came looking for me, and called me back to Brookfield. I've been in the world less than twenty-four hours, and *already, my demons welcome me home. I don't need this shit.*

25 August, Wednesday - Chicago, IL. O'Hare Airport

Back on another corporate patrol. Sitting in O'Hare, waiting on my connection to Omaha. I thought I was coming out here for a workshop, but my boss sent me here for another 'reengineering' meeting, like the one in Cranston. Another 'rollout' of another new software program supposedly ready to launch. We'll see? Slept in this morning. Got the kids off to school, spent some time with Gloria and then flew out of good ole White Plains International Airport.

Slept well last night. I wasn't sure I would, after tripping out staring into the woods. O'Hare is the epicenter for people watching. You see everything on two legs the world has to offer. I never mind a layover here. Hard to imagine just two days ago I was enjoying peace on the French River. That's a long way from here.

People are rushing everywhere. All playing the games of modern life, just like me. A growing number of people are chasing rainbows through airports, down the concourses, from city to city, desperately trying to reach an ever moving finish line. Our country is changing, and not for the better.

Sometimes I think of life in Nam, as good as it gets. It was so simple. You ate what was available; you slept when you could; you bathed when you had the opportunity, and if you woke up in the morning, you were a winner. We lived, or we died. What could be simpler? Life in the world, at times, is not all it's cracked up to be. They called my plane. *Wish it was a rescue chopper.* Later.

26 August, Thursday - Omaha, NE. Airport

Hard to believe I get paid to do this shit. I'm at the airport waiting on an earlier flight. My boss met me here for breakfast. Told me the project we are here to review is a bust. The meeting lasted all of ten minutes. Ten minutes. Cancelled the charade, another piece of the 'reengineering project' bites the dust. Corporate nonsense played with funny money. What's wrong with people? I flew out here; my boss flew out here ... for a ten minute meeting. Go figure. Corporate America is alive and well, and going down the tubes faster than Wiley Coyote can run.

Hope my flight connections are good today. Flying home to do a workshop on 'Personal Effectiveness' for women at church. I should have taught it to the crew here in Omaha. It's days like these when you realize there's a whole lot of money in that sugar water we sell. If not, we'd be broke by now. I remembered when I was in a dinner meeting with Mr. Lay, of Frito Lay. He's the man. A nice gentlemen. He was laughing at dinner and said, "The only thing more profitable than snack foods is prostitution and rock music." Apparently, he was right.

Time to go.

28 August, Saturday - Brookfield, CT. Home

Had an interesting experience today. I went to Stew Leonard's, the largest volume grocery store in the world. It's a class act. It has musical characters around the store, live animals outside, sampling and a carnival atmosphere. A unique place for sure.

Cortney was walking with me; Whitney and Gloria were somewhere else in the store. We were walking through the store *when I was startled, turning a corner I ran into a Vietnamese man and woman. They were the real deal, small, wrinkled with very bad teeth. I know this sounds mean, but these two were original rice paddy daddies from my days in Nam. It was like I knew them.*

My daughter came over and grabbed my arm. "Daaaad! What are you staring at?" I turned, as she is pulled me down the aisle, *and said, "Cort, I think I may have shot at those people"*. She quickly told me she thought that was terrible, and weird, too. She told her Mom, who quickly moved our entourage outside.

It wasn't weird in my world. To bed.

30 August, Monday - St. Louis, MO. Hyatt at Union Square

Hot and muggy here today, *like Nam.* Meetings all day, then home on an early flight tomorrow. Pepsi's building a new $40 million plant here. I'm here to work on the startup. Corporate thinks our reengineering work will help them. Sure it will.

I know it's weird, but I love my new shoulder bag. It converts from a carry on laptop bag to a backpack, my favorite part. I can now have one carry on for overnighters. Simplify. Gloria calls it, my purse. That's a bit strong. To me, *it's a civilized rucksack. Perfect for stateside corporate patrols.*

My Canadian R & R is fast disappearing in the rear view mirror of my life. I can feel the black, but it hasn't smothered me yet. So not turning on the TV tonight. *Don't need to get caught up on Slick Willy. Man, it's hard to call him President.*

31 August, Tuesday - Brookfield, CT. Home

Home from another patrol in corporate America's bush. Dead tired, but compelled to write. I feel better when I do. It's after midnight. I got in from St. Louis this morning, went to work, left late, and had lots of work waiting on me here. Paid more business bills, getting the debt down.

Last night, I was feeling fine, a little tired. I kept my no TV pledge and went right to sleep. Somewhere around 0400, *prime time for a sniper in Nam, I wake from a deep, deep sleep.* I'm not at the Hyatt *but on Hill 51 in the Co Bi Than Tan Valley. I look around, my heart racing, unable to make sense of what's happening around me.*

I hear the pop of a mortar tube. Incoming! I roll to the floor, and realize, there's carpet there. Where am I? What am I doing? I just got back from Canada. *My adrenaline's pumping. I want to be in the valley right now, taking out the mortar crew. I know we can do it. We own this valley.*

I climb back in bed and pray for sleep. Confused, I toss and turn. Then the alarm went off. I'm back at the Hyatt in St. Louis. I have an early flight. Get up. Get ready. Why did that happen? I'm confused. *Was it the gooks I saw at Stew Leonard's coming back to haunt me? My new backpack? Or my permanently imprinted psyche?* God only knows.

I need to get to bed, but I hate to. I need to sleep. I really need to sleep.

"Death is my business, and business has been good"
Found on a Zippo lighter in the War

SEPTEMBER

03 September, Friday - Brookfield, CT. Home

Today's the end of summer hours, and summer too. It's nice to have half days on Friday. We get them Memorial Day to Labor Day. Got home about two this afternoon. The drive was tough. Lots of traffic. *I'm still strung out from my trip to Hill 51 the other night.* It's been a difficult week, transitioning back from Canada. Maybe I disengaged a bit much.

Shortly after I got home this afternoon, the girls were fighting. We have lots of pets, a dog, cat and four ferrets. It's the kid's job to take care of them, not mine or my wife's. We're having a work stoppage of sorts; the girls don't want to clean the ferret cages. Just home from the road, *the rebellion tripped my trigger.*

To me I see, *don't disobey orders, people die.* "Stop the grab ass, girls, clean the cages, right now!" I surprised them. They didn't know I was home. They scattered in the direction of the ferret cage. I walked upstairs to change, and got into it with my wife. She'd been fighting with the girls. I tried to catch myself, and apologize, *but the blackness smothered me. It hit me like a sucker punch from downtown. I never know where the blackness hides, but it chokes the life out of me when it sneaks out.*

It's sad, *but the family knows to leave me alone when I go to my bad place, it takes center stage.* Instead of going out as a family, as we planned, *I went to the garage. I worked alone, setting up my wood shop. I needed space. I needed the little bastards running around in my head to straighten up. Get back in formation, line up, and stop the crap. You never know what they're up to. Once they escape it's tough to round them back up. Like herding chickens.*

We all made amends by dinner time, and happily went out to eat. Looking forward to a better weekend. Later.

06 September, Monday - Brookfield, CT. Home

The weekend improved after my outburst on Friday. It turned in to a nice weekend. Today's Labor Day. It's also my brother Randy's 39th birthday. It was on this date, in 1967, that I earned my second Purple Heart. That was twenty-six years ago today. I hold this day as a second, or in my case, third or fourth, birthday. Maybe I should remember it as my, 're-birthday'.

I always reverence this day. Its one of those days; that should have been my last. There were several times I should have met my Maker, but this one stands out. I always take a little time alone on this date, just to sit and think. It's a special day to me.

I call my brother to wish him happy birthday, then go off to contemplate my second chance. One of many. *"Hear that? Hood whispered. I did. It was someone chopping wood. It was mid-afternoon, our patrol was skirting what we called the 'Booby Trap Ville'. The place was supposed to be deserted. It was thick jungle from one end to the other, laced with well worn trails, making a labyrinth inside.*

The five of us had been working the valley for four days. As we headed back to Hill 51, we heard the chopping. Red and Hood were crack troops, our other two snipers, were green. They just arrived from stateside. I was short two snipers; both wounded in action, or the two new guys wouldn't have been with me.

The Booby Trap Ville was a deadly place. When the grunts swept this old village it was the 4th of July, explosions everywhere. A nasty place. One thing we knew, the woodchopper didn't belong there, especially in the middle of the afternoon. "There it is again", Red motioned in the direction of the noise. We carefully, and quietly crept along the outside trail, silently moving towards the noise. It was too tempting to let be. They were in our valley.

The old village was about a hundred yards long, and fifty yards across. Once a thriving village, the people were relocated long ago. It now sat in our Free Fire Zone. It was our territory. We reached the middle trail that led inside the village. The chopping continued. It could be a trick. They could be trying to lure us inside, but I didn't think so. I huddled with Red and

Hood. We decided to leave the two new snipers at the trail junction. I told them if they heard a single shot or two, no worries. If they heard a firefight or an explosion, call Hill 51 for back up and come inside to help.

The three of us dropped our heavy gear, loaded up on M-14 ammo and grenades, repainted our faces and started inside. Red walked point, with me in the middle and Hood on tail. We moved slow, one silent step at time, stopping to listen after each one. The chopping continued; the pace even picked up a bit. It was hot, getting hotter and more humid the deeper we penetrated the palms and undergrowth.

We reached a familiar trail junction. I motioned Red to head to the left. The jungle growth on either side of us stood about five feet tall. There was no direct sunlight penetrating the heavy canopy thirty feet above our heads. The chopping sound grew louder with each step. We were creeping deeper into the suffocating humidity that was smothering us.

Another twenty yards we reached a second trail junction. Red looked for direction. I put my hand to my ear, knelt, cupping it from behind, to magnify the sound. As I did, my gut told me to get out, now! The jungle fell silent. I could smell a gook. He was close. Adrenaline filled my body. I motioned Red to take another left. I knew it looped around and would lead us back, outside the village.

Red took a step, as I turned to tell Hood what we were doing. When I did, I saw a short, tough looking gook, pop up in the jungle grass, about fifteen feet away. I let loose with a blast from my M-14, as he tossed a grenade. It exploded between Red and me. Hood emptied a magazine into the jungle. I yelled, "Red! Go!

The three of us ran down the trail. As he ran, Red yelled over his shoulder, "I'm hit!" About twenty yards down the trail, we stopped. Hood covered our rear, as I checked Red. He took shrapnel in his right shoulder. My knee hurt, but I didn't know why. There wasn't time to worry about it. Bullets whizzed overhead as I told Red where to go. The fire picked up, so we returned fire. We could see three gooks firing from the area behind us. Hood stood up and let loose with a blast that took down two of the three. Is there more? When the two went down, I told Red to move it out. As we ran down the trail we heard American voices; they were yelling for us.

Following Red, I could see his jungle jacket, soaked in blood, running down his back. I could hear the grunts outside the village, calling for us. They couldn't return fire to support us, we were between them and the guys chasing us. I decided to go straight to them. I grabbed Red, told him where to go, as we did; bullets again cracked overhead. I could tell it was one rifle firing, so we kept going. We cut through the thick jungle and ran into a bamboo thicket; it was a wall of bamboo, but it was small stalks. We could barely see through it.

Red was slowing down from shoulder his wounds, blood covered the back of his jungle jacket. I told him to step back. I took the lead. No time to waste. I put my head down, rifle at port arms and plowed through a thicket. Felt like I was mowing down corn stalks in Dirty Dorothy's corn field back home. I knew the grunts were on the other side. When I busted free, I fell forward onto the ground. I got up and saw a grunt squad lined up about ten meters away. They motioned for us to get to them.

A ditch and the perimeter trail stood between us and them. I took off to cross the trail and on my first step I heard a 'ping'. Not good. Life slowed to a crawl; I was in slow motion, running for my life. I looked down it was an American grenade that had fallen from a C-rat can. It landed on my right foot, and rolled into the ditch. I'd tripped a damned booby trap. I yelled, grenade as I jumped forward, covering my head with my hands, like that mattered. Red ran to right behind me, and Hood left, both sprawling on the ground.

The silence was deafening. I lay there, hands over my head, when I heard a grunt say, "You're cool man. It was a dud". A dud? I stood up, looked around, and knew, I was one lucky dude. I walked back to the trench, and there it was. An American grenade, pin pulled, spoon gone. The ping I'd heard was the spoon flying off the grenade. My luck continued.

Our two new snipers had done good. They'd connected with a nearby grunt patrol with a Corpsman. He called a Medivac for Red. Turns out I had a six inch, by half inch, twisted sliver of metal sticking out of my right knee. I'd be on the chopper too. As we waited for the Medivac, I see Hood, standing nearby, naked from the waist down.

"Hood! What the hell are you doing?" I yelled. He turned; his wry smile pasted on his dirty face, and said, "Come on Kug. You two are gonna' get Purple Hearts. I gotta' have a scratch here someplace". That was Nam.

09 September, Thursday - In the air to Cleveland, OH. Northwest Airlines

Short flight tonight. Leaving Detroit, always a good thing, heading to Cleveland, the city where the river caught fire. Spent yesterday in Jackson, Michigan, working on the reengineering project. Spent the night at the Hilton at Detroit Metro Airport. Quick out and back.

10 September, Friday - Brookfield, CT. Home

It's the middle of the night. Can't believe it. Woke up from a deep sleep. Clap of loud thunder that rattled the windows. More storms. *It might be thunder but I hear a mortar drop down the tube. I was great at hearing them. Why am I hearing them now, tonight? Things have been pretty calm. I don't know, but that thunder brought me bolt upright. I mean straight up. As I did, there was a lightning flash outside. Adrenaline poured through my tired body like the flooding Mississippi. It's been twenty-five years since I heard a mortar fired, why on earth did I hear one tonight? Don't understand it, just live with it. Nothing's particularly bothering me.*

I was pissed about stopping in Cleveland for a forty-five minute meeting, but what else is new? Planes ran on time. Home at a decent time. *I guess some questions have no answers. Why I hear mortars in the middle of the night is one of them.* Tired. Need sleep. I'll try again.

11 September, Saturday - Newtown, CT. Dog shopping.

Spent the day taking Cortney dog shopping. We love having pets, but with all the stress of moving, we weren't sure we wanted another one right now. But, she's turning sixteen in a few days, and that's what she wants. We rode out in the country to a farm that had poodles. Gloria and I had them early in our marriage. Cort wasn't impressed. I think we've decided not to get one right now but not sure?

15 September, Wednesday - Brookfield, CT. Home

Big day at the Kugler house. Cortney's sixteenth birthday. Our neighbor's daughter is her first friend since we moved here. She had a surprise party for her here at our house. I was assigned to get her out of the house so the kids could come. Easy enough. She and I both enjoy the book store, so off we go. We pull into the book store, and Cort sees a pet store. I remind her we decided last weekend to wait. "But Dad …", She pleads. "Let's just go in and look". We do.

We're now the proud owners of a miniature, white, Bichon Frise. She fell in love, and I couldn't say no. She only turns sixteen once, and it's cheaper than a car. Cortney was surprised by her party; the partygoers were surprised by her new dog and my wife was left wondering what I might do next.

Cortney had a nice party. When everyone left, we found out two of the boys lifted a few cases of water from our food storage. A weird thing to steal. Could be worse. Our neighbor told us we were lucky, at the last party someone stole a stereo system. Wonderful young people these days.

Hopefully, after such a good day, sleep will come.

16 September, Thursday - Brookfield, CT. Home

Kids were off school today, so I took off work to be with them. I needed it. Had a rough night. We slept in, then had a late lunch together. Family sure beats playing golf. Don't get the attraction. The girls went off to play together downstairs. We lay, listened to the rain pounding on the skylight above our bed and fell asleep.

We woke up, after about an hour, and went downstairs with the kids. Life is good. Gloria put her tea in the microwave, always a problem for me, but today I'm determined to stay right here at home. The rain outside is so heavy *it brings monsoons in my mind*. But, we went to the living room to play some games and the demons disappeared.

It's been a great day. Hope it will be a great night.

19 September, Sunday - Newtown, CT. Church & Home

In Sunday School, the lesson was supposed to be on Church History. The Instructor works for the government and escorts foreign delegations around Washington. He went a different direction and *brought my Black Bastard out of hiding*. I came home from church early, been struggling ever since

He started out by saying, "I feel compelled to tell you about my week and issue you a challenge." He tells us that he took a visiting Chinese delegation on a tour of DC. He said they loved the historic sites, especially the Washington Monument and the Lincoln Memorial. Being a cynic before my time I'm thinking 'interesting, but not relevant', get on with the lesson.

Then he says, "I have to tell you, all the monuments in Washington are impressive, but seeing the Vietnam Memorial was overwhelming." It was his first time there. He said he and the delegation were taken aback by the shape, the symbolism and the overpowering list of names, all young men taken in the prime of their lives.

His comments were very heartfelt. He concluded by issuing us all a challenge to go. He said, "The place has a spirit all its own. It's very different from anything I've felt before." He eventually went on with his Church History lesson, *but I'm doing a headlong dive to my bad place. I knew he was right about the spirit there; it is different. It's overwhelming, as I drift back to a visit there with my wife. I feel the smog of blackness descending over me, choking out the spirit of the Lord.*

I gathered the family and went home. *I didn't tell them I was depressed, just said I wasn't feeling well. Buried me.* It's time for bed.

21 September, Tuesday - Providence, RI. Marriott Downtown

First night of two, here in Providence. Three hour drive over. I know when I'm depressed. I break out my Harry Chapin music, and trip out. Did it all the way here. Trying to fight my way back from my fall off the black cliff Sunday. Didn't see that one coming. Irrational response on a rational day.

No late night tonight. Need some sleep. Miss the family already. If I'm not with them, I'd rather be alone. *Thinking, pondering, observing and seeking my own peace. Twenty-five years ago? Seems like yesterday. I'm learning my triggers as I go. If I live long enough, I may figure this out. And yet I know, I'm doing better than most. I don't know about others, but my wife is my guiding light. I remember years ago, she told me to take the good from my Vietnam experiences, and leave the bad. My filter for the bad doesn't always work, but every single day I'm upright, is a good one. Just like Nam.*

26 September, Sunday - Brookfield, CT. Home

Our house was full tonight. Had eighteen youth from our church over for a Fireside. The Bishop asked me to teach Stephen Covey's Seven Habits program. I modified it for the kids. We did it in our living room. Gloria provided the snacks. We had a good time. The kids were engaged and responded well.

The last week's been tough. Things like tonight, help me chase the dark away. Everyone's gone now. Gloria's getting ready for bed, Cortney too, and Whitney's in bed. *The black's not smothering me but I can still feel the dark cloud hovering nearby.* Work tomorrow. Time to wrap the night up.

27 September, Monday - Somers, NY. Pepsi

In the office early today. Went to sleep last night to the beat of the monsoon rains. Been raining a long time here in Connecticut. It poured all the way in to work. It's nice here in the office before everyone arrives. I couldn't sleep. Up at 0500 and here I am. At least I'm in town all week.

Sad site on the way in this morning. Near the I-684 junction, there was a bad accident. It was very foggy. When I passed by the scene, two bodies lay in the rain, covered up on the side of the road. I remember it well. As I sit here this morning, *I'm with Crutch; we're hitchhiking a ride out of Dong Ha. Finished a Force Recon patrol, and need a ride to our platoon, sixty miles south, in Phu Bai. The Air Force and Marines both fly supply planes in and out of here. The Marine pilots wouldn't give us a ride without an approved chit from our command. Our command isn't even here. The Air Force pilots were more laid back. They were flying out of Da Nang, a hundred-twenty miles south, they fly right over Phu Bai on the way. They'd stop, drop us off and pick us up in the morning on the return. Very cool.*

An Air Force C-130 was sitting nearby, engines warming up. We found one of the pilots, he told us to hop aboard, as they were about to leave. We grabbed our packs and climbed in the back. The Crew Chief told us where to sit for takeoff.

The plane soon taxied to the end of the runway, revved those big engines as we rattled and clanged down the steel matted runway. Once in the air, we made a big sweeping turn over the South China Sea. Our ride to Phu Bai would be a short one.

I laid back to catch some Z's. Crutch punched my shoulder. "Check it out". The cargo area where we were sitting near the front, began to fill, with what looked like, fog. It was cool. The red combat lights inside made for an eerie feeling. I closed my eyes and lay back once again.

"Kug, check it out. We're in an airborne meat locker". Crutch stood up, walked in between the racks filling the inside of the planes cavity. They stretched from floor to ceiling and ran the length of the plane. The fog now filled the entire plane. Crutch motioned me to join him where he was standing. I walked over next to him. In the glow of the red lights, I struggle to see what he's grinning about.

"Get with it brother. We're on a plane load of misery. Those are dead Marines. Get it?" I looked around, the racks each contained a green body

bag. Bodies were stacked from floor to ceiling, left to right. Damn! Heavy losses.

The realization of our cargo shrouded in a white fog filling the inside of the plane, brought the war home. Fifty, probably sixty bodies, not long ago someone's Son, Father, Brother and Friend, are now dead. Their families are just finding out their world will never be the same. We sat back down, looked over at the Crew Chief, he just shrugged his shoulders.

The plane landed and taxied to a stop. With the engines still running, we hopped off. The Crew Chief yelled, "Need a ride back in the morning?" We said we did. "Be here at 0600. We'll pick you up". We walked off in search of our sniper area. As we walked, Crutch laughed, put his arm around me and said, "Isn't this a wonderful place. Let's get drunk with the SeaBees". That we did. 0600 would come too soon.

28 September, Tuesday - Brookfield, CT. Home

Weird day at the office. Amazing amount of money we're spending to 'reengineer' the company. I don't believe in this 're-engineering', but I love change work. It keeps me doing different things, and I don't get bored. If I just run a normal operation, I'm bored in a heartbeat.

I continue to struggle with life. I'm often conflicted. I came to Christ in 1976. For ten years, I read nothing but the scriptures and religious books. During that time, I rarely had a flashback. *As I immersed myself more in my business life, the flashbacks have gradually come back. Not as bad as when I first came home, but frequent. At least I don't buzz out for days on end anymore.*

Gloria was up this morning when I left. She was in the kitchen making her tea, *and the smell got me again. Demo Dean and I were interrogating an old Papasan. I threw a bagel in the toaster. Thoughts bounce around inside my head. It's like a laser light show in there.* Gloria's talking to me but I don't hear her. "Ed, I'm right here". She brings me back to Brookfield. I spread some cream cheese on my bagel, give her a kiss and leave.

In the car, on the highway, I grab the tape. It's a John Conlee morning. The first song that comes up is, *As Long As I'm Rockin' with You*. That's my Gloria. The fact that I didn't grab Harry Chapin means, I must be feeling a little better.

30 September, Thursday - Somers, NY. Pepsi

It's Noon. Just shut my door for lunch. *Need to be alone.* When I came in this morning, the VP of Purchasing stuck his head in, and told me the senior team had validated my decision to scrap the inventory project in Cranston. I didn't know they had to validate it, but glad they did. My boss stopped by to congratulate me on how I handled it. Good decision, a little late, millions down the drain.

The waste we see is amazing. Fads are a big problem. People at the top, far removed *from the grunts life, making decisions to solve problems that don't exist. Just like the friggin' M-16. McNamara and Westmoreland crammed that piece of shit down our throats. If I'm to stay sane, I'll have to use the 'monsoon method' of survival. After twenty-seven days and night of rain, you laugh or you go crazy. Rain, rain, go away and don't fuck with us another day. It's been raining for three weeks. I'm with three snipers working with the grunts. We have to stay in the mountains, the flatlands are muck, and the rice paddies are lakes, and dangerous. No way to know where the dikes are, which makes walking slow and treacherous. Life in the monsoon is misery in human form.*

The sky's dark and gray during the day, and charcoal black at night. It never stops raining. We just slogged on. It may drizzle, downpour, or rain so hard you can't see. But it never stopped. Leeches in the monsoon were as plentiful as mosquitoes in the dry season. You couldn't feel them on you. You'd see a blood trail, running red with the raindrops down your body.

We're on patrol, but we weren't fighting, just existing. Moving in and out of the jungle, searching tired villages long ago deserted. The toll on all of us was high. Many came down with immersion foot. If they were lucky, they'd be evacuated when the rain was light, and the skies lighter. If not, they dragged themselves along with the rest of us, living in our own special kind of madness.

Some were afraid of drowning. Crossing paddies was treacherous. Crossing the rivers was worse. We carried fifty, maybe sixty pound packs on our backs. We carried heavy ammo belts, and harnesses that seemed like they weighed a ton. And the poor grunts, they wore flack-jackets. Heavy, bulky and cumbersome flack jackets. If you slipped and went under with all that gear, you'd better hope another Marine was close by, or you were going down for the count.

More than a few Marines simply couldn't stand the incessant, nerve rattling, rain. With ugly gray muck up to our knees, we often scaled hills on all fours. It was the only way to get to the top. A few Marines lost it, and disappeared when a chopper finally arrived. Then there were the few, and they were few, who shot themselves in the foot, just to get out of the rain. That was one desperate way to do it.

We had four more days left to play games in the sewer of our lives. That's what it smelled like, a sewer. Insanity didn't do it justice. There was only one way to cope. You had to laugh. Dark humor. It was a Brotherhood built of adversity. Laugh. We had to laugh. We'd turn the whole experience into one good time. We laughed, pouring water from the barrel of our rifles. We laughed when a buddy disappeared in the deep water before you. And we laughed when we pulled him out. It was all insane. Especially when you're a sniper and your scope is fogged blind, and you know you're living out here never to shoot your rifle at a target you can't see. Laugh. Laugh or you'll cry, or worse. Just laugh.

> "A sucking chest wound is nature's way of telling you that you've been ambushed"
>
> *Found on n a Zippo lighter from the War*

OCTOBER

01 October, Friday - Brookfield, CT. Home

Can't think about work right now, even though I should. *It's crazy. The events unfolding in Somalia are royally pissing me off. I see red, and that's not good.* That dumb ass in the White House is clueless. Putting troops in places like that and then tying one hand behind their backs. Our country's screwed when we elect people like this guy. Unbelievable!

03 October, Monday - Orlando, FL. Marriott Hotel

Can't believe it? America is swirling in the toilet bowl of history. Just saw the news, reporting on the string of 'random' murders here in Orlando. Something new, 'drive-by' tourist shootings. That's a new one. Never heard of that before. Ten shootings so far this year. *What crap. That would be a pisser. Make it through Nam, and then have some crack head blow you away for kicks. They better not miss.*

Here today meeting on what else, reengineering. Can't seem to shake that disease. Now they want me to lead another project. In Orlando today, out tomorrow. We travel whether we need to or not. I am grateful for my job. I know it's a good job. I just struggle with the waste, the nonsense and the money wasted that could be put to good use. *I want a no-nonsense environment. I want order, not grab ass. I still miss the Marine Corps.* And oh yea, I want sleep.

04 October, Tuesday - Washington, DC. National Airport

Flew out of Orlando this morning. Been reading magazines all the way here. Not good for me to read Time and Newsweek in one sitting. Here at National Airport waiting my connection to White Plains Nairobi. Going home. Need to be home with my wife and family. That's my peace.

Read Slick Willy's latest assault on morality. One of his new appointments is changing some of our child porn laws. He'll also let some pervert in Harrisburg, Pennsylvania out of jail. He's been in for receiving naked pictures of small kids. *The guy should be shot and save us all a lot of money.* And our President pardons him.

Read a worse story. It was on the organization in NYC called NAMBLA, I think it stands for something like the National Man Boy Love Association. Can you believe that's even possible. Incredible. *Makes me want move to Canada or somewhere, or worse, start shooting some of these people.* The guys leading this perversion are NYC school teachers, and they don't think they should be fired. *Why should this even be a question in America? You're fired. Leave or be shot. Millions of people died for our freedoms, and we have to put up with these perversions on our kids. No way.*

I'm appalled we have a President who's a draft dodger, liar, empty suit and pretender. And this Somalia charade, keeps my adrenaline levels off the chart. Waiting for my plane to be called right now, watching the TV monitor. CNN's reporting live from Somalia. The number of dead Rangers is growing by the minute. *It's all bullshit. It's an absolute shit hole of a country, yet the Media's bitching about collateral damage.*

They're calling my plane. As I leave they're talking about Ranger bodies being dragged through the streets by these neanderthals, parading around like they just had a big victory. Ignorance abounds in this administration. Worse ignorance than is being displayed in the streets of Mogadishu. Gotta go.

***

Airborne now. *People around me talking about Somalia. Get the hell out now, that's my opinion.* At least when Bush went to Kuwait he had a plan, an objective. He got international support, in the form of money, and he lets the military do their thing. Swartzkopf and Powell applied lessons learned in Nam. What happened? We had it done in five days. Beat the *vaunted Iraqi Army in five friggin' days. We were in battles in Nam that lasted longer than five days. Now Slick Willy has us in this dirt bag country with no objective, unimaginable restrictions and no clear objective.*

I'm livid. That poor excuse for a human being, Les Aspin, Secretary of Defense, is arrogantly calling the shots over there. Like he would have a clue as to what to do in combat. I read a story that he requires anyone who wants to see him, to have an interview with one of his lackeys to decide if you are worthy of Aspin's time. Somebody needs to bitch slap some sense into him. And get this, if you pass the pre-interviews you have to take a number. And this pompous ass denied, as in refused, the field Commander's request for tanks and armor in Somalia. He seriously needs his ass kicked. Apparently he didn't want to damage any of that classy Somali architecture. Wood buildings held up by nothing more than dirt blown into the crevices by incessant desert winds.

My head's killing me, I want to sleep.

07 October, Friday - Brookfield, CT. Home

Still outraged over Somalia. Our brave young men wasted, for nothing. First time in my life, I called the White House today. As if they give a shit what we think. Just saw footage of one of our Blackhawk pilots, shot down and captured. The guy is giving an interview with some bongo bozo who acts like he's king. What the hell has happened to our military? An interview? On TV?

Can't sleep. Fired up. I wanna' go help. Pisses me off I'm getting too old to do it all over again. More headaches. Gloria's mad at me. Says I'm losing it. My boss asked me today what was bothering me. I told him. He said good luck with that. Felt like hitting him. I need to lie down.

08 October, Saturday - Somers, NY. Pepsi

Feel the full weight of the world on me this morning. I must have slept at some point; I don't know. *I spent the night in Somalia. I wish I was there with those young guys. Always wanted to go and do it all again.* Woke up early, came in here at 0500. Always something to do. Gloria's still upset. Told me to get a grip. She's tired.

I can't focus. It's hard to believe what's happening over there. Coming to work Imus said, "How are we getting our butts kicked by a bunch of thugs in grass skirts with rocket launchers?" Good question. The lessons of Nam don't apply to the Draft Dodger and his merry men. I called the White House yesterday when Imus gave out the number. *I hate how I feel.*

I teach people every day how to work in their circle of influence. I know how to do it. It's the right thing to do. But with all that shit going on, I just go off. Gloria reminded me last night; *it's been twenty-five years since Nam, and I still have the red rage. At least it's not every day anymore. I'm seething over that shit in Somalia. For what?* The poor excuses we have for leadership in DC are embarrassing our great nation?

Heard an interview with Colonel David Hackworth, America's most decorated, living soldier. I read his book, "*About Face*"; it's outstanding. I love the guy. He's now a correspondent for New York *Newsday.* He said it best. "You can't sit on your fat ass in the White House and second guess your field Commanders". Of course the incomparable Les Aspin's now saying if he had the decision to make again, he'd provide armor. No shit Sherlock. Drop troops in the middle of Mogadishu, think a column of reinforcements will get through on the ground without armor, I can't think of a better word for him but asshole.

My mind's filled with the M-16 debacles years ago, rules of engagement, zipping bodies in bags, Perl and Greek. My soul aches. I need to go home, make amends with the wife and settle down. It's a war I can't win, just like the last one. Fucking politicians.

10 October, Sunday - Brookfield, CT. Home

Came home from work yesterday after lunch. I don't usually work on Saturday, but lots going on. Spent the rest of the day with Gloria and the girls. I thought about how I'been on the drive home. *I've been out of it.* I needed to apologize and restart. At least at this point in our lives, the family can call me out. They let me know when I've retreated to my bad place. *I needed to get a grip.*

Slept better last night. Vowed to give up TV for awhile. No news. *I feel mentally wounded right now. Violated by this President and his administration. That makes twice for my government, Nam and now.* But I have a family that loves me. I'm blessed to know God lives, and Jesus is the Christ. Church today helped my healing.

Gloria got the unwanted call today. Her Mom's not doing well. She'll probably have to head back out to Ohio soon. Doesn't sound good. Not a good time, but then there never is a good time. It is what it is, deal with it.

11 October, Monday - Brookfield, CT. Home

Off work today. Some holiday or other. Gloria and I are back on track, thanks to her. She's the stabilizing force in my life. I know her, and I know we were meant to be. When I came home from Nam, I had no intention or interest in getting married. Wanted to party the summer away, then head to Europe in search of mercenary work in the Congo. When I met Gloria shortly after Nam, I wasn't sure what I was feeling, I'd never felt that way before. The voices in my head were even silent. I knew if I was going to have a chance at even a half-way normal life, I had to marry her. She thought I was crazy. I was.

Today we had a great day together. I hit the road on another corporate patrol tomorrow. Gloria's leaving for Ohio on a flight before mine. She needs to be with her Mom again. We'll ride to the airport together; that's a first. I'm heading to Indianapolis. Speaking at a meeting of the American Society of Quality Control, or ASQC. Corporate America has more acronyms than the military. Indianapolis is also home to Demo Dean and Tomo. I asked the meeting sponsors if I could have one of them attend the meeting with me. They were more than happy to accommodate.

I called Demo Dean and he's on board. I can't see them at the same time. Tomo hates Dean. We worked together for months in Nam, but Tomo is Tomo. In his mind, Dean grew up on the rich side of town, and that don't fly with him. I'm seeing Tomo for breakfast on Wednesday morning. Haven't seen either of them since the early 70's when they came to visit me in Ohio, separately of course. *We're brothers; it doesn't matter.* I better go. Early morning.

12 October, Tuesday - Pittsburg, PA. Greater Pittsburg Airport

Waiting for my connection to Indianapolis. Gloria got off to Ohio okay. We have a lady from church staying with the kids while we're gone. Looking forward to seeing my two Rogues, even if it's *at different times. They're oil and water, and the oil's on fire.* Can't help but think of old times. *"Kug! Don't let him toss that grenade!" Tomo didn't trust Demo Dean to go fishing with a hand grenade. Raid and Red had each dropped one in the river already. Now Dean wanted to do it. We were paddling the muddy river in the Co Bi Than Tan valley, picking up stunned fish from the last two grenades. Red wanted fish for dinner.*

"Come on Kug. I'll be careful". Demo Dean was our fifth teammate. A member of Mensa, he was smart. I had to ask him what Mensa was; I wasn't that bright. He was smarter than an MIT Professor, but when it came to common sense, there was a void the size of Alaska. He taught himself Vietnamese after just a few months in country. I used him as my interpreter, not my point man. We were never sure Dean knew the depth of our situation. The team once played a trick on him. They removed the primer from one of our hand grenades, put it back together and pretended to drop it next to him. The spoon flew across the tent. Dean just sat there looking around, as everyone else, who knew about the 'joke' ran screaming from the tent. Some things he just 'didn't get'.

On this hot afternoon, we'd been on patrol for a few days, paddling our fourteen foot aluminum swamp boat around the river and the flooded valley, looking for targets of opportunity. It was my second monsoon; I knew that the valley would flood. I requisitioned a rubber boat; the kind Force Recon used. It was denied. The Marine Corps bureaucracy said, only Recon could have rubber boats. Our Colonel loved us, so he ordered the engineers to provide us with this flat bottom boat.

Dean kept begging, and Tomo kept threatening. Our boat held five. Tomo and I were in the back, Red and Raid, in front of us, we all had paddles. Dean was in the bow. His job was to motion right and left so Tomo, and I could make us move when we needed to turn. For night operations, we put fluorescent tape on the back of his hands so we could see what direction he was motioning. The boat was our only way of transportation in the monsoon, the only way we could get from hill to hill, because of the flooding.

Red wanted more fish; he was egging me on to let Dean toss a grenade. "What's wrong with you? That dumb ass will drop it". Tomo was furious, but then, he was always furious. Demo Dean, we called him Demo Dean because he loved to blow things up. We were all trained in land mine warfare and demolitions. We were all trained to set and disarm booby traps, but Dean loved doing it. The rest of us did it as a matter of course, he lived for it.

"Okay, toss one grenade, out there", I said pointing off the front of our boat. When you tossed a grenade into the water it would blow up with a muffled explosion, followed by a big water bubble, then stunned fish would float to the top. Simple and fun. Easy enough. Tomo sat next to me, looking like he sat on a mound of fire ants. He was pissed.

Dean, who looked like a young Tommy Smothers, stood, grinning, grenade in his right hand, pin in the other, as he looked at me for approval. I nodded. He turned to toss it, and when he did, he dropped it. The bow of our little boat was tied together with a triangular plate of aluminum on top of the bow. The grenade fell with a thud onto the plate and into the water next to our boat.

Tomo and I watched in horror, as we frantically paddled backwards, desperately trying to get us away from the blast that was coming. We didn't get far when a muffled boom went off below, and slightly in front of our boat. The boat rocked backwards from the blast. The bottom of our boat showed dimples pop up, from the shrapnel hitting it. No one was injured. Miraculously we had no holes in the boat.

Dean was still standing, looking about the same as he did before the blast, and Tomo yelled, "Duck!" He swung his paddle in a circular motion, left to right, hitting Dean in the ass, knocking him head first into the muddy waters. "Asshole!" Tomo was irate. "Guess I should have listened to you?" I said laughing.

We paddled the boat to shore. Red and Raid were hiding and camouflaging our boat. We needed to get ready for trouble. Dean slogged out of the water, smiling, as he did. "If I see you in civilian life, you're dead," Tomo growled, with his finger in Dean's face. "What's he so upset about?" Dean had been in Nam nearly two years, six months longer than me at the time. He was a trip.

I came back to the world when the voice over the PA system called my flight. It was about to board, time to button things up. I'm excited to see these guys. Tomo told me yesterday, that if he saw Dean, he'd make good on his promise. Love these guys.

12 October, Tuesday - Indianapolis, IN. Holiday Inn East

What an evening. I'm tired. It's nearly 0100, and 0200 in body time. But what a night. Speaking engagement went well. About three hundred people in attendance. Speaking is something I'm beginning to enjoy. The entertainment tonight was meeting Demo Dean again. As educated as he is, he sure does some stupid things.

As the dinner meeting was about to start, there was no Dean. I was wondering if he was going to show up? About five minutes before I was to speak, I see Tommy Smothers, weaving through the tables from the back of the room. He's got on a plaid shirt and Levi's. I told him a suit and tie. He looks exactly like he did twenty-five years ago. I don't. Apparently that shocked him.

"What the hell happened to you?" he yelled, walking between the last two tables he stopped, bent down, as he looked me up and down. "Really, what the hell happened to you?" We were at the head table; I had, fortunately, prepared them for anything that might come from Dean.

I got Dean settled down. It was time for me to speak. He made himself right at home, smiling like he did in the boat years ago. He hadn't changed at all. He was oblivious. I hadn't seen Dean since he and his wife came to Ohio for a visit in the early seventies. They divorced after two years. I found out why after the meeting, back at my room.

Back in the day, Dean would talk incessantly about the coming revolution in the United States. He told us about powerful people in Europe and the United States, old money, who controlled all the shots. We'd humor him and keep on going. He's still talking revolution today. Sleeps with a loaded 45 under his pillow. Said it upset the wife. I can imagine. Said he used to have dreams. Opening his mouth to show me his teeth he said, "I dreamed a gook kicked me in the teeth. I snapped off my two front teeth in the process". Sure enough, they were half the size they should be. Said his wife couldn't take it and left.

I updated him on the comings and goings of the Rogues since we returned stateside. I'd called him about Greeks passing. He'd visited him in New York before, and knew his family well. He now has two Masters Degrees, he's still a member of Mensa, and the one above that, whatever that is? He works driving a pizza delivery truck and lives with his Mother. I asked him the obvious, why are you driving truck with two Masters Degrees? He laughed. "The revolution is coming Kug. I want to be in shape."

As crazy as he is, I still love the guy. The brotherhood surpasses the nonsense. I reminded him of his night in the valley, all alone. That's about the only thing that takes the smile off his face. *We were on patrol, on a very, very dark night. Dean walked tail-end Charlie. We'd stopped to check our bearings, and walked off while Dean was doing whatever Dean does. We'd left him standing there. We quickly realized he wasn't back there, and held tight on the trail. He never caught up. The next morning we found him. It's the only time I saw him upset. And he still can't laugh about it.*

I'm tired. I got Tomo at 0700 in the restaurant here. Later.

13 October, Wednesday - Indianapolis, IN. Holiday Inn East

Started the day with Tomo. Loved every minute of it. Wish I had more time. Then spent the day with the folks at the local bottling plant. I hired the Plant Manager there a few years back when I worked for Frito. Great young guy. Doing well with Pepsi. Frito didn't want me to hire him; I hired him anyway; he was good. Their reason? He was from the University of Pittsburg. They wanted people with logistics degrees only. And they wanted them from the University of Tennessee, Ohio State or Indiana University. What a crock. Tim is outstanding.

My breakfast with Tomo did my heart good. We laughed about the time he came over with Suzie, his wife, to visit us in Ohio. Danny, their son, was five at the time. Trevor was two. Danny's hair had a Buddhist look, or maybe it was a Moonie look. Little circle of hair in the center, front of his head. The rest of his head was shaved, just like his Dads. I said, "Tomo, that's cruel". He grunted, "It'll make him tough". He called Danny over, and told him he's tough. Danny would tighten up his little stomach, and Tomo would give him a little punch. He'd fall on his butt laughing, get up and go play. Tomo's my man. I'd go through hell for him.

He wanted to stay connected to the military, so he joined the Indiana National Guard. His first summer camp was his last. When they were preparing for camp, his Captain challenged him to a contest. The fact Tomo was a Marine bugged the Captain. Wrong thing to do with him. He told Tomo he would be on the 'opposing' force for the exercise. His challenge was 'you will never be able to capture me'. Poor guy.

They arrived at the training area, got their marching orders and prepared for the 'exercise' which started the next day. Being a creative fellow, Tomo considered the 'next day' to be 1201 midnight. He snuck into the Captains tent, bound and gagged him, then carried him out and hid him in the woods. He kept him there for the entire three day exercise. Tomo said, "I captured his ass." He was asked to leave the Guard, for 'acts unbecoming an Indiana National Guardsman'. Now that's funny.

We compared notes on our experiences in corporate America. Both of us are successful, but we know it comes at a price. We both hate working for others, especially those we don't respect. We both need order, can't stand bullshit and would rather be alone. It's interesting how similar we are.

When we parted company, we were talking about the phenomenon of the brotherhood of war. Tomo said it must be that, "male bonding thing, or some other shit'?. I laughed, as he reached out his hand. I ignored it and gave him a hug. I felt him tense up as I did. As he's pulling away, he said, "Kug! Don't take this male bonding shit too far!.'

It's been a great trip. Too late to call Gloria so not sure what's happening in Ohio right now. Time for bed. Early flight in the morning. I lay down to sleep but *my mind raced from seeing my brothers. It's Friday night. It's September 1969. Gloria and I are in Indianapolis for Tomo's wedding tomorrow. We drove in from Akron today. I'm his best man, according to him, his only friend. We had a brief walk thru tonight. Then the four of us went out to dinner. Before dinner, I went with Tomo to grab something at the Drug Store.*

Sue, his wife to be, asked him to go buy her some Midol. Tomo motioned for me to come with him. He's 5' 7" tall, 210 pounds of muscle and mean. He shaves his head, has a fu manchu, wore knee high moccasins with fringe around the top and a muscle shirt. If he was black, he could double for Mr. T, from the A-Team. He was quite a sight.

Outside, we climbed into his little Triumph two-seater convertible. He had the top down. We must have looked like two clowns, hanging out of our clown car. After a short ride, we pulled up next to an old wooden building, looked like the original drug store in the neighborhood. Tomo jumped out of the car like he meant business. I had to hustle to keep up. The counter was right inside the door. A smiling teenager greeted us.

"Give me some Midol", Tomo growled at the kid. The young clerk grinned, cocked his head to one side, and all I could think was 'don't do it man'. "What's a matter? Is it that time of the month?" Before I could step in, Tomo reached across the counter, grabbed the kid by the shirt with both hands, pulling him close and off the ground as he screamed, "I told you, I want some fucking Midol!"

He got the Midol, from the shaking kid. Tomo slammed down his money and stormed out the door. "He's a little irritable tonight", I said, walking quickly out behind Tomo. Back in the Triumph I said, "Tomo, man, crank it back a notch". There was a long pause as we drove. "Kug, I'm having some trouble settling down since Nam". I nodded my understanding and agreement to that understatement. "And, you know I hate punks", he said bellowing his patented evil laugh, as he threw his head back and raced down the street.

16 October, Saturday - Brookfield, CT. Home

Got in late last night. Gathered the girls at the babysitter this morning. Gloria's still in Ohio with her Mom. She's flying in tomorrow night, an hour before I'm leaving. I'm heading out for another week on the road. Tough times with the family apart. The girls and I had fun today. They're in bed; I'm about to settle in for the night. Hopefully, I can sleep. It's been pretty good, even after seeing the guys in Indianapolis this week. Love those guys. Later.

17 October, Sunday - Philadelphia, PA. Marriott Airport

Home one night, gone the next. Gloria and I met at the Nairobi Airport, went off site to Burger King, then back to the airport. She drove and dropped me off. I'll be away all week. It's bad when Flight Attendants recognize you, and you recognize them. The flight crew that's flying today recognized me. Amazing.

At church today. I got asked to present another Fireside for the youth. One of the other Marines in the Ward is a youth counselor, he asked me. That's cool. Present a workshop tomorrow, then a late flight to LA. Cross country and back this week.

18 October, Monday - In the air to Los Angeles, American Airlines

I'm tired, and the week just started. Slept well last night. Looking forward to getting home for the weekend. Heading to LAX as I write. Meeting tomorrow with Taco Bell. In PepsiCo, Taco Bell is said to be the company that knows how to successfully reengineer. When I'm handed something new, I start by talking to people who've already done it. That's how I learn. We'll see what they have to pass on. *I love turning operations around, and then move on. Reminds me of life in Nam. Gives me an adrenaline rush. Get bored doing the same thing. Need the work hard and play hard culture.* Right now I need to sleep. Later.

19 October, Tuesday - Los Angeles, CA. Marriott Airport Hotel

Very tired tonight. Time zone's got to me. Great meeting today with Taco Bell. It was a pretty good drive to their headquarters. Should have flown into John Wayne Airport, instead of LAX. Oh well. Sharp people at Taco Bell, who've, as we used to say, 'been there and done that'. Learned a ton. Whether Pepsi will listen to their advice is another matter.

It's worth documenting a couple things. First, they discovered when they bring field people to headquarters to work on a project; they become like the people in headquarters, out of touch. They decided to run their projects in the field. The headquarters people involved in the project have to live in the field. It worked. Love the idea. *Reminds me of my time in Nam. People in headquarters generally had no clue what went on in the field. Always pissed me off when they tried to tell us what to do.* Same in corporate Pepsi.

The other thing I found interesting was their approach to timelines. They were quite committed to the principle. They take their best and brightest, have them calculate the time line, apply contingencies to it, and then double it. They found in reality; that's how long it will take. I have found that to be very true.

But today we have higher ups who think challenging people to impossible goals and ridiculous timelines is leadership. *It's not leadership; it's bullshit. Saw that in Nam too. Zipped thirty-five people in body bags because of that asshole McNamara's timelines on the M-16 implementation. We should have zipped his pompous ass in a body bag alive.*

Enough of that tonight. Been doing good. Not up to any old firefights of the mind tonight. Not even hump day yet. Heading north to San Francisco in the morning.

20 October, Wednesday - In the air to Indianapolis, IN. US Scare

Easy day thank goodness. Flight went well. Meetings went well. It was a good day until I had to fly US Air. At the gate, they told me the plane was full. I decided to upgrade to First Class, so I could get on, and sleep. I have the miles, so it's not a cost issue. The gate works with me; I'm finally on the plane. No problem.

I board the plane, take my seat when I notice hardly anyone is boarding. I ask the Flight Attendant what's up, thinking we're delayed. Not a good week for delays. She tells me we'll be leaving shortly. I turn, stood up and looked, there were about ten people on the plane. I wasted an upgrade. The Flight Attendant told me she couldn't help. I hate incompetence, and this airline could be appropriately named, 'Air Incompetence'.

I get up, walk off the plane to the check-in agent, I tell her I want a seat in Coach, and my miles refunded from the upgrade. She tells me that the plane is about to leave. I tell her that's interesting, but not relevant. She's irritated. What else is new? She quickly keypunches something into the computer. Then tells me it's handled, and hands back my folder. When I get back to the plane, I don't have a seat assignment.

The Flight Attendant tells me she can't help me. I go back out and get a seat assignment. I get 19D. I re-board the plane. There isn't one person within ten feet of 19D, but somebody is in 19D. I take another seat, far away from everyone, only to have the Flight Attendant ask for my Boarding Pass. She tells me I'm in the wrong seat. She makes the dude in 19D move, and I end up with a whole row to myself.

I got that nonsense off my chest. It's better than hurting someone. *My red rage was simmering.* Meetings tomorrow morning. Then on to Detroit for afternoon meetings, St. Louis tomorrow night. Crazy schedule. I'm exhausted. I need sleep. Later.

21 October, Thursday - St. Louis, MO. Stouffer's Hotel

My last night on the road. *Another corporate patrol nearly down. Not near as much fun as Nam.* Left the meeting in Detroit early. The bureaucracy got to me. When I arrived at Detroit Metro, I find out US Air has canceled my flight. Blamed it on computer problem's. Sorry, they said. Sorry, my ass.

Got one of those US Air 'union stewards' again. Detroit style. Told me there was a 'plane' leaving but no way I could get on it. It's full. *A combination of being exhausted and my inability to handle pricks well, I told him to standby. I fought to hold the demons at bay. I went over to the pay phone and called the President's office of US Air. I got a nice Administrative Assistant named Ivy. Said she worked for the President. Took about five minutes, and I was on the flight.* I now had another name of a US Air union steward, screwing with customers, that I could pass along. I have no idea how they stay in business.

I'm struck by the way bureaucracies perform. It's sad, on the one hand, and amazing that people put up with it on the other. *In Nam that bullshit killed people. Stateside, it just kills hopes, dreams and careers.* What do you mean we aren't authorized to have camouflage *uniforms. We're snipers. We're not authorized face paint and bush hats. Here's the deal, you're not authorized. Life in the Corps. We bought stuff on R & R and traded the friendly gooks for tiger stripe uniforms and bush hats. My Mother sent us archery face paint, and we burned wood and carried burnt shavings in plastic bags to rub on our faces. Solve the problem, quit bitching.*

What do you mean you don't have jungle boots? We live in the jungle. We're out. How can you be out? We're just out? We wore the same tired, torn and worn jungle boots for six more months. Make do. But the bottoms are worn flat. Make do. You have no socks? Mom comes through again. She supplies our team with socks for six months. Bureaucracies are the worst. And petty pricks operating in them without thinking trip my wires.

Workshop in the morning, then home, finally. Too tired for a Nam night, I need to sleep Dear Lord.

22 October, Friday - In the air to Washington National, US Scare

One more Corporate Patrol down. Heading home. I need my family. I realize more and more; those of us working in corporate America are Olympic class hamster's running wild on the treadmills of life. Chasing something, we're not sure what? Our leaders are chasing the latest buzzword, one that will get them promoted the quickest. They're doing anything to drive up short term profits in search of next quarters bonus. Happening all through our society. We're living in a time of the quick fix and little if any accountability.

At lunch today, I sat next to a fellow who's been in the bottling business since 1950. He works for one of our franchises. In his forty plus years, he's done almost every job in the business. I asked him how the business has changed over the years. He had some interesting thoughts we should listen to.

He said, "The technology of manufacturing has improved. Highways have improved. Trucks have improved. But the business itself hasn't changed at all. It's a simple business. The route salesman still has to go door-to-door. Plants still have to make it. Warehouses still have to ship it. And drivers still have to deliver it." He's so right. Our motto should be 'we make the complicated simple'.

He shared with me that their franchise operations, as do ninety percent of franchise operations, makes more profit per case than corporate operations do. I asked him what the biggest challenges of franchise bottlers were. He said, "Like all businesses, getting good people. The next biggest problem is not participating in the latest corporate programs". We got a good laugh, but I know from experience, it's true.

I know in my heart unless drastic changes come to America, it's heading down a slippery slope. It's becoming an America unrecognizable to most. Today, everyone has an excuse for their nonperformance. Everywhere I look, people have an excuse for being fat, for why they steal, why they kill and why they can't keep a job. I'm fat because I eat too much of the wrong foods and never exercise. Be accountable for goodness sakes. It's a question of accountability, not what's your excuse.

In the Marine Corps, I was held accountable. My Drill Instructor made it clear, every minute of every day, that I was personally accountable for my performance. In Vietnam, our leaders, Gunny Dubai and Staff Sergeant Rider, held us accountable. It was clear. At Frito Lay, I was held accountable. My boss made that clear. It's not quite that way at Pepsi. I can feel the changes in our country. It started in Vietnam. Mr. McNamara was not accountable for the thousands of deaths his decisions caused in Vietnam. Mr. Johnson was not either. The Perfumed Prince General Westmoreland was not accountable. The pukes who went to Canada rather than serve their country were not accountable. I see much less accountability in corporations today than just a few years ago. As for our country, we're now led by a President who has never been accountable for his actions. Ever.

Traveling is taking a toll. Been traveling for the past ten years. Missing so much of my kid's lives. I have a great job, but I'm not

happy. I can't stand the lack of leadership, the bureaucracy or the bullshit. I'm tired. Really tired. When you live on the road, and have a blitz week as I've had, and return home, your life lens is distorted, just like returning from patrols back in Nam. I dozed off.
"*It's crazy as hell, but we'll do it*". *Tomo proposed a prisoner snatch. He wanted to capture one with his bare hands. Not exactly sniper work, but it'll be a trip. I'd been in country now for eighteen straight months. Sometimes, it felt like a lifetime? It was surely an adventure. If Tomo wanted to wrestle a gook with his bare hands, then he deserves a chance.*

We spent the day working our way up the hidden river bed, about fifteen clicks from our previous location. We didn't want to be seen by anyone. We knew the gooks moved in and out of the village we targeted for the snatch. There were five of us. We hid in the river bed, a click away from the village. It was 1600 hours when we got as close as we could. We had at least three more hours to wait before we'd have the cover of darkness.

Tomo and I huddled to plan the execution of the snatch. We knew the gooks in the area traveled in groups of three to five, maybe six. If only one happened by, it would be simple. I'd let Tomo do his thing. If more came by, Tomo would tackle the last guy in the column; hold him on the ground, while the rest of our team took out the rest.

"You know, you're out of your minds", Red smiled, calling us out on our plan. Tomo grunted, "Fuck you. It'll be fun". I figured the heat was screwing with our brains, or we've been in country too long. We kicked back and tried alternating sleep sessions, but that wasn't happening. The heat was at its peak, stifling our thoughts at this point.

I sat up and took the map, working on pre-plot mortar targets. If things went bad, we'd need to abort the mission and beat feet. If we aborted and ran, I wanted us covered with some incoming of our own. When I had the coordinates and code names ready, Hoss, who carried our PRC-25 radio, communicated them to the grunt mortar crew nearby on Hill 51.

At 1900, it was time to rock and roll. Red led the way, me second, Hoss, Tomo, Butch, and Raid in the rear. It wasn't as dark as I'd like, but everyone was antsy so we moved out. We climbed up out of the river bed, crossed a dry paddy and into the jungle's edge that surrounded the village.

We skirted the village on a small trail when Tomo stepped around Hoss and grabbed my pack. He told me we'd arrived where he wanted to execute the snatch. We set Hoss off the trail and behind us. The remaining four of us sat near the trail's edge. Hoss had the radio and I needed him nearby. He slid down behind me. The five of us knelt in the jungle, about five feet off the trail, ambush style. We hid in four to five foot jungle growth, and began camouflaging one another with bushes, and rubbed our homemade charcoal on our faces, necks, arms and hands.

Total darkness descended around us. The night was clear; stars began to shine bright, it was a moonless night. Sweat streaked our black faces. To pull this off we needed to be unseen, unheard and undiscovered. I told Tomo to quit grinning, his teeth were shining in the night. He was pumped for his upcoming tussle.

An hour went by and nothing, no action, it could be a long night. My sixth sense meter began rising. It just didn't feel right. I could feel gooks nearby, and I was feeling them right now. I leaned over to Tomo and whispered, "What do ya' think?" He shrugged, urging me to be patient. It wasn't about patience. Nervous, I carefully slid back near Hoss. I glanced over my shoulder past Hoss, and the small rise behind him, where we would normally be. The rise was silhouetted against the night sky. I checked my watch; it was 2230 hours.

Sweat poured down my forehead, adrenaline filled my veins tight. My nerves danced with anticipation. Let's get it on. We sat tight. It was 2300 hours. My pucker factor went off the charts when I heard a scraping noise. It sounded like somebody walking with corduroy pants. It was a sound that didn't belong, I instantly knew we were in trouble. I cupped my hand to my ear and heard it much clearer this time. It's movement. Movement through the bushes behind us. Its more than one walking through the scraggly branches burned in last months napalm strike. I knew gooks were behind us.

Tomo looked my way; he wasn't smiling now. I slowly turned, not wanting to make noise and Hoss pointed behind and over his shoulder. I raised my head about a foot above the grass and saw the outline of several figures, bent over, trotting along on the skyline. We were 'had lads'. It was show time. Abort!

I turned to Red, "Time to di di". He jumped to his feet, looked around and took off running across the dry paddies, away from the bad guys encircling us. We had fifty yards to the base of the bare hill that led out of here. There was no cover. We trotted in single file. About half way across the paddy, our quiet night turned ugly.

Automatic weapons fire erupted from the AK's behind us. Raid was on rear guard, returning fire. Red reached the base of the hill first, me second. Bullets ripped into the ground around us. Red and I returned fire to cover Raid and the other snipers. Hoss knelt next to me with the radio. As I took the handset to call mortars he dropped down next to me and started firing. "Give me Romeo and Juliet now! Walk them south slowly." Raid and Tomo stayed at the bottom of the hill providing cover fire while the three of us climbed as fast as we could. The pace of the incoming fire picked up, the gooks were closing in.

We cleared the top of the hill onto a forty yard plateau. We formed a line and began returning fire until Raid and Tomo joined us. "Where the hell are the mortars?" Tomo screamed. I wish I knew. I told Hoss to raise them on the radio. Before he could reach them, mortars began landing on the gooks. We ran across the plateau in a column with Raid and Tomo taking up the rear. By the time we reached the edge, to head down to the river and safety, I'd had it. I was tired of running, and seriously pissed off. Red, Hoss and I spread out, and waited on Raid and Tomo to join us. As they did, the gooks in pursuit cleared the top of the hill and were on the plateau with us. There appeared to be seven, maybe eight or nine of them. We opened fire.

Hoss was telling mortars to walk towards us. We blazed away until all the bad guys disappeared from view. Raid and Tomo stayed behind, covering us as we raced down the safe side of the hill. As we did, mortars continued to walk right where we needed them. I'd guessed right with my pre-plots. Artillery from Camp Evans began dropping illumination rounds on top of the hill. Raid saw a few gooks buy the farm as the AK's fell silent. We reached the river bed, regrouped, and made a hasty crossing. Climbing up the river bank on the other side, Tomo, laughing, said, "That was close". "That it was, Tomo, that it was". As we walked to the safety of a grunt squad nearby, I realized I'd been here a long time, maybe too long. But then again, it's been a fun ride.

27 October, Wednesday - Brookfield, CT. Home

Finally sitting down to write again. Landed in Nairobi just before midnight Friday night. Quite a whirlwind week. Tough transition home, my life lens is seriously distorted. The family functions fine without you; then you're home. Who fits where? It's great to be home, always great to be home. But a major adjustment at times. Cannot come close to imagining what it would have been like to be married in Vietnam? It woulda' been tough.

Took Monday off to be with Gloria. We slept in, went out for lunch and had fun for a change. We always have fun, but not when I'm on the road. This morning, driving into work, I was listening to Imus in the Morning. He was on the radio, live, with an ironworker on the Brooklyn Bridge. He encountered a knife wielding guy, heading to the top of the brIdge carrying a sign that read, "fed up". Aren't we all? The ironworker is cool. He said he told the guy, "Let's go have a beer and talk this thing over". What a world. I'm listening to a guy on the radio who is on top of the Brooklyn Bridge, on a cellphone, with a guy wanting to jump. Live, no less. America. What a country.

29 October, Friday - Somers, NY. Pepsi

End of the day. In my office waiting for Friday night traffic to lighten up. Tough day. Meeting on top of meeting on top of meeting. We're now actually meeting to decide on meetings. Keep sharp objects away, I might do something awful to myself. I can see the young MBA's are learning that meetings are work. Hardly.

Looking forward to getting home and having the weekend with the family. Travel is heavy this time of year. We're making a profit and meeting our numbers, so we're not burning any furniture this year. Travel's not been restricted so onward and upward. It's after 6, I'm out of here.

> **"The only thing I feel when killing a person is the recoil of my rifle"**
> *Found on a Zippo lighter from the War*

NOVEMBER

05 November, Friday - Somers, NY. Pepsi

    Been awhile since I've written. Been traveling and run down. Been in Cleveland, Dallas and Orlando. Sometimes it's all a blur. It was another monsoon morning driving in this morning. Sitting in my office. It's quiet, lots of other folks on the road today. I'm sitting here, looking out the window of our headquarters, flags waving wildly in the morning winds. The Pepsi flag's flying next to our wonderful American flag. Guess it's growing up in a small town, surrounded by World War II vets, but I love this country.

    For the first time in weeks, no meetings today. My boss is out of the office. As I look out the window, people are scurrying into the building, umbrella's of every color, protecting their heads from the downpour. Suddenly, *I'm with Perl. Leading a platoon of ARVN's, troops from the Army of the Republic of Vietnam, on patrol. None of them spoke English, Perl and I didn't speak gook. A Green Beret Advisor, a Captain, was supposed to go with us. But when we met the ARVN's at midnight, he told us he didn't go on operations less than company level. Rank does have its privileges.*

    Perl walked point, me second followed by thirty so-called, 'allied soldiers'. We didn't have to speak the language to know they didn't want to be in the bush. For starters the three man team assigned to walk point for us, refused. Played dumb and acted like the three hear no evil, say no evil and do no evil monkeys. They coughed, clattered and clanked their way through the night with Perl on point and me second. They wanted to make sure we didn't surprise anyone. The highlight of our patrol came when it started raining. Without a word, every one of them broke out raincoats. Raincoats! Not just any raincoats, raincoats in various colors like they were on a picnic. It was surreal.

    The phone rang and brought me back to the office. Need to get to work on my reengineering turnaround.

07 November, Sunday - Brookfield, CT, Home

Got a surprise at church today. The Youth have a monthly meeting on a Sunday called a 'fireside'. I've spoken a few times, always on gospel topics. Since Veteran's Day is coming up, they invited me and two other guys to share our stories. I'm sure it's good for the kids.

The Marine chopper pilot was away, flying for work. He's in Anchorage. The other guy served with the 173rd Airborne, in the Central Highlands of Vietnam. He was wounded, shared some tender feelings about America, and what it means to be an American. He shared his difficulty coming home after the war. He shared his concerns over Somalia. And he closed by sharing that he'd never again go to war without a purpose. His words come from the heart. The kids were engaged

As he's talking, I decide they don't need war stories tonight, he covered that well. I like to share what life was like over there. While it shocks them to hear what we ate, how long we went without a bath, and the millions of unique bugs, they like it. It turned out to be a fun evening. A nice surprise. Leaving for Seattle tomorrow. Time to sign off.

09 November, Tuesday - Seattle, WA. Embassy Suites Hotel

Here for a week working with a large franchise we bought. I'll be working as part of a team to bring them into the Pepsi fold. I hope our bureaucracy doesn't ruin them, like we usually do. Good people. It's nice working with them.

I'm excited for tomorrow. It's not only the Marine Corps birthday; it's one of my re-birthdays. I also made contact with one of the Rogues, who lives here. Harley always told me he'd either be in Dallas or Seattle. Twenty-six years later, I found him. It's unbelievable. We're going to Ruth's Chris Steakhouse tomorrow night. Still can't believe I'm going to be with him after all this time.

We talked for over an hour. I hung up with my adrenaline pumping. I feel like our days in Nam. When I heard his voice, I knew immediately it was him. He is one of the most unique people I've ever met. A serious biker. I need to go to bed, chances of sleep are slim. I lay down and hear him talking. *"Give me some fucking paper", Harley growled as he grabbed a piece of paper from the pad I was writing on. As he tore it off, he nearly broke my makeshift, ammo box table. "What are you so pissed about?" I fire back. "Look at this shit, Kug". He hands me a polaroid picture he'd got in the mail. I'm looking at a big green Harley sitting in a driveway. "So what?" "So what my ass! My old lady let her loser brother paint my fucking bike green. I told her no one could touch it".*

He was irate. His outbreak was drawing a crowd, now gathering in our squad tent. We were between patrols on a day off. "Give me your fucking pen". Before I could hand it to him, he ripped it out of my hand. He leaned down on my rickety table, placed his left hand with the middle finger out, in the 'flipping the bird' position, and drew an outline around it. Inside the hand, he wrote, 'Best wishes Bitch!'

"That's a little harsh, Harley", one of our snipers observed. "Harsh my ass. I just married her three months before coming over here. Screw it. We're done. I told her, no one, and I mean no one, touches my bike while I'm gone". I quickly handed him an envelope before he took one. He addressed it and stormed out of our tent heading to the mail drop.

I got up, walked around the room. Got a drink of water, and laid back down. Morning would be here soon.

10 November, Wednesday - Seattle, WA. Embassy Suites Hotel

It's 0400. I'm awake again. I don't know if I slept or not. *My adrenaline rush won't let up. Minds jumbled; I've been tossing all night.* Breakfast's at 0700. Today's November the 10th. I lay down one more time. *"Perl! Look". Gooks moving in the bush. 400 meters. Perfect. We were on a two-man sniper patrol, ten clicks south of Camp Evans. We hid on a small hill; a river lay between us, and the NVA soldiers. We saw* four, then three more. They had no idea we were about to strike. It's perfect; our dream come true. They were moving right to left through tall grass and spotty jungle underbrush.

We carefully moved to a sitting position, shoot on three. One, two, three, Boom! We fired in unison dropping, two. We ejected shells from our bolt action Winchester Model 70's, fired again dropping one, as they disappeared into the green hillside we began receiving return fire that hit all around us.

"Let's get the hell outta' here!" I yelled above the bursts of AK fire coming our way. "I'll cover you, go!" Perl yelled, as he began firing as fast as you can with a bolt action. I spun to my right, crouched, and began a low crawl to the rear of the hillside. As I did, my right foot caught on something. Bullets whizzed overhead. My pucker factor was wound tight.

I kicked with my left foot, motivated to get out of the line of enemy fire. As I did, a muffled explosion went off between my legs. My world slowed to a crawl. Blue grey smoke rose between my legs, as I fell forward on my left side. Perl, unaware of what happened, scurried by me. I jumped up and followed him.

We hid on the backside of the hill; the AK fire stopped. I quickly called artillery on the area where the gooks had been. After two volleys of artillery fire, Perl and I carefully made our way ten yards back to the top of the hill. I found a Chi-Com grenade that had been placed in a Y branch of a low bush. I'd tripped a booby trap smack between my legs. It fizzled, and saved me from the full explosion. If the grenade had gone off, I'd be four feet shorter, or dead. I checked it for secondary charges; there were none. I untied it from the bush, tossed it in my pack, and we started back to Evans. When they sent us out here after ten days in the bush, they promised us a chopper to extract us after the hit. We knew that was a mirage. We just wanted to get back in time for a piece of birthday cake and our two beers.

It's 0645. Time to head down for breakfast. I'm pumped to see Harley.

***

Just finished lunch with the group. Got ten minutes before afternoon meetings. Had to write this before I forget. I probably wouldn't, but it's too funny. Hadn't thought of this for years and years. I was thinking about tonight at lunch. *I remembered an unforgettable exchange between Harley and Wiener.*

They were on patrol with the grunts. On a break, they were sitting side-by-side when Weiner snatched a Praying Mantis right out of the air. The grunts thought snipers were crazy, and we liked to perpetuate the image. Holding it up in front of his face, Weiner looks at Harley and says, "Do you want the head or the ass?" Smiling, Harley says, "Ah, I'll take the ass, I had the head yesterday". With that, Weiner tore the Praying Mantis in half, and they ate it.

Didn't want to miss that flash of inspiration. Back to work.

***

It's just after midnight. I'm toast. Dead tired but pumped. Forgot to call Gloria last night. She'll understand, she knew I was meeting with Harley. Today's been a blur. I have to be at the airport at 0530 in the morning. So tonight is going to be a very short night. Coast to coast flight, I can sleep on the plane. That is if I can slow down the adrenaline pumping out of my eyeballs.

Harley brought his wife, Joan. She's very nice, kind, pretty. I asked him, how the hell he got her? I'm sure when people meet Gloria they think the same thing. Turns out, it's his fourth wife, but looks like she's a keeper.

I haven't seen him since he was shot in August of 1967. He got his bush hat shot off, leaving a graze on the side of his head. Just like in the movies. He's a Jerry Reed look alike today but sounds like John Wayne. He looks good. Still slim. I'm maybe the only Rogue who pigged out?

He's been a biker, riding with gangs, for over twenty years. I asked Joan if it was okay to talk about the years since we'd seen each other. I was dying to know what happened to wife number one, the one he wrote the creative Dear John to back in Nam. Joan was good with it.

After sending his first wife the middle finger salute, he never wrote her again. When he returned, she understandably had a restraining order against him. One down. He met and married again, stayed straight for five years until he got bored. He came home one day, threw some clothes in a grocery bag, got on his bike and went back on the road. When he told me about the third one, it was funny. I thought he'd have a fit when I told him I'd become a Mormon. He laughed the way I remembered. Turns out wife three was a Mormon. He said she was nice, and wanted him to join the church. He said, "Hey, that's no problem. Those missionaries were nice guys. So I joined. When we got married, damned if she didn't want me to go to church". That one didn't last long. I could tell it was different with Joan. I was happy for him.

What a wonderful evening. A world away from the last time we were together. People don't understand what we have. The bond is indescribable. The feeling of being together again was magnificent. I love this guy. I love all our guys. We fought side-by-side, for each other. You're never the same again.

Harley left the biker life behind when he and Joan got together. He's a cement contractor now. I congratulated him on having his own business. He said, "Hell, I had to. I couldn't work for anyone. Between wanting to rip their faces off and my falling asleep all the time. I had no choice". Since he took a bullet upside the head, he's had narcolepsy. The VA can't explain it, and at this point, they don't care.

He couldn't believe I put up with the corporate bullshit. It wasn't easy. I have real problems working for people, but do it for the sake of my family. I make it work. I updated him on Crud's suicide, and Greeks recent death from cancer and all the other Rogues. We committed to have a reunion. I'd had a small one, right after Nam, but since then all communication has been through me. We laughed the evening away, reminiscing about our 'good times' in Nam. The only thing missing was a can of C-rats to share. Ruth's Chris was a little better than a dirty foxhole.

I'm tired, but so excited. It does my heart good, just knowing Harley's doing well. What a day. I have a couple of hours to sleep. Over and out.

11 November, Thursday - In the air to Chicago, IL. American Airlines

Just left Seattle. It's 0630. So many feelings. So much to write. I was talking to Harley about my journal. Hope to turn it into a book. I told him I also want to write a book about the Rogues. We were unique and had so many individual characters. We're like the TV program, MASH. Only we didn't save people, we killed them.

Harley loves the book idea. Told me I have to do it, no one else had a brain. That's not true, but it's in me, and has to come out. Ironically, at Seattle Pepsi, I met a retired Army Colonel. He told me about a friend, another retired Colonel, Michael Lee Lanning. Lanning has written five Nam books. One I read, "A Company Commander's Journal". Good stuff. He gave me his phone number. I'm going to call him. See what I can learn about the process.

I'm so ready to sleep. Nearly fell asleep a minute ago. It's early morning here, as I sit by the window, looking out as I type. It's dark behind me with signs of sun rising in the east, where I can see bright blue skies, and wispy clouds. The patchwork quilt on the ground must be eastern Washington.

I have a headache. Probably jet lag and no sleep. Must put this away.

12 November, Friday - Somers, NY. Pepsi

Got into Nairobi last night about 1930 hours. Slept most of the way from Seattle. Did a little people watching on my layover at

O'Hare. Always fun. I'm still on my adrenaline high from Harley. Have to call the other Rogues, update them on our resident biker.

Gloria and I stayed up late, talking. She brought me up to speed on the goings on at home, and I debriefed about my visit with Harley. She's so cool about it all; she always loves my guys. Always opened our apartment or home to them any time they needed it. I'm so blessed to have her. She's someone who loves, and understands me, regardless. She's been my built in therapist since we married. Neither of us knew it at the time, but it's true. She was never surprised by anything I told her about my life in Nam. That made a huge difference.

Driving in this morning caught more news on Haiti. I'm sorry, but that place isn't worth one American life. What's this all about President Bubba? As I drove along this morning, listening, I knew for certain why I'd not been watching the news lately. *Too irritating. I thought of Private Benware, in Santo Domingo. The poor kid was the first person, a Marine; I'd seen killed. I can still see his face in front of me now.* As I drove to work listening to war reports on the radio I knew the demons were restless.

Santo Domingo was twenty-eight years ago, and there was his face. He looked peaceful but dead. Eyes wide open, he was sitting right where he'd been stitched by a rebel machine gun. Benware was gone, less than a year out of boot camp. One hot afternoon a lifetime ago, and the images are still deeply embedded in my psyche.

"Ed. It's time for your 9 o'clock". My Assistant broke the silence of my Friday morning. Come back to the world Kug, back to your new reality.

15 November, Monday - Somers, NY. Pepsi

In the office early. Lots going on. The project from hell, reengineering. But it does get my juices flowing, love to fix things and stop the bullshit. I hoped to catch up on my rest over the weekend. Still beat, but feeling better than when I got home from Seattle.

Saturday night, our boss had a department meeting on a cruise boat in Manhattan. A dinner cruise around New York. Very cool. Gloria loved it. I was tired, so I had little interest. Boss gave out some bogus awards. Hate that bullshit. When I was up front for mine, my boss says, "And Ed & Gloria will soon be celebrating their 25th wedding anniversary". One of the guys in the group blurted out, "To the same woman?" Everyone got a laugh. Sadly, being happily married is a novelty today, a sign of our times.

Sunday we found out about a party Cort wouldn't attend. The girl next door's mad at her. It was a 'co-ed' sleepover that parents didn't know about. Lots of drinking at the party. Neighbor girl got drunk, her parents found out, and she blames Cort for not going with her. Times are getting tougher for kids.

16 November, Tuesday - Brookfield, CT. Home

Things are good for a change. Of course, that's always the case when I'm home. Had a few 'Greek' moments, but other than that, catching up on my rest. Supposed to be in Orlando tomorrow, but cancelled. Need to be home for a little while. Besides, tomorrow is my second re-birthday.

17 November, Wednesday - Brookfield, CT. Home

Stayed home today. Saw the kids off to school. Went out to lunch with my sweetheart, to dinner with the whole family, and relaxed for a change. Good day. Then, I was gone. *I was with Perl when I tripped the booby trap. November 10, 1966. I vowed I wouldn't go on patrol the next year on that date. I'd take the day off. Which I did. I went out with the Rogues a couple days later, and a year and a week later, it happened again. Another near miss, that I honor every November 17th. Another re-birthday.*

I remember it well. That's the day the NVA soldier pulled the trigger of his AK about three feet from my stomach. It misfired. Advantage Kug.

After that one, Greek was convinced that God was really, really saving me for something. Still an Atheist, I laughed. So glad I cancelled Orlando this week and stayed home. I need rest.

25 November, Thursday - Uhrichsville, OH. Grandma's House

We're at Gloria's Moms for Thanksgiving. Our first visit for all of us in two years. Took a couple days off. Got here late last night. Cortney's learning to drive, so she helped with the driving, which was nice. We had an early Thanksgiving dinner and then participated in the shopping wars. That's insane.

Brought in all the spoils from shopping, got settled down, and Cort yelled to tell me I'd left the back window down. It's pouring outside. When I got out there, the Suburban was soaked inside. I got the window up, went back inside for some towels. On the way, I realized I'm not upset. That's unusual. I guess I found peace in the rain tonight. Go figure.

No ghosts, while we've been on the road. Feeling pretty good.

28 November, Sunday - Bloomsburg, PA. EconoLodge Motel

Drove here this morning. We're spending the night with Trevor. He worked the holidays. We talked into the night. He's attending Bloomsburg University. We lived an hour and a half north of here for six years when I worked for Frito. Pennsylvania is crazy about hunting. When I worked here at Frito, we had to shut the plant down on the first day of hunting season. No one would show up for work.

When I was unloading the car, I looked at the surrounding hills, shrouded in fog. A light rain fell, and *I was back in Nam. Monsoon in the DMZ.* Not today. No more trips back in time. *I realize it's the resemblance to Nam that's getting me. A trigger. I have lots of triggers. Maybe one day I'll begin disabling them, one at a time.* But not today.

Driving home tomorrow morning, heading to Orlando Tuesday morning. *Saddle up.*

30 November, Tuesday - In the air to Orlando, FL. US Scare

Off to work on my new project. Had a great Thanksgiving. Nice trip to Ohio. Heading down here to evaluate part of the reengineering work. This part is floundering too. Talked to Harley over the weekend, great to be reconnected. Later. Need a nap.

"There is no gravity, the world sucks"
Found on a Zippo lighter from the War

DECEMBER

01 December, Wednesday - Melbourne, FL. Holiday Inn

Drove here last night. Met with the Pepsi folks in Orlando when I arrived. Got up at 0 dark early this morning. I wanted to ride a Pepsi route truck here in Melbourne. Needed a first hand report on the new computer system. Need to know what's driving the bad reports. The feedback's not good. I'd already heard that in Orlando. My boss is not in to hearing bad news. He'll have to get used to it on this project. All the news is bad.

Driving down last night was a trip back in time, one I didn't expect. The area was low; the highway lined with palm trees on both sides, the night dark. *Suddenly, I was on Highway 1, north of Hue, heading to Quang Tri. Our convoy's hit. Tracers light up the night. Explosions break eardrums, and maim, as the ambush rips through our lives.* I hear the car radio saying the Space Shuttle launch is in five minutes. I'm back in Florida, making my way to Melbourne. Life's good.

I'm surprised; I slept well last night. Heading back to Orlando in the morning. I have a meeting; then I'm flying home in the afternoon.

04 December, Saturday - Brookfield, CT. Home

Made it home from Orlando in one piece. You never know when you fly US Air. The holidays are coming; something great to look forward to. Gloria always makes Christmas special for everyone. It'll be the first time in two years that we'll be in one place for the holidays.

We don't like Connecticut, but moving again would suck. I was shocked when we moved back here last year. Hadn't been here in over ten years. When we went to license our car, they made me pay nearly a thousand dollars in penalties for not turning my old license plate in when I left. *That was a trigger. It's bureaucrats screwing with your life. I was furious. I went in to the tax office and demanded to see the law that said I had to return my plates. They could not show me. I even drove to the capitol in Hartford. Couldn't show me. Visited a State Senator, no luck. Bottom line, it's a game to make money. I was pissed and decided when we leave, I'm mailing those friggin' plates to the Governors office, certified mail.*

Church in the morning. Done.

05 December, Sunday - Brookfield, CT. Home

Not much happening today, but a good day at church. Today was our Fast Sunday. As members we commit to fast for two meals the first Saturday of the month and donate the value of those meals to our church welfare program. I couldn't help but think of the long odds of my being A Christian. Our family had no religion growing up. My parents were good people but no interest in religion. My Mother was raised in a church orphanage. Her Mother died at the age of thirty-five giving birth to her eighth child. I assume the orphanage experience was the basis of her dislike of all things religious. To her dying day she never talked to me about it.

Then an odd thing happened. One day, Mom dressed us up, loaded the three of us kids in the big Buick and ushered us off to a local Moravian Church to be baptized. She didn't really tell us what baptism was nor why we were doing it. After being sprinkled, we headed to a local Dairy Queen for a treat, never to hear of it again. Our home had no Bible and I never again stepped inside a church until Parris Island, Marine Corps Boot Camp. My mind drifted *to my first weekend in boot camp. June 1964. Hot and humid South Carolina. We didn't know how to march yet, and our Drill Instructor wasn't happy with us. We half-marched to a church near the parade grounds. I didn't know what was happening, sounded like a break from the screaming maniacs we met a couple days ago.*

"*Protestants to the right, Catholics to the left!. Fall out!" The DI screamed, pointing to each of the buildings behind him as he did. I stood frozen in fear. I knew what a Catholic was, I grew up with a few. I had no clue what a Protestant was, so I remained standing at attention. There were six others standing with me. "Kugler! What are you doing here? I know you're not a Jew! The DI stood in front of me, his face about an inch from mine, screaming.*

"*Sir! I'm not either one of those, Sir!" I screamed as loud as I could. I remembered my simple baptism at the Fry's Valley Moravian years ago. "What the hell are you then?" The DI screamed back. Our uncomfortable exchange continued. "Sir, I'm a Moravian, Sir! With that, the DI stepped back, eyes popping out, looking like a raging bull about to charge. "What on God's earth is a Moravian, Kugler?" Now he had me. I had no clue. "Sir, I don't know Sir." The DI was incredulous. He started cursing as he walked around me in circles spewing swear words I hadn't heard before and I'd heard more than a few. "Give me twenty bends and thrusts" he bellowed in the air. I immediately dropped and pumped out twenty bends and trusts amidst serious badgering by the crazy man.*

Sweating profusely in the Sunday morning heat, I jumped to my feet, standing at attention. Naively, I thought my charade was over. "What the hell are you now Private Kugler!" Shit. What do I do now? I was sure I couldn't be a Protestant, whatever that was. "Sir, I guess I'm a Moravian, Sir!" Stunned, the DI berated me for not knowing what a Moravian was. "Twenty more bends and thrusts Private Kugler!" I dropped to the deck and pumped out twenty more bends and thrusts, slower than the first set. Tired and scared, I was again back at attention.

Two more boot platoons arrived, marching in on either side of me and the Jewish recruits. My DI went berserk. "Twenty more Kugler!" Down again, I gutted out my assignment. I stand as he starts screaming like we were under attack. "Hey, come over here and see Private Kugler!. We got us a fucking MOWWW-ravian!". The other DI's came over and had some fun with the resident Moravian, me. I didn't remember reading this in 'The Story of the U.S. Marines' I'd read in Fifth Grade.

"Twenty more Private Kugler!" I got them done, painfully. As I again rose to my feet, the DI walked over, laughing and stood before me. "Kugler, I'm anointing you a fucking Protestant. Get in there!" As he said 'Protestant' he slapped me upside the head. I guess that was my anointing.

I had to laugh to myself thinking about my encounter over twenty-nine years ago. The journey from there to here has been a memorable one. Time for bed.

06 December. Monday - Somers, NY. Pepsi

In early. Catch up time. Cortney had her first date. School dance. Turned out it was very unsupervised. Several kids drinking beer, amazing, it was on the school premises. Stopping by to see the Principal this afternoon. I just want to make him aware; it's not his fault. Parents were supposed to be supervising the dance. So much for that idea.

07 December, Tuesday - Somers, NY. Pepsi

Still in the office, wanted to catch up before driving home. Traffic's hideous, might as well write now, rather than midnight. Met yesterday afternoon with the high school principal. Told him I wasn't there to complain, simply inform him of the situation. He was a young guy, very professional and sharp. He listened intently. Then he told me, "Mr. Kugler, I appreciate you informing me of the situation". It wasn't his first rodeo. "Let me tell you my problem. The parents let them drink at home, and when they supervise a dance, they see nothing wrong with it. First time it happened, I invited parents in to discuss the matter. Bottom line, they approve of their children's behavior. I will address it on our property; that is wrong. Otherwise, my hands are tied". At least he was honest, but what a sad state of affairs.

The meeting with my boss was interesting. He handed me another new project. Our illustrious leaders want to collect employee data from every single store Pepsi serves, across the entire US and Canada. We have over 650,000 customers. Pepsi's developing this new, 'super', handheld computer. They want to use the data base so our route drivers will be able to walk into any store and be able to say, "Hello Barb, how are you doing today?"

I told my boss to think about that for a minute. Imagine say, Seven Eleven stores. There's thousands of them. One of their major problems is finding and keeping good people. Their turnover is fifty percent or more. How will we ever keep the data up to date? It will be out of date by the time we finish gathering the data. It's going to be like painting the Golden Gate bridge. He told me he personally agreed, but the project was already underway, and he wanted me to fix it. "Fix the Titanic? The damage is done."

He smiled and I said, "Have you ever ridden one of our routes with our sales guys?" He said he had, and while it's a difficult project, he knew I could make it happen. The work was to travel around the country, to every sales area, teaching our sales crews how to collect this data. They would collect the data on paper forms. The route drivers would fill out the information about every store. Nothing could go wrong with that. *A plan like this one was as bad flying into Ashau Valley years ago.* My mind flickered.

His next few words made things more unbelievable. The plan was for each sales area to collect the data, aggregate the paper forms, and overnight them to our new data center in North Carolina. That was a new one. "We have a data center in North Carolina?" As far as I knew, ours was here in our Somers headquarters. Turns out, as part of our 'reengineering' the corporation project, we were building a new $11 million dollar data center in Raleigh for the sole purpose of running this new data base and support the new handheld. A handheld, I learned that wasn't even in beta test yet. "I will do everything in my power to make this successful. But Steve, just between us, you do realize this is not possible?" He said he was not in a position to change anything.

I'm not the fastest bullet in the magazine, but I knew this was one big waste of time and money. I took off to check out my new disaster. The handheld they were designing didn't work, and worse, didn't exist. I went down to where the reengineering group was set up, in PepsiCo headquarters in Purchase, New York. When I demanded to see the handheld, it was still a balsa wood model three months from launch.

Frustrated and disappointed, I left knowing we were all just pulling up a chair, waiting for the coming train wreck. I think the Vietnam War, and its aftermath, will prove to be an important vehicle for those wanting to destroy America. Our morals took a dive in the Sixties; LBJ's Great Society was a magnificent bust, and since Nam, no one is accountable for anything. In the business world, it's no longer about enabling your people to do their jobs, like we did in Nam. It's now about getting along with your peers, smile screwing your boss, and playing along. Sad.

09 December, Thursday - Brookfield, CT. Home

Got a surprise at work today. Bad timing, with the holidays coming up. Pepsi made a mistake with my pay; they didn't stop my car allowance I was getting in my previous job. I got a raise to come here, so with direct deposit I didn't notice the difference. Now they want it back, which I understand. There goes $3,600 right before Christmas. Timing is everything, this sucks. Add that to our mortgage increase, which went up $200 a month, just to live over an hour from work. Tie a knot, and hang on.

10 December, Friday - Somers, NY. Pepsi

End of the day. Staying here awhile to miss Friday night traffic. Lots of travel coming up before the holidays. Kicking off our data collection project. Charades; nothing real's going to happen. It's not a question of, if it will all blow up, it's only a question of when.

Heading to Orlando next week, then to Detroit. Have to squeeze in Dallas, Birmingham and St. Louis before Christmas too. *More corporate patrols.*

11 December, Saturday - Brookfield, CT. Home

Been a long and difficult day. Rumblings from the past rattled my mind. *It's been a year today that we planted Greek way out on Long Island. As I sit here tonight, his loss is as deep as it was when we lost him in Nam. My mind is flickering, an old movie with clips of our lives. I remember a time in Canada when he insisted he could paddle a canoe across the bay. I can still see him getting into it in shallow water, then flipping over the second he got in. He did that several times. When I waded out to help, he was adamant he didn't need any help. After some time, he concluded it was a balance problem. With one leg missing, he was a bit light on one side. He had a good laugh, as did everyone watching. Fun times with him and his family.*

The bond I feel with him and his family is unbreakable and surprising. Combat changes lives, welding them together forever. He struggled with drugs for years, me with alcohol. He struggled to hold a job, I held one that often drove me crazy. He was from Brooklyn, New York, 'the city' as he called it. I was from Lock Seventeen, Ohio, 'the country'. The two of us were raised in two different worlds; combat in the Marine Corps brought us together.

The experience of risking your life with others changes you. Our brotherhood's built on the common experience of not knowing if you'll come out of a situation alive. Combat changes your mind. It's not always visible, but it's very real to the user. When you return home you feel alienated, even though, you and those around you are often unaware. People don't understand you, and in the beginning, you don't want them to. The adrenaline filled world you left behind, followed you home and drives you every day. You chase the high you felt in combat.

I am grateful to know, that he is home with Christ. That wasn't always the case with me. I talked with Harley and YaYa yesterday. They're my brothers too. I'm grateful for the experience in the Marine Corps and of fighting in Nam. Without it, I would not be the person I am today. I wouldn't have my brothers; they are closer to me than my own brothers and sister. If you weren't there, you don't understand.

It's 0130, time for bed. Church is early. My mind's jumbled as I lay down. I drift to the spring of 1966. *"I'm getting a map, you pump the gas", Greek said, climbing out of my 396 Chevy Super Sport. He'd been driving since we crossed the border to Indiana. We'd pulled off the Interstate, near Terre Haute, on the western edge of the state. We'd been on the road nearly ten hours. I had a few days left on leave, before reporting to the Reserve Center in Fort Wayne. Greek flew out for a long weekend. On a whim, we decided to run out and see Stu, who lived in a couple hours west of Des Moines, Iowa.*

It was a warm spring night; I was chatting with the kid pumping my gas. I looked up at the starlit night. It wasn't that long ago Greek and I were staring at that same sky, only ten thousand miles away. I heard the door of the station open. Then I heard Greek yell, "Kug, do you know where the hell Iowa is?" I paid the guy at the pump as Greek walked towards us.

"Don't worry about it", I said, climbing into the driver's seat. "I'll drive, you sleep". Greek slid in the bucket seat next to mine, staring at the map he'd just bought. "No, I mean, like Indiana and Illinois is between Ohio and Iowa?" I laughed; he was always terrible with maps. "Yea, I know that. We've got another ten hours to Stu's house". I went through the gears and up the ramp, jumping on I-70 West. Greek sat speechless, mouth wide open.

About a mile down the road as I was cranking 80, he regained his composure, he ordered me to turn around. "You didn't know it was a day's drive out there?' I asked. He said he didn't know Indiana and Illinois were there. He'd never driven outside the city. It was pretty drunk out earlier in the night, it seemed like a good idea at the time. I still had a week's leave left, why not? I turned around at the next exit after Greek realized his flight back to New York, was in the morning. I knew it, but didn't care; I wanted to go see Stu. We drove a couple hours towards Akron, got a motel, and slept it off.

I woke up about three to go to the bathroom. I was as tired as I was years ago with Greek.

14 December, Tuesday - Orlando, FL. Hyatt Regency

Flew in yesterday, to deliver a short workshop on data collection, to the route sales people here. It went over like a pregnant pole-vaulter. When I told my boss, he thought my attitude was questionable. I can only imagine how the union drivers in Detroit are going to receive the news.

Need to sign off. One of the route sales guys, asked me to ride a route with him in the morning. They start work early, hopefully I can sleep tonight.

15 December, Wednesday - In the Air to Detroit, MI. US Scare

Upgraded to First Class using my miles. Need to sleep. Restless night. Up at 0500, on the route at 0600. Rode them before, so no surprises. The guy tried to collect data along the way. Some cooperated, most didn't. The drivers have enough to do, without adding this joke of a project. On one of our rural stops, I had to use the bathroom. It was a backwater place; they had a makeshift outhouse. It was a two-seater. I sat down and *was immediately back in Camp Carroll. I was sitting in a six-seater outhouse, all alone. It was made of plywood, vented with a small screen around the top. They were tall with a slanted metal roof, and a plywood door on either end. I'd barely sat down when a machine gun blast stitched ragged holes above my head. I dove face first onto the floor, pants around my ankles and moon shining bright. Not a good way to die. I lay there, listening, waiting to see what came next. I could hear running outside; Marines heading to the perimeter. I got up and ran out of there. Apparently, a rogue gook was out having fun.*

I hadn't thought of that for years. It made me smile. *When I came home from Nam, every time I sat down on the John for five or six years, I heard that machine gun. Weird how it's all still in my head.* Need some sleep.

December 19, Sunday - Brookfield, CT. Home

A week to Christmas. Fun times. Kids are excited. Trev let us know he's working Christmas Day, so he won't be home. Said he's doing it for the double time he'll get paid. It is what it is. Deal with it.

We get lots of those sappy Christmas letters? The ones where they bought a chinchilla farm and all the chinchilla's are in heat. Or their Orthodontist said the kids have the straightest teeth he's ever seen. Being a reformed whack job, my wife questions the reformed part; I convinced the family to send a funny, but truthful, Christmas letter. Gloria was a dissenter. I'll never do that again.

I wrote a creative letter filled with the truth. I told our friends I was fired from my great Frito job, Cortney's struggles in high school and the craziness of two moves in two years. Then of our son's blowing off college, where he was set to play basketball, to go on an Alaskan, fish cannery adventure. And it wouldn't be complete without the story of our business going down the tubes. We all thought it was pretty funny.

The calls started coming in yesterday, even more today. They're calls of condolence. One lady called to offer money. When I told her it was a joke, she got mad, told me what she thought about our joke. She was German, raised during the war. No sense of humor. We sent out fifty letters. It appears only one in five got the joke. Guess I should have listened to my wife.

December 21, Tuesday - Somers, NY. Pepsi

So much for the holidays. It's 0645, I'm at work. More bullshit meetings today on the data collection fiasco. It's a shame we waste money on this crap. It's a tribute to our workers in the field that we make money at all. If the stockholders ever knew how we piss money away, they'd bail.

Trevor mailed me my Christmas gift. He bought me a new Marine K-bar. Sent along a note, explaining it was to replace the one of mine he lost, back when he was eleven. A million dollars would not have meant as much to me as his gift. I was pretty hard on him at the time; it was the one I carried in Nam.

As I write, Vietnam pulls me away. *I'm on Hill 51. We're being attacked. Grunts are locking and loading, running to the perimeter, rounds begin streaking into the valley. This group of grunts had just flown in to replace the one's who'd been here for a month. What's worse, these guys had only been in country a month. They were jittery.*

"*Kug, what's up?*" *Red woke from a deep sleep. We lived on Hill 51 when we weren't on patrol in the valley. It was 0100; we were due to leave on a sniper patrol at 0300. I was up because I couldn't sleep, so decided to cut some holes in my bush hat. I used the holes to put small bushes on it for camouflage. My K-bar was well worn. "That thing ain't gonna' cut hot shit". Tomo was now up. As we talked, we could hear M-14's firing about twenty yards away on the perimeter.*

Marines yelled back and forth, sure the NVA were charging their lines. We'd lived on Hill 51 off and on, for nearly six months. We knew it was a phantom firefight. Worst case? A couple bad guys probing our lines. The new grunts were spooked, firing wildly into the night. Suddenly the night lit up like high noon; the grunts were dropping illumination rounds over our heads. Each illumination round burned bright for four, maybe five minutes, as it floated down in its tiny little parachute. Maybe they'll see the ghosts better now?

Fear is a funny thing. The longer you're in country, the more fighting you've seen, the more callous you become. Combat is crazy, frightening, chaotic ... the first time. A little less the second time. And soon, you learn that fear rides on a sliding scale for each individual. We'd go back to sleep if we could, but the noise bothers us.

"*I need one more illumination round, I've got one hole left to cut*", *I said. Tomo grunted, "Get done. We can leave early, get away from these clowns". Pop!* The illumination round created a silvery light that showered down around us. I held my bush hat in one hand, lifting it high, as I pushed hard with the point of my K-bar, I needed one more slit in the brim. It was so dull it was tough going.

The point of the K-bar went right through my hat and into my index finger. It didn't hurt much, but I was bleeding like a stuck pig. I held my finger up in the fading light as blood poured down my hand and onto my wrist. "Marine! You're wounded! Corpsman up!", a grunt walking by saw my hand, and sounded the alarm. "I'm not hit. I cut myself". Before I could slow down the emergency brigade, a Corpsman slid down beside me like the air was filled with bullets. "Where you hit?", he asked, breathing like he'd just finished a marathon. "Cool your jets. I just cut myself". Undaunted, he whipped out his first aid kit, about to bandage my hand. I declined got a small piece of gauze and told him to tape it tight. I can only imagine the war stories that'll come out of this 'enemy' encounter.

When the excitement subsided, we got out of there, early. It was 0200 and …

"Ed! You're late for your first meeting", my Admin brought me back to Somers. Long day of meetings ahead, got to go.

December 23, Thursday - Brookfield, CT. Home

Whitney told me Santa's so close she can smell him. It's a fun time of year. My daughters are excited; our son bought them something this year. What's the world coming to? Work is hectic. *Booby traps going off all over the place. It's like a bad day in a minefield*

Driving home tonight, *Greek came to me. Like a baseball bat to the side of the head. If he'd lived, we'd only be an hour and a half apart. Damn it! Pissed me off. I try to put him out of my mind, but he keeps coming back. And I'm glad. I miss him and his New York sense of humor. Sometimes, I long for my life in Nam, with the Rogues.* Sleep is nowhere to be found tonight. It was a simple life.

"*Kug! You gotta' do something. That asshole LT is gonna' get us killed". Greek and I were on a ten day grunt sweep with elements of the 1st*

Battalion 9th Marines. They were all riding the same crazy bus. They'd moved up here from Da Nang. Had to get them out of there after the gooks hemmed them in with Bouncing Betty mines. Bouncing Betty's were American mines. When tripped, they flew three or four feet in the air, then exploded. They'd cut you in half, and make quite a mess.

A shipment of 10,000 Bouncing Betty's, destined for our 'allies', the South Vietnamese Army, happened to come up missing. Hundreds of them turned up around the perimeter of the 9th Marines. One element of the 9th Marines, the survivors of the massacre, were those we were now with. They'd suffered over 50% casualties, ugly stuff. Disfigurement, loss of limbs and sight, the lucky ones, died. The dead and wounded were the result of trying to run patrols by day and ambushes at night. Brilliant move. Pure bullshit.

"Letem' do what they wanna' do, Greek". I didn't give a shit. The grunt survivors were bitter survivors of the carnage. The other half, brand new boots from stateside, FNG's. The LT, or Lieutenant, was right out of OCS in Quantico. He was from Brooklyn, New York. When he talked; he sounded exactly like Deputy Dawg, 'Da you knaw wheeere we arrrrre?'. There was little respect for this guy, and he had little control over the crusty survivors now under his leadership.

He was always lost, and did whatever ever Sgt. Thigh Bone told him to do. We didn't know Thigh Bone's real name, but everyone called him Thigh Bone. We assumed because he had a human thigh bone hanging from his cartridge belt. He was my age, but looked like he was in his late forties. As we were moving along, we took a sniper round from a nearby village. Thigh Bone wanted to go in, move all the people outside the village, and burn it. The Lieutenant wanted to call artillery. It'd be interesting who won this debate.

"Kug, he's over there trying to call in arty. He's going to kill us. Go tell him where we are". Deputy Dawg was clueless. Greek and I were set in on a small knoll, about seventy-five yards from the grunts. The plan was the grunts to sweep the village and we would cover the escape routes. If he was trying to call arty, the plans had changed. My money was on Thigh Bones plan.

Greek had a point. I'd been trying to tell Deputy Dawg for a week where he was, but he wasn't fond of listening to me. "Kug, get the hell over there!"

We were crouched in the bushes, sweating buckets, in the hundred degree heat. I decided he was right. I got on the radio, advised the grunts we were heading in. We didn't want these burned out cowboys blowing us away.

I barely clicked off the radio, when a freight train whistled through the air, vibrating our fried minds. It soared over our heads landing nearby with a loud thud. I jumped head first, flat on my stomach. The moron called in a spotter round. The thud we heard was the unexploded round burrowing into the ground. It was what we called a dud; it didn't detonate. I grabbed my radio and called the grunts. "This is Rogue One. Cease fire! Cease fire! Cancel artillery! You nearly killed us! Do you copy?"

Greek was wandering around, looking for the location where the spotter round landed. He found it, thirty feet from our position. It left a hole, about ten inches across, deep into the ground, so far we couldn't see the end of it. Greek once again shared his resolve that the Lord was saving me for something, one more time. We made it safely back with the grunts. I went straight to the LT. He was a pitiful looking guy. Most Officers were very good, always there for us. This guy, I wondered how he ever passed OCS? I explained to him how he nearly killed us, Thigh Bone told him to listen to me. I showed him where we were. I told him I could call in artillery for him if he'd like. He didn't like. It was a miserable time serving with these guys.

The sun went down and darkness soon followed. We were on the move, tired, worn out from the heat, wondering what madness we'd get into tonight. We snooped and pooped the bush most of the night, looking for people to ambush. It was a twist on Force Recon's 'ambush at will'. At around 0500, just before dawn, we found 'will'. We heard movement ahead, jumped off the trail and ambushed a group of NVA moving our way. A heated firefight erupted. It was black as a chunk of coal, tough to coordinate our defense amidst the chaos surrounding us.

It was a quick, close, intense firefight. When the early dawn fell silent, the scene wasn't pretty. We'd killed six bad guys, but they'd killed Sergeant Thigh Bone. He went down guns blazing, but he was gone, KIA. Another man down about to ruin a few lives back in the world. He was tough. He was a Marine, a wild one at that. Living through the 'Bouncing Betty' war had taken its toll on him and the others. The Marines he led were in *mourning. They would never listen to what the LT said now. We had four days left; it was a long and wicked four days.*

24 December, Friday - Somers, NY. Pepsi

In early. Half day today. Looking forward to some time off. *Couldn't sleep last night. Spent too much time in Nam. It's weird. Amidst the insanity of war, you can feel peace. Your mind plays tricks; you're sure that death is something that happens to someone else, not you. You're young; you're invincible. Not me. It won't happen to me.*

Work will be low key this morning. *We'll grab ass around*, have lunch with the boss, and then head home. I am lucky to work with some great people. Too bad we're so poorly led.

25 December, Saturday - Brookfield, CT. Home for Christmas

Christmas. It's that time of year, almost everyone treats each other the way we should the rest of the year. My wife makes Christmas special. We've been very blessed in life. It's been seventeen years since I found Christ. I always laugh, when I think about calling Greek to tell him I'd found Christ. Then, when I called to tell him I was being ordained a lay minister, he laughed, "It'll be a cold day in hell when that happens". The day I was set apart, it was ten below zero and we had eighteen inches of snow. I guess he was right.

It's afternoon as I write. The girls are enjoying their presents, and Gloria is taking a nap. It's a little bittersweet, Trevor didn't make it home. Turns out the joke was on him. The Manager decided that it wasn't a double time day after all. Told him he doesn't have enough 'hours' to qualify for overtime. The games they play in Corporate America never cease to amaze me.

The blatant stupidity of managers is on the rise. He cooks in a Truckstops of America facility on I-80. He never misses work, speaks English, can put more than one sentence together at a time, and you can't pay him double time for working Christmas. He once walked five miles in a snow storm to get to work, because all the roads were closed. Our country is losing its moral fiber. In a few more years we'll be swirling in the toilet bowl, about to go down.

I miss my Nam brothers today. Can't believe Greek, Crud and Perl are gone. Way too soon. After twenty-four years, Gloria's finally getting some of my feelings out. It's been a long road. In Nam, I perfected having no feelings. No reaction to anything. No emotions. It worked well. I've compartmentalized my life. Only now is my core beginning to crack. On days like today, it's tougher. Sometimes, I'm not so sure I should open the personal, nuclear waste dump housed in my mind.

Gloria's up, time to leave for Christmas dinner. We're driving to some friends. I am back in the world, I think.

***

Home. Late. Everyone's in bed. Don't know why, but tough dinner, as well as the drive home. It's such a neat time of year. We sang carols. The Spirit was warm and comforting. *Then I started to think about how lucky I am to be here. Maybe God was saving me for something.*

"Wait up Marine! Coming around". We walked in a long column, zombies, making our way from village to village in the Street Without Joy. The voice behind me was a grunt Gunny, moving to the front of the column. We'd been walking in the sand dunes for days, occasionally interrupted by a village, we plodded on.

I stopped, and stood aside, "There you go Gunny". He passed by, walked about eight feet, and one step into a five foot high hedgerow. BOOM! Dirt flew everywhere, as the Gunny contorted in the air like a scared cat. I flew backwards, sprawling on the ground. He'd tripped a booby trap, a concussion grenade, right where I would've been.

I sat up, dusting myself off, trying to get my head on straight. The Gunny was in bad shape. He landed in a heap a few feet from where he got launched. The Corpsman was already there. My head ached, but I was otherwise unharmed. I sat up as the Gunny moaned, and rolled on the ground in pain, severely wounded. The bottom half of his right leg, and the foot on the left were missing. It was the Street Without Joy. Just like the French, we knew it was a bad place.

Time for bed.

27 December, Monday - Brookfield, CT. Home

Today seems like the longest day of the year. Nothing big going on, *but one bad night last night.* I thought I was doing better, *but the year's not ending well. Vietnam is like Hallmark,* "The gift that keeps on giving".

28 December, Tuesday - Somers, NY. Pepsi

In early. Working on my latest debacle. It's a shame how good, hard working people, sell their souls, for the sake of being seen as a team player. Preach the party line, in the name of bogus loyalty. People today don't know the meaning of loyalty. *It's a struggle for me. The parallels with Nam are clear. We don't learn from history in America, or in corporate life either. We plod on with happy faces while we complain in the bathrooms about things we'll never say in public.* I'm thankful my current boss is into what he calls 'good work', and not a quick fix most leaders want today.

I presented to our President this morning. He's a good guy, buffaloed and creatively lied to by his direct reports. I delivered the bad news on one of my turnaround projects. They thought the project would rollout in six months. I delivered reality. It will be another two, maybe three years before it's completed. The bottom line, his people, have been 'smile screwing' him for the life of the project. At least he didn't kill the messenger. He thanked me. That's as good as it gets.

While I was presenting to him and the Senior Team, as they're now called in the 'new' Pepsi, *my mind flickered, like an old 16 mm movie years ago. Images flashed in my mind. I'd answer a question between frames. I got a glimpse of President Johnson, standing before the American people, lying through his teeth about troop increases and the progress of the war. And Nixon announcing more bombing, like bombing people into submission ever worked.* It didn't hold me today; I came back to my meeting.

Heading into 1994, I'm struggling, big time. I sit here, no college degree, made it near the top of Pepsi, a major corporation, only to find the same bullshit we put up with in Nam. *People don't die here, as they did in Nam, but their careers do, their families suffer and businesses fail. Why? Often because people sit back, make no waves, go along to get along. The bullshit grows like weeds in early summer.* Sad.

This stuff has haunted me for years. Since I left Nam. Leaders in corporate America manage play money, not real money. *There's no longer a connection between real results, and rewards. It's the peons, the grunts in these companies, the ones working out in the plants, warehouses and up and down the street jobs, who make these companies work.* Their work enables the Kings and Queens of corporate America, to play their silly games. It's getting worse every day as the distance between the peons and the perfumed princes grows and grows.

I'm frustrated, but as I sit here today, waiting for traffic to clear, I lead a very blessed life. I'm certainly grateful for my blessings. I'm blessed with a great wife, great kids and a great job. *But sometimes, like right now, I can't help but wonder, why me? There are nearly 59,000 names on a granite wall which represent young human beings, just like me. Each and every one, frozen in time in the minds of their loved ones, who wonder what might have been. Why? I'm seeking answers to questions that have no answers, at least in this life.*

Just looked up, it's six thirty. Need to call Gloria, and head home. Cortney and I are speaking at a baptism tomorrow night, in Pennsylvania, Where we used to live. Need some sleep tonight. Hope it comes.

29 December, Wednesday - Mill Hall, PA. A Friends House

Long day. Kids are asleep on the living room floor. We're sleeping in one of the kids rooms. I'm sitting at the kitchen table, trying to keep my journal going. We woke up early today, packed, and hit the road. Took just over five hours to get here. It'll be a quick trip.

Every year this time, *I think back to 1973. In October, the second Arab Israeli War took place. I was still drinking heavily every day. It would be three more years before the love of my life gave me an ultimatum. Quit drinking or leave. It wasn't easy, but I quit. But when the war broke out, my adrenaline came on like a new volcano. I wanted to fight for Israel. I admired their fighting prowess, and their incredible spirit. The ceasefire came quick, but I knew it wouldn't last. On a business trip to Chicago just before Christmas, I found myself a bit under the influence, standing in the Israeli Consulate, asking how to enlist. They didn't want me, and I didn't blame them. I wasn't presenting my best side.*

It's been a wild ride, and I've loved every minute of it. *I still don't fully understand the indelible imprint Nam left on my life. My two years are deeply imbedded. A flashback is always a thought away. Triggers are everywhere.* As I've learned more about the gospel of Jesus Christ, I often wonder about the lives lost, on both sides, and how it will all work out one day? I don't know.

We were both fighting for a cause we believed. I've never had any hard feelings about the Vietnamese. My anger comes from the contempt I feel for Jane Fonda, Lyndon Johnson, Robert McNamara, William Westmoreland and the commies who incited the riots we experienced. Leaders on both sides put us into battle, and then played games with our lives. In the end, I have to think justice will come from God, not from us.

Gloria's support is a blessing. Her love, feedback and coaching are indispensable. Without her, I wouldn't be sitting here having just spoken at the baptism of our friends daughter. It was a great evening. Church, the one place outside of our cottage in Canada, where I have peace. I'm thankful for that. Tomorrow we're hanging out, visiting friends, and getting ready for a small New Years Eve get together. Time for bed. It's 0100.

31 December, Thursday - Lock Haven, PA. Friends Cabin

We've had a nice day with friends. A few couples and their kids. We were at a friends family cabin outside of town. The Allegheny Mountains surround us, trees as far as you can see, and deer everywhere. Beautiful. It snowed this morning. The cabin is neat. A great place to bring in the New Year. Most of the adults are engrossed in board games, kids are upstairs playing, I'm off in the corner. I have a serious need to be alone. It's New Years Eve. *I think of the only New Years I can remember in Vietnam. New Years 1966.*

My Gunny asked me to go with a Green Beret, a Major, who was heading to his headquarters, in the old Imperial capital of Hue. He wanted security for the ride down Highway 1. The rain was blinding. We bumped along for twenty miles or so in our jeep. It was better than spending the night in a flooded bunker in Phu Bai. We arrived without incident. Their Headquarters was in an old French compound inside the Citadel. The rooms were aged, with high ceilings, and furnishings the French left behind. The Major had a small apartment with two bedrooms and a small living area. At least it was dry.

He apparently came here often; there was a little Christmas tree on a small table. He didn't say much to me, so I took the hint and went into the spare bedroom. I laid my gear on the floor and hopped on the old bed. A bed, it felt but good, odd but good. It was rickety and lumpy but wonderful. Safe, dry and comfortable, I dozed off.

I woke up when the door slammed when he came back in. I didn't know he left. He must have retrieved his mail. He walked over, and quietly closed my door. As he did, he whispered, "I have a tape from my wife". I could care less. Glad I didn't have one to worry about. Wouldn't be needing one, ever.

I had C-rats with me for dinner, but I was enjoying the moment, relaxing on my bed. The walls were apparently not insulated, as I could hear his wife talking on his cassette player. I heard whimpering, then crying. It was the Major, crying, as he listened to his tape from home. A frigging Green Beret, crying. And a Major at that. A Major wimp. I didn't get it.

I heard football on the TV in the cabin. I got up and joined the guys watching Ohio State and BYU. I grew up a Buckeye fan, even got to go to the Horseshoe a few times. I sat down with the others, but I was fighting the clips playing in my head. I watched a couple of plays, couldn't get into it, so I went over to watch the board games. I decided to join in, anything to keep my mind occupied. It'll soon be 1994. Unbelievable!

"When the power of love, overcomes the love of power, only then will we have a chance for true peace."
Found on a Zippo lighter from the War

EPILOGUE

There it is. One year in the life of one vet. Written in 1993, twenty-five years after the war ended for me. My service in the Marine Corps was the fulfillment of a Fifth Grade dream. I'm grateful for it. It was a dream that changed my life, for the better. It came at a price, but everything good comes at a price. It was worth it, even with the bag of demons I unwittingly brought home. In the old days, World War I, they called it Shell Shock. In World War II, it became known as Battle Fatigue. In those days the vets were told to go home, don't talk about it, just forget it. Most of them did. More then we'll ever know were put away in institutions and forgotten. I've never read what they called it in Korea. I have a feeling those forgotten vets were not allowed to have any problems when they came home. After Vietnam, it became known as PTSD, Post Traumatic Stress Disorder. Since then, there is at least a recognition that warriors may come home different than when they left.

In spite of the year I chronicled in this book; it would be another fifteen years before I admitted I might have a problem. My family knew; I wouldn't hear it, I knew I was fine. Until one day, one of my fellow Marines decided it was time. He personally took me to his counselor at the Vet's Center in Spokane, Washington. That day I had to admit it to myself. The counselor in Spokane connected me with a great counselor in Missoula, Montana, a Navy Seal in Nam. He was able to help me begin the journey to reassembling Humpty Dumpty.

It's my hope and prayer, by bearing my soul and sharing my journey, that my young brothers and sisters, veterans of our current debacles, will realize you're not the Lone Ranger. I'm living proof, as are my fellow snipers from Nam, that you can succeed in life, in spite of the demons that followed you home.

In spite of the progress we've made in understanding the problems of today's veterans, our current culture is again turning its back on the military. Yes, we had a brief resurgence of patriotism after

9-11; the fervor is now gone. The only people aware of the current war in Afghanistan are the servicemen and women who are fighting it, and their families. We have lost our patriotism, our resilience and our appreciation of history. We have become a selfish people in America. We've lost the history of the greatest nation the world has ever known. We were a nation filled with a diverse group of people who came together to work for, and die for, an idea known as America. Without America, there is no freedom in America, and the entire world. We are living witnesses of America's demise.

I believe that today's returning veterans, suffer a further complication that fuels the development of PTSD for six reasons.

1. First, they must fight under the most ridiculous, restrictive and damaging rules of engagement warfare has ever seen. Today's ROE's put those we fought with in Vietnam to shame. The risks to our warriors deployed today are treacherous and nonsense, dreamed up by lawyers who wouldn't know a bullet from a testicle. When you send people into hostile environments without the ability to instinctively respond, it messes with the mind. To be seriously threatened without the right to defend yourself shakes the very roots of the human psyche.

2. Second, being expected to fight, while having the most minute decisions made not by direct leaders, boots on the ground, but by their so called leaders a few time zones away; fuels the demon of rage many bring home. Further, being second guessed by lawyers, now deployed at the least provocation, disempowers our troops, feeds distrust and cynicism. The resentment and anger build, a trigger is developed, and when tripped, sends the warrior into a rage.

3. Third, coming home to an ambivalent nation, downright hostile in many cases, and a media that constantly questions

your every move, causes a feeling of separation between the veteran, society and the government. The current state of our culture makes the veteran feel betrayed and separated from the society and the government they just risked their lives to protect. The veteran begins to feel a disconnect from all he thought he was fighting for. One veteran who tried college told me he had students in class with him who did not know who bombed the World Trade Center. The 'thank you for serving' many receive today rings hollow for many.

4. Fourth, the political correctness overwhelming our society manifests itself in absurdity. That absurdity messes with the minds of warriors. I can only speak for the Marine Corps. We join the Marines for many individual reasons. One of those reasons is because you want to fight our nations enemies. You are intensely trained to kill 'the enemy'. You take an oath to defend our nation from all enemies foreign and domestic. You graduate boot camp with a single focus. Protect our nation or die trying. Today, the military is pressured into providing cultural sensitivity training, legal briefings, accept any yahoo that shows up, and are accompanied by embedded reporters, who by their own admission, are not there only to report the war to our citizens; they are there to expose the military's secret society. If you're even a semi-rational person, think about what that might do to your mind. Do you feel proud to serve today? Do you feel supported when your pay is withheld by our Commander in Chief? Do you feel supported when every move is open to judgment by those not even present? Hardly. And that messes with the mind.

5. Fifth, the rapid decline in our societal standards is being pushed on the military. We now accept people in the military who are surprised when they deploy and find themselves in

a real war. They're shocked when they see people killed around them. When the true ugliness of war hits them between the eyes, it's a blinding shock. They joined for the great benefits of our all volunteer force, for the fake notoriety at home, and not to serve their country with whatever it takes. We send people to the war zone with cell phones, allow texting and video games. I speak from experience; you can't live in two worlds and not suffer consequences. Our young generation is sitting around wasting their lives on video games, sitting next to their date, and both are texting, are not ready for combat. The new reality for kids is not outside, it's imaginary, it's a video war game. As a nation, we no longer have the 'stomach' to defend ourselves as our forefathers did. Being placed in that position messes with your mind.

6. Sixth and last, the length of our current 'so-called' wars overwhelms many. Deploying individuals and units time and again with no end in sight and no purpose is damaging to all involved. We currently have no clear purpose or strategy on where we place troops and why. Even I know we can't change the culture of the Middle East in less than a century. Yet, we continue to play with the lives of our young people. Furthermore, it's not our job to do so. For a warrior, a lack of purpose messes with the mind.

The problem we know today as PTSD is not new. Its just been revealed, and it's getting worse because of the six reasons above. The decline of America began during and after World War II, although most didn't see it. During my era, the Vietnam War, the 60's as it were, the decline picked up speed. Today, we've reached Mach 3, speeding towards Mach 4 as we speak. Its a leadership problem.

Its been over forty-five years since I was last in combat. It has been about a week since I had a flashback. I now expect them, understand them and know many of my triggers. That's quite an improvement from the early days. I've not only had counseling, but I've done a great deal of self-examination and reflection. Most of my demons were positive. I rarely had a nightmare; I had many flashbacks wanting to do it all over again. The negative experiences I've had started around 2003. That's when my anger surfaced again over the pathetic leadership our troops were experiencing in Iraq and later in Afghanistan. Regardless of what the 'experts' say, Afghanistan is Vietnam. We learned nothing. And today, with the total decline of America under our current leadership, it is a daily chore to manage my anger.

Along the way, I've learned a few things. I'd like to share them with our current vets, their loved ones, and those with loved ones and friends who are struggling. They represent my journey. Yours is probably similar, yet all of us are different. I personally struggled because I wanted to go back, to do it all one more time. I'm one end of a wide spectrum. The other end is those who have nightmares, are disabled and don't want to think of it or ever do it again. Somewhere on that continuum is the anger you hold for our leaders in the Pentagon, the White House, Congress and the media, who play with our lives everyday in pursuit of more power and money. Wherever you fall on the spectrum, there is hope.

As warriors, we're trained to never leave a brother behind on the battlefield. I'm here to tell you, that commitment extends beyond the battlefield, to your brother, the one wrestling with the demons that followed him home. Whether your demons are lurking right beneath the surface or reveal themselves after a dozen shots of whiskey, deal with them and help others do likewise. We have a lifelong commitment to each other. The irony of it all, the irony you never imagined, you returned to a new battlefield of cultural change, estrangement and in some cases, downright betrayal. The old saying, 'If it is to be, it's up to me' applies to all of us.

We must remain close to those we served. In the Marine Corps, we call that Semper Fidelis, always faithful. It cannot be just a motto; it must be a way of life. It is my hope, and prayer, something in this book will serve you well. I pray something I said will make your journey home, your quest for a 'new normal,' a little quicker, smoother and meaningful.

"You've never lived, until you've almost died"
Found on a Zippo lighter from the War

"Everything can be taken from a man but one thing: the last of human freedoms - to choose one's attitude in any given set of circumstances, to choose one's own way."
Viktor E. Frankl

AFTER ACTION REPORT - ADVICE FROM MY JOURNEY

1. It Is What It Is:

I know that's a popular cliche, but it's true. One of the best things you can do is accept how you feel. Don't bullshit yourself and those close to you. I've heard it said that PTSD, like crazy, is a normal response to an abnormal situation. It does not mean you're a nutcase. You may feel crazy at times, but you're not. You're living with a new normal in a world where you are not yet comfortable. Recognize it. You can't change that which you don't acknowledge and confront.

It is what it is, deal with it. You're not the person you were when you went to war. That's expected and it's okay. It doesn't mean you can't get better and live a normal life. It doesn't mean you're right, and everyone else is wrong, or vice versa. It means you're a different person. One who's a much better person than the one who went to war. The only way out of a problem is through. 'Through' begins by admitting where you are and deciding to confront your situation and become better.

You all know maps and compass, or today I guess, a GPS. The first thing you must do is be certain where you are right now. You can't get to where you want to be if you don't know where you are when you start. If you were calling mortars, artillery or air strikes you'd tell them where you were. It's not rocket science but it is tough to do. I couldn't stop drinking until I admitted I was a drunk. I couldn't lose weight until I admitted I was fat. You can't fix what's broken in your life until you admit you have PTSD. Your future success depends on learning 'it is what it is' deal with it. In the end, whether we like it or not, changing is a choice only you can make.

2. Reactions:

Once you know and admit where you are, you can begin your war to fix it and get your life back. The war of PTSD is a war you can win. And like the war that brought you here, you have to understand the enemy. The enemy buried deep inside what we call PTSD, is your reaction to events that happen. Your reaction to certain events manifests itself in the behavior that's interfering with your life. A few things I experienced are listed below:

- Difficulty seeing the positive in anything. *Still wrestle with it a bit.*

- Burying myself in work and booze. *I used to bury myself in work. I haven't had a drink in over 40 years. Never did drugs, many do.*

- Difficulty sleeping and concentrating. *Still do. At this point in life, age becomes another factor.*

- Emotional numbness. *Still suffer this at times. Got my relief by traveling to a family cottage in northern Canada. Funerals still shut me down.*

- Irritability, anger and rage. *Mine is primarily under control, although my wife might disagree at times.*

- Feeling not understood or misunderstood upon your return. *Had the problem, but it's gone.*

- Chasing an adrenaline high. *Spent days 'chasing' it early on. Age took care of this one, for the most part.*

- Depression. Fought it without admitting it for years. *I manage it well now with journal writing, medication and activity. You should find what works for you.*

- An inability to tolerate any degree of bullshit. *Still operating full tilt on this one. Thus my one website 'nomorebs.com'. I decided this one served me well - most of the time. I kept it.*

- You seek 'truth' in the black and white world you live in, because you've been lied to and screwed with so much while deployed in the war. *I'm aware of it now so I can deal with it better. Learn how it may impact you.*

- Don't tell me what to do, cause' you ain't got your lion. Let me explain. You'll get it when you hear the story. There's a story said to originate in Africa. In at least one village, the story goes that when a young boy turns a certain age he is expected to go out and bag his first 'lion'. When he does he becomes a man. Think about your experience. Ever been furious when you have a leader or a boss who has done nothing more than party his way through a college degree or an MBA and he starts telling you what to do and he or she obviously doesn't have a clue. At that moment you feel the anger simmering. What you're feeling is 'he ain't got his lion'. *It was a problem for me for many years until I understood this principle. And let me note, not all people deployed to a combat zone ever get their lion either.*

Your behavior, exhibited by your reactions, represents your PTSD. You need to develop your list, one by one. It's not about sitting down with paper and pencil. It's about recognizing your 'symptoms' repeated over time. It's about your feelings and emotions and how they're exhibited. Knowing your 'symptoms' leads to the next step ... discovering the triggers that set off your reactions. Your trip wires.

3. Triggers:

You can and will be successful, by taking charge of your life as you did in combat. The value of looking back on your life is to draw strength from your past. Tell yourself, if I could do what I did in combat, I can do anything! Your next step is to discover the triggers, hiding like an IED, behind your reactions to certain events. Why do you now behave as you do? What is driving your behavior? It won't happen all at once, but you have to know.

One of the things that helped me most was learning I had triggers that were setting me off. I was walking into mental booby traps not knowing they were there. It was someone else's problem, not mine. The second thing that helped me was learning to tie my behavior, my reaction, to a specific trigger. What sets you off, or what drags you down? You gotta' know.

I shared an experience earlier in the book when I painfully learned one of my triggers. It was painful and there was collateral damage. It started with a stereotypical reaction to a seminar leader. The guy walked in the room and tripped my wire. It wasn't his fault. But I ruined his first seminar with a new company. After a sleepless night I traced that trip wire to the booby trap. What I learned helped me immensely down the road. It will do the same for you. It's important. Understanding your triggers is an important step on the way to living a better life. Your triggers are key to keeping your mind out of your 'bad place'. Your 'bad place' can show up as a positive or a negative. Either way, learn your triggers and live a better life.

There's one thing that separates man from animal. It's the power of choice. We can rarely choose what happens to us, but we can always choose our reaction to what happens. The power of choice is an important life skill, especially when you struggle with PTSD. The important thing about tying your triggers to reactions that stem from PTSD, is that only then can you take the next step to understand what's driving your behavior. It means learning to become proactive and not reactive. Refuse to be a victim of whatever happened in your life.

Once you know and admit where you are, learn your reactions to events, tie your triggers to those events, then and only then can you begin to establish your 'new normal'. Go back and reread my year, see my triggers and the reactions I had. Your triggers could be a smell; a backfire, a firecracker on the Fourth of July, a date on the calendar, or any number of things that take you back to a traumatic event, a death, or one filled with high danger and adrenaline that fires you up.

You're never going to feel the normal you felt before the war. I have found over the past 40 plus years since the war that PTSD is not something you cure or heal. It's something you learn to live with. The process outlined above is how I learned to live with it - you are establishing your new normal. When you return from war, your reference points in life are out of balance. You're looking for stability but don't know where to find it - except back in the war zone with your brothers. What's serious, what's funny, what's threatening, your definitions are all different now.

To establish your 'new normal' is going to require help. I was blessed with a wonderful wife who loved hearing about my war experiences. She has never been shocked, by anything, our entire marriage. She tolerated my drinking to a point, then put her foot down and helped me get over my alcoholism. If you have a wife like me, cherish her.

Whether you're blessed with a great companion or perhaps a close and caring family or friend, that's great. I was also blessed to stay close to the men I spent the war with. It made such a difference. We are close to this day. Many years later I also humbled myself and sought professional help. However and whatever you choose, you're going to need help, support and love from your circle of life.

The next thing that helped us, as a family, was learning how they could help me correct my course without offending me. They needed to tip me off that I was actually in my 'bad place'. Because telling someone with PTSD that they're acting badly isn't easy, those close you know what I'm talking about.

4. Find a Metaphor:

In the early days I was sure the world around me had a problem. There was no good way to let me know I'd go off. I really didn't want to talk to anyone but my wife. I was learning as I went but the on the job training required great patience from my wife and others. My bullshit meter had a very short range. The space between stimulus and response had to be measured in milliseconds. Many years went by before I unwittingly discovered my 'Bees'. A metaphor that changed everything for us.

For many years, I became upset if my wife, and eventually my kids, challenged or reminded me I was acting a bit irrationally. Like wanting to join the Israeli Army was irrational? Or setting booby traps for the kids trashing my mail box was a bad thing? It pissed me off. Over the years, as I began reflecting, trying to figure myself out, I realized most veterans compartmentalized their war and lives. I discovered I had a bad place. When I went there, my life lens was distorted, my adrenaline started flowing but I could never express how it felt inside my head. But the family picked up on my referring to 'my bad place'. I began to hear, "Dad, you're in your bad place". It began to work. It wasn't offensive, it wasn't challenging to me and it began to allow me to build a space between stimulus and response. The space that started out in seconds was now up to an minute or two, maybe. At least it was a start.

As the years went by, in February 2011 to be exact, I discovered my 'Bees'. My wife and I were staying in our motor home at the time. I was talking on the phone with a colleague when he received the news of a purely bullshit decision on a project we were proposing at church. I went off. I hadn't shot off the charts that bad for some time. My wife reminded me I was in 'my bad place'. She asked, "What are you feeling right now?" Good question. I didn't know.

We were in an RV Park, so I went out and walked a few miles, thinking about what happened. Why did that happen? What was I feeling? How could I put it in words? By the end of my walk, it came to me. It felt like bees were swarming inside my head. The noise, the buzzing blinded me to the actual reality around me. My anxiety shot through the roof. I returned and explained it to my wife. The next day she went shopping and returned with several bumble bee items. A cell phone holder, several different bees of made of cloth and plastic. "I'm going to set these around to remind you of your 'bees'. It worked for us. We shared it with the kids. When I have an episode and go to my bad place, they say 'the bees - the bees' and walk away. It's a small thing but it helped. Never stop learning. You must learn to manage your PTSD, you're not getting rid of it.

Now let's look at a fact you need to accept.

5. No, They Don't Understand: *Let it Go*

One powerful and enduring feeling you'll have when you return is, 'they don't understand'. You're right. They don't understand, but that's okay. How would you expect them to understand? They have not traded lead with people trying to kill them. Or lived through an IED blast or picked up the pieces of friends who weren't as lucky as you. The only people who understand are people who have been through what you've been through. Think about having a baby. If you've never had one, you don't understand what it's like to give birth. Most of us have not lost a child, we do not know what that's like either. It's okay. Forgive them and move on.

Remember, the only person you control is you. There's a theory called the Circle of Influence and Circle of Concern. I have a lot of experience with this theory, and it works, as long as you apply it. It means in each of our lives we have things we can influence, or control, and things that we have concern about, that we cannot control. If you're taking your family on a picnic and it rains, you have a choice. You can be pissed off, or you can take them inside to an arcade. The choice is yours.

In the above example if you chose to be pissed off, you're living in the Circle of Concern. If you chose to take your family to the arcade, you're operating in your Circle of Influence. I made that a thought process in the late 80's, and it made a remarkable difference in my life. I'm perfect at it, but I'm better because of it. And choice by choice I got even better at not allowing events I didn't control, control me. When you think someone doesn't understand, before you respond think about your Circle of Influence - Circle of Concern. Exercising your power of choice can change your life.

John A. Parish, M.D., in his book *Autopsy of War*, says, "The same group identity, carried to its extreme, makes each person in the unit important. Rather than leave a dead or wounded Marine behind, the entire group may take heavy additional casualties to retrieve him. Loyalty to fellow soldiers prevails over everything. By comparison, patriotism, captured land, spoils, treasure, or any concept of winning the war means little". That's one of the reasons you're different and that's okay. But take charge of your situation and make choices that make you better.

What's important once again, is recognizing, it is what it is. It doesn't make people bad that they don't understand. They may be jerks, rude, obnoxious and stupid. So what? Understand you're not going to change them and if you go off into a rage you're simply justifying what they think of veterans. Spend your time with people who care about you, want the best for you and are there to support you. Stay in contact with your fellow warriors. They understand. Compare notes, support one another and remember, we leave no one behind on the battlefield. Your life is now your battlefield for some time to come.

Another must do is next. Keep pumping air in a tire and it will explode. You're no different. Hold in all those experiences and one way or another, you'll explode. I did.

6. Let it Out:

Author Stephen Covey in his best-selling book, *The Seven Habits of Highly Effective People,* taught that unexpressed feelings come forth in uglier ways. Let me repeat that. Unexpressed feelings come forth in uglier ways. Think about that for a minute. You know it's true. In our minds we have a core, where we've compartmentalized our experiences, experiences well out of the norm. These experiences are imprinted into our psyche. From our core, leaps the demons who followed us home. In my case, that's what I call 'my bad place'. That is where my demons live. Those demons are tied to triggers who produce a reaction when provoked. The reaction comes out as your bad behavior that is self destructive and disliked by those closest to you. If you're just controlling your behavior on the outside, pressure builds up in your core. If we don't let the pressure out, it will come forth in uglier ways.

It's imperative that we find someone, hopefully a spouse or a fellow warrior, a close friend or family member you can reach out to; people who care about you and love you. Build a small circle of supporters–a team. A team like the one you were with in the war. A team you can trust. You didn't get where you are alone, and you're not getting out of it alone either.

You can reach out to a counselor too. When you reach out, they don't have to understand, they just have to care, to listen and not be judgmental. Look for someone who isn't going to be shocked by what you share. You need someone who has empathy, and preferably a Counselor who is a vet. If not, find one who has worked with vet's and can relate to the military life and combat. Admittedly, sometimes that's difficult to do. But you must do it.

Another thing I've found helpful is journaling. I was challenged to write by a great friend, Keith Holdaway. At the time, April, 1976, Keith was a young nineteen year old missionary. I've been writing ever since. I just passed 10,000 pages. Will anyone ever read it? Probably not. Does it matter if they do? No, because writing makes me feel better and helps me come down from an adrenaline high and makes me come up from my depression. Neither began working over night, but they helped me immensely over time. Instead of punching out the driver of the car that honked at you, come home and write what you'd like to do, rather than doing it. That lets off steam, and helps you to understand yourself. Will it work for you? I don't know, but it did for me.

A few other things I've seen work for others, working out at the gym, running, shooting, hiking, anything physical. I've met a few who turned their energy to painting. I know an Army vet, a survivor of the Ia Drang Valley, who writes poetry nearly every day. There are no right answers, only the answer that relieves the stress your demons create. You need to find a way to manage each demon living in your bad place. You must find a way to release the pressure and don't turn to booze and drugs to do it. Deal only in reality.

If you're not buying it yet, think of a boiling pot on the stove. If you don't adjust the heat, or take off the lid, at some point it's going to boil over. If you boil over things are damaged, and in some cases people are hurt. That's what can and will happen to us, too. We have to let off steam driven by our demons.

A long and painful story made short, I once had to walk away from a high six figure job to keep my sanity. In a meeting, I actually stood up and made one step toward my boss with the absolute intention of tossing his ass out of his eighth story window. I could see him flying out and hear the glass tinkling to the ground. One step into it, my mind shut down. Completely shut down. I walked out never to return. My boss didn't have his lion and I was done dealing with his petty bullshit.

During a particularly challenging time shortly after that, I took my youngest daughter to the movies. We saw "Liar, Liar". A funny movie, my daughter, thought, until I burst into tears. Why? I'm not sure. Something seeped through a new crack in my core and exhibited itself in sobbing. The older you get your 'core' develops a few cracks. If there are demons lurking there, demons you have yet to deal with, they will come out in uglier, sometimes unusual ways. Be proactive, don't allow yourself to be a victim, take charge of your life, and you will succeed.

Now let's look at another skill. You need to rejuvenate, humor.

7. Humor:

The military has a brand of humor all its own; combat has an extension of that humor that is unique to all who've experienced it. I know Doctors call it 'ER humor'. We used to call it 'black humor' or 'dark humor'. In times of stress, people use humor as a stress reducer; many not even realizing why. The point…don't lose it. That doesn't mean using it at the expense of others or at inappropriate times. It means using it for you. Is it appropriate? It is in your world, and it's a key to reestablishing your new normal. Now let's look at a skill that will mean the most to your posterity.

8. Be a Filter:

We've talked a lot about the power of choice. Your PTSD brings with it certain behaviors, if left as a part of your life, will impact those closest to us. Our families for instance. Your children if you have any or plan to. Some choose to try and hide their PTSD. Some choose to ignore it. Some succumb to their PTSD. Others, like me, deny they have a problem. It's all a choice. If you choose to deal with it using booze or drugs, that too is a choice, at least in the beginning. Your PTSD driven behaviors cause collateral damage to those around you.

Each of us has a past and a future. We need to choose to invest our past into our future. We need to use what we've learned from our past to build a better tomorrow. In the first five years of our marriage, I put my wife through a lot. A lot. Between my drinking, my Marine sniper reunions, my flashbacks and my activities chasing adrenaline, it was tough on her but we were committed to each other.

One day she said to me, "Ed, use your strengths from the incredible things you did in Vietnam, to do good. Work to leave the bad things behind". While that is easier said than done, I can attest that it's possible. It's another big key to your turnaround and success. And its a key to not allowing collateral damage to destroy those close to you.

When you've faced war, it demands things of you that you'll never experience again, as long as you live. You most likely did things you never imagined you could do. Things you may despise, hate, be surprised that you love and you may have seen things no human being should see. You need to capture those feelings. You need to use those feelings to invest in you and your family's future. Know that you can do anything, after what you've already done.

In the end, you can become a better person than the one who went to war, by becoming a filter in your own life. Take all you've done and filter out the bad, those things that don't serve you well; and choose to permit your good experiences, the ones that serve you well and make you stronger, to pass through your life filter. Make them part of your life, your skills for success. What we do everyday is what we believe … all the rest is just talk. Choose to pass down to your family a future of strength.

Let me illustrate with a personal experience from my life. When I came home from Nam, my wife would not marry me unless I agreed to go to work. That didn't make sense to me at the time. I wanted to be a mercenary, but that seemed to conflict with her idea of a happy life together. I went to work as a mechanic and truck driver. Using what I learned in the Marine Corps and

Vietnam, I went from where I started to Vice President of Compaq Computer, with no college degree.

I share that only as an example of using your strengths to build a better tomorrow. After Vietnam, I knew I could do anything. If I got a job that I didn't understand, I either bought a book or met with someone who'd done something similar and learned from them. In the Corps we say, 'improvise, adapt and overcome'. You know the drill so do it. You can overcome by being a filter, by using the good in your experience and build a better tomorrow for you and your loved ones.

Now let's get serious about dealing with PTSD ... don't cop out.

9. Do NOT Self Medicate:

My advice comes as a recovering alcoholic. I know the military culture is heavy in the work hard, play hard culture. I was too. I started drinking at the ripe young age of 14. I used to gather up pop bottles, cash them in for five to twenty-five cents each. I'd get enough to buy a quart of Black Label beer and off I'd go. I was leading edge at the time, few if any kids were doing it. Today, everyone has an array of bad choices.

When you drink to excess or do drugs, you're masking what's bugging you, you're self medicating. You're dealing with the demons by burying them in the fog you create with booze or drugs. It's that simple. You may be like me and not know or want to admit what you're doing, but you are. As we talked about before, there is always collateral damage. If you're single it's more limited than if you're married. But behaving badly is an insult to those close to you who love and support you. You're a veteran and in to truth, that's the truth.

Let me share a painful, personal experience to make an important point. My drinking came to a head one Sunday morning after a very bad night. My wife and I were living near Camden, New

Jersey. We'd driven to Ohio for the weekend. Our company office was there.

I was into racing at the time and was picking up a new panel van that I was going to pimp out for my racing equipment. My wife's parents lived an hour south of the office in Akron. I was picking up my new van near the office, so I told my wife I'd go to the office in the morning for a couple hours, pick up the van and be down with her in the afternoon. That is truly what I intended to do.

I picked up the van and went to the office. At noon, I headed south to my in-laws. On the way, before leaving Akron, I decided to stop for one drink. One! The problem was I'd never been able to stop at one. I assured my wife I didn't have a problem. After all, I could go two, maybe three days without a drink. But if I had one, I'd drink until I fell over. That was a serious problem about to come to a head.

My wife went through a great deal in those five plus years. She loved me, cajoled me and begged me to quit drinking. I promised I'd quit and even meant it at the time. But like any addiction, once my drug of choice took over, nothing mattered. What mattered in my case was one more drink so I could trip out on my adventure in Vietnam. My mental burst of adrenaline fueled by my desire to relive Vietnam is what drove me.

On that fateful day, my one drink turned into two and three and four. My last memory in the bar was at 4 PM. I'd stacked twenty-seven mixed drink straws in a pyramid, in front of me. The bars in Ohio at that time closed at 0230 in the morning. That's when I had to leave. My next memory came somewhere around probably 0300 trying to find my way out of Akron, Ohio. Akron had only two Interstates. One running north and south, one running east and west. I was trying to go south. At times, I saw signs indicating all four of those directions. All I wanted to do was sleep. I really needed sleep. As I later looked back, I saw how pitiful I'd become, as well as how much I'd hurt the girl of my dreams, the only person who stood between me and a life on the bottle.

My story of self-medication ended on northbound I-77 near Fairlawn, Ohio at around 0400. I was frustrated seeing all those signs and somehow not being able to get out of town. Horns had been blaring at me for a long time as I swerved my way around Akron. It's weird; I have a perfect recollection of climbing in the back of my empty van while driving down the Interstate at fifty or sixty miles per hour. I gave no consideration to the fact I was about to crash. It didn't matter in my shitfaced state. All I wanted more than anything was sleep.

My next memory was waking to flashing lights, red ones, and people yelling to me. "Are you okay?" I just wanted sleep. Of course I was okay? I found I was laying in about a foot of water, inside the van. What the hell? I didn't know it at the time, but when you quit driving and lay down, you crash. My new van, with about forty miles on it, went through the guardrail, through the air and landed back first in a small creek about twenty feet down from the highway.

The next bit of consciousness I experienced were the red lights again. I was sitting alone, in the front seat of an Ohio State troopers car outside a Union 76 station. The wrecker pulled me into the gas station. While I could barely see him, my images were fading in and out, the trooper was walking my way. My first thought, 'you're in deep shit my friend'. In Summit County Ohio, drunk driving was an automatic three days in jail at the time.

I felt my head bobbing and weaving as the Trooper entered the car. He said, "Where were you going?" I sat there a minute, grasping for normalcy and losing. I said, "Sir, I don't even know where I am". He wanted my driver license, so I handed him my wallet. There wasn't a chance I'd find my license. He'd already found my registration and insurance card in the glove box.

"You know your information gives three different addresses". I didn't. Turns out my driver's license showed my parents address. I hadn't bothered to change it since we married. My new van had my wife and my old address in Akron. My insurance listed our new address in Jersey. The Trooper asked, "Tell me what's going on in your life". Before I could answer he found my Marine ID card in my wallet. It had a picture of me, taken in my jungle fatigues in Nam looking very dark and Pancho Villa like. "Were you in the Corps?" I answered as best I could.

He sat there for what seemed like a long time looking at my Marine ID. Then he turned to me and said, "Mr. Kugler, you look like a guy with a problem. I'm a Marine. I'm going to give you the break of your young life. You see your van over there?" I nodded that I did. It was parked beside and behind the gas station. He continued. "I'm taking you over to your van. You're getting in your van and sleeping it off." I nodded. All I wanted in the beginning was sleep. "The attendant at the station has your keys and my number. If you try to leave here before morning, he will call me, and I will throw the book at you. Do you agree?" I nodded that I did. He then told me I'd get a bill in the mail for the guardrail, and I'd better pay it. He drove me to the back of my van. Helped me out of the car and over to the van. I climbed in the back and crashed, getting the sleep I desperately needed.

I woke up to a hot Sunday morning and a massive hangover. I'd done a lot of drinking since the age of 14, but I'd never have a hangover like this one. I got out, got my keys from the attendant and decided to drive over to the office and call my wife. I hadn't talked with her since I'd left her parents house the previous morning. We were supposed to go out to dinner that night with friends. The collateral damage had begun.

I pulled out of the service station without checking my van. The tires screeched, splitting my head in two. I stopped on the ramp before getting on the Interstate. My front wheels were so out of line it was visible with the naked eye. They were also bent a little outward at the bottom. No choice, I got back in and endured the screeching for the ten miles to the office. I could only go twenty-five miles an hour, people were again honking at me.

Gloria was an hour away, when I called, the anger and hurt in her voice poured through the phone like hot lava rolling down a rugged mountainside. It would turn out to be the longest hour of both our lives. I locked up the office, and went outside to wait. We were supposed to drive back to Jersey today. We'd driven our car over, and were going to drive both vehicles back. That wasn't going to happen now. I climbed up on one of our trailers that were sitting in the yard. It was loaded with steel pipe; I climbed up and sat on top of the pipe. Not sure why, seemed like the place to be? Sitting in the hot morning sun, sweating the booze out, I pondered my fate. Would she forgive me, again?

I'll spare some gory details of our meeting, but the most important thing she said was, "Here's the deal. It's the booze or me, now! Your choice". She'd bent before, many times but never broken. I had broken her this time. Her face and emotions bore witness to the deep hurt and embarrassment I had caused. My actions reverberated to her parents, to her friends and mine. It was the end, unless I changed. I've never had another drink since that day.

The reason I have shared an ugly part of my life is for all of you who are exactly where I was in this story. I know there are many of you out there. I'm not talking about a drink now and then, or an occasional party. I'm talking about doing something stupid, again and again and again. I know you're a different person when you are sober, than when you're drunk or high. I know you don't think you have a problem, just as I was sure I didn't have a problem. You cannot change that which you don't acknowledge. You may not recognize it because your'e living it. If it's a problem for those around you, it's a problem for you. You're tossing artillery into friendly towns and villages, wantonly causing untold damage to innocent victims. It is what it is. Deal with it. Now!

Let's move on the last tip I have to offer. Humility.

10. Be Willing to Seek & Accept Help:

Warriors are tough. Mentally and physically. If you've been a warrior and lived through combat it's in your DNA, never to be removed. When you return from combat you view life through the lens of 'being tough'. Yet, when it comes to problems with your head, no way. Don't talk to me about that stuff. I'm tough. I can handle it.

But ... think about it. When you were in the heat of battle and a brother went down, you didn't hesitate to yell, "Medic or Corpsman Up!" And if they didn't show up on the spot you were pissed. Or if the Medivac was late, you wanted to slap the pilot around. So tell me, why, when your wife is yelling for help, or your son or daughter, or a fellow warrior, why do you hesitate? You wanna' know why? Because you're a warrior and you're tough. And that's your paradigm. It's in your DNA.

Let me share another experience in our family. One of our daughters went through an incredibly difficult experience that far too many women experience in America. She suffered from a violent crime while a senior in high school and attempted suicide. I had yet to progress beyond 'I'm tough'. I told my wife I would counsel with her. She didn't hesitate to tell me that wasn't happening, we were seeking professional help. We did.

We went through four different therapists to find one who had a clue. She was wonderful. She counseled her individually and with us as a family. I saw changes in my daughter and in my attitude. A step towards knowing what I didn't know, humility. Then she got crazy. She told us my daughter needed medication to get through the crisis. Medication? Not in my family. I'm a Marine. She tripped a wire that said 'I was weak', not strong like a warrior. How dare you!

My great wife wasn't backing down on this one either. But the therapist sensed my 'problems' and took me on. She confronted me, privately and directly. She wanted me to go down the hall and see the shrink. She said, "He will understand you. You will like him". Me like a shrink? I doubt that. She said, "Do you trust me with your daughter?" I said I did. "Then why don't you trust my advice for you?" She had me there.

Turns out the shrink was a Flight Surgeon in Vietnam. He had his lion! I grew to love the guy. But medications? He changed my paradigm with one exchange. He said, "Ed, if your daughter had a broken arm would you treat it?" Of course. "Then understand that her head is broken from her experiences. Treat it". Umm?

He explained, in layman's terms, that she was in severe depression. When a person experiences depression the chemicals in their brains are not being produced in the way they're designed to work. He placed his hands together with fingers nearly touching each other. He explained that the chemicals are required to make the synapses snap back and forth to allow us to function normally. When depressed, the synapse aren't snapping like they should and the medication he prescribes serves to enable the brain to work properly until my daughter begins dealing with some of the issues in therapy and the natural chemicals start working again. He moved my needle. I agreed. While she spent three years in therapy, often times medicated, she is married, a great Mom to three wonderful kids and living a wonderful life today. That would not have happened without therapy and medication. And me being humbled enough to accept I didn't know what I didn't know.

Why did I share this story. In hopes of moving at least one needle like mine was moved. I pray it will impact at least one warrior, one family who's led by someone 'strong' like I was back then. May you 'get it' long before I did. You weren't a shrinking violet in the war zone, don't be one now. Deal only in reality. Some of you are 'surrounded' by your demons. As we used to scream in Nam, "Gooks inside the wire!". Don't be afraid to yell "Corpsman Up!" for yourself.

It doesn't make you a wimp; it makes you smart, it makes you brave, it makes you humble, and still tough. If you broke your leg, you'd see a Doctor. If your son broke his arm, you'd take him to the Doctor. Well, I didn't back in the day, but I should have. War can break your head; you may need to see a Doctor, and that's okay. Be strong. Get help when you need it. Don't suffer in silence, or make those around you suffer. Before you do something stupid. Before you slip so far down the muddy, smelly foxhole in your mind that you do something you'll regret or worse, harm yourself or others. Reach out for help. Corpsman up! You can do it!

Besides what I shared above and being blessed with a wonderful wife, there is one other thing that helped change my life and make PTSD manageable. Finding Jesus Christ. While in Nam I was an atheist. Vietnam sent me on a journey to find 'meaning' in my life. I never considered that to be 'religion'. It's a story I share in another book, *Through the Darkness Comes the Light,* but I can testify that finding my Savior made a tremendous difference in my life.

I share that not to preach to you but to be honest about what helped me. What I do know is that finding meaning in life is a key to a better tomorrow. How you find that meaning is up to you, it's a personal quest.

A NOTE ABOUT THE VA

When we came home from Nam, the VA sucked. We hear a lot today about the awful VA Healthcare system. I don't doubt that is true, in some State systems and hospitals. Trust me, it's all relative. If you want horror stories talk to your Nam vets who were wounded. What they did best then was dispense pills to shut you up.

Today, while it's far from perfect, it's a lot better overall. Don't get me wrong, there are still issues. Much of it depends on where you live. What I hear is that great service is very spotty. Large cities like Dallas, Houston and Phoenix are still operating in the Vietnam era. Many locations, like here in Montana, are outstanding. I have also heard positive things about the VA in Indiana, Washington and Northern California. I was flown in an emergency to the Salt Lake VA, and my two weeks there were a real bad comedy of errors. Administration cared less. I've been treated there since and it was fairly good. I've found it's not the people in most VA's that are the problem, but the system and top leadership. It's a large bureaucracy, and few bureaucracies perform well.

When it comes to psychological issues, it's a mixed bag at best. I worked with a young Marine, with two tours in Iraq, who held off a SWAT team for over two hours. He has some serious issues. He was threatening to harm himself and others. His Father contacted his psychiatrist in the Tennessee VA Healthcare system. His response was an email, telling him to make an appointment. Hardly comforting or appropriate. I once had to go, as an emergency, to the walk-in PTSD Clinic at the VA hospital in Salt Lake City. I was jacked up. It's in the eyes. The thousand yard stare returned for a spell. I was out of town, off medication and needed some immediately. It wasn't my first firefight of the mind. After the fifty minute hour with a young Social Worker, she asked me if I could come back next week. I asked why? She told me I needed to see someone who could prescribe me the medication. As you can imagine, that tripped one of my wires that sent a volley of fire her way like I'd just seen Osama bin Laden. I got my medication that day, but it was ugly. It shouldn't have to happen that way.

In my experience, there are three major issues with the VA when it comes to psychological problems.

- First, the system is overwhelmed. After a decade of war resulting in catastrophic physical injuries, the introduction of Traumatic Brain injuries and an incredible rise in psychological issues such as PTSD, they are having major trouble coping. Remember, it is what it is. That's not the people who work at the VA's fault. Don't take it out on them. It's a bureaucracy and it's overwhelmed for sure.

- Second, specifically in the area of psychological problems, they're buried and understaffed. You cannot produce psychologists overnight; there is currently, in my opinion, little chance of providing adequate care, especially in large cities. Where do you come up with the number of Psychologists and Psychiatrists necessary to deal with today's volume of veterans? I don't know if this number is accurate or not but it sounds right. I have been told that since the early 2000's when our current Middle East wars started the uptick in Vietnam Veterans PTSD at the VA is about 30%. I know mine got new energy and caused problems since then. Very difficult to cope with from a VA perspective and 'it is what it is'. It's not the people, it's the circumstances and the system.

- Third, I've noticed that today, I'm sure in an effort to 'keep up,' the VA has a philosophy of using people with Social Work degrees to counsel veterans with PTSD. The feedback I hear and my personal experiences tell me that's not working. I've worked with one local lady, a social worker and psychologist, not VA referred, who was outstanding. I worked with another,

VA referred, where I spent my first three sessions filling out government paperwork. I called the VA and told them it was a waste of my time, as well as our tax dollars. It doesn't make these folks bad, but it does make them misplaced and places both the Social Worker and the vet in a lose/lose situation. So where does that leave the vet? Good question. We should continue to work within the system where it works. If it doesn't work for you there is one other solution I have found that usually works well. Your local Vet Centers. The Vet Centers receive funding from the VA, but they operate independently and are staffed by Veterans. Therefore, they are Veteran friendly. Most of the people you're talking with 'have their lion'. The local vet center in Missoula worked in my life where the VA didn't for my PTSD. They worked for a couple of my Nam friends. I've referred several OIF/OEF vets to their local centers and the feedback was positive. They can make a difference and are well worth trying. Whatever you do, understand there is no right answer, only the answer that works for you.

Every organization is perfectly designed to produce the results they are getting. That's not the fault of the people working in those organizations. Take the high ground and treat the people with respect. The problem is not the people, it's the system. Systems are the responsibility of leadership. I consulted turning businesses around for ten years. In every organizations I worked, the problem was not the people, it was always a leadership problem.

CLOSING THOUGHTS

The problem with war is, it's the greatest adventure for a young man, and the greatest tragedy for mankind. We fight wars for many reasons: for land, over artificial boundaries, ideals, religion and politics. In the end, that means little to the warrior. The warrior doesn't know it in the beginning, but he'll be fighting for the warrior beside him. When the warrior comes home, they're seen as damaged goods. Fewer and fewer citizens even care about the plight of the veteran. Veterans and their families care about other veterans. Many people at the VA are there because they care about veterans. Our leaders in the White House and Congress, pretend to care, all the while sending more troops to faraway places, with no purpose, with unclear objectives and rules of engagement the size of the Obamacare bill, and just as ridiculous.

Marine legend, General Smedley D. Butler, recipient of two Congressional Medals of Honor and Author of *War is a Racket* said, "War is a racket. It always has been. It is possibly the oldest, easily the most profitable, surely the most vicious. It is the only one international in scope. It is the only one in which the profits are reckoned in dollars and the losses in lives."

May we always stand vigilant to protect our loved ones, our way of life and our nation. May we always stand for freedom. May we put God back in America. May we pray that General Butler is not right, but if he is, may we band together and build a better tomorrow, for ourselves, our families and our nation.

God Bless America and all of you!

Most Richly Blessed

by an Unknown Civil War Veteran

I asked God for strength, that I might achieve.
I was made weak, that I might learn humbly to obey.

I asked for health, that I might do great things.
I was given infirmity, that I might do better things.

I asked for riches, that I might be happy.
I was given poverty, that I might become wise.

I asked for power, that I might have the praise of men.
I was given weakness, that I might feel the need for God.

I asked for all things, that I might enjoy life.
I was given Life, that I might enjoy all things.

I got nothing that I asked for, but everything I had hoped for.
Almost despite myself, my unspoken prayers and true needs were fulfilled.

I am, among all men, most richly blessed.

***

May you all be, Most Richly Blessed

Ed Kugler

ABOUT THE AUTHOR

Ed was born and raised in the thriving metropolis of Lock Seventeen, Ohio, along with its seventy-four other residents. He graduated from Gnadenhutten High School and entered the Marines Corps two weeks later. He served a four year stint where he saw action in Santo Domingo, Dominican Republic and two years in the Vietnam War. He shared the details of his life as a Marine Sniper in Vietnam in his first book, *Dead Center - A Two Year Odyssey in the Vietnam War.*

After the war, Ed met and married Gloria Patterson. They have now been together for forty-five years. He began his working career with various jobs in the trucking industry, moved to Frito Lay where he spent thirteen years, then Pepsi Cola for three years and rose to the position of Vice President of Worldwide Logistics for Compaq Computer, all without a college degree. Along the way, Ed started and operated several business's, the last his own consulting company, Direct Hit, Inc. He provided Fortune 50 companies with operational turnaround services.

Ed is the Author of several books. A couple great ones, a few good ones and a few bad ones. He and Gloria are the parents of three kids, have four grandkids and live on a peaceful mountainside in Big Arm, Montana. The Last Best Place.

CONTACT ED

edkugler@icloud.com

www.edkugler.com

www.nomorebs.com

www.facebook.com/ed.kugler

www.twitter.com/sgtkug @sgtkug

www.amazon.com/Ed-Kugler/e/B001KHMJX8

www.amazon.com/Ed-Kugler/e/B001KHMJX8

www.ezinearticles.com/search/?q=ed+Kugler

Made in the USA
Middletown, DE
09 May 2015